Strength and Weakness

William F. Stone   Gerda Lederer
Richard Christie
Editors

Strength and Weakness

The Authoritarian Personality Today

Springer-Verlag
New York Berlin Heidelberg London Paris
Tokyo Hong Kong Barcelona Budapest

William F. Stone
Department of Psychology
University of Maine
Orono, ME 04469-0155
USA

Gerda Lederer
55 Barksdale Road
White Plains, NY 10607
USA

Richard Christie
Department of Psychology
Columbia University
New York, NY 10027
USA

With two illustrations

Library of Congress Cataloging-in-Publication Data
Strength and weakness: the authoritarian personality today / William
    F. Stone, Gerda Lederer, Richard Christie, editors.
        p. cm.
    Includes bibliographical references and index.
    ISBN 0-387-97698-1 (alk. paper).—ISBN 3-540-97698-1 (alk.
paper)
    1. Authoritarianism. 2. Authoritarianism—Cross-cultural studies.
3. Authoritarian personality. 4. Authoritarianism (Personality
trait) I. Stone, William F. II. Lederer, Gerda, 1926–
III. Christie, Richard.
    [DNLM: 1. Authoritarianism. BF 698.35.A87 S915]
HM271.S74 1992
303.3′6—dc20   92-2178

Printed on acid-free paper.

Production managed by Bill Imbornoni; manufacturing supervised by Jacqui Ashri.
Typeset by Best-set Typesetter, Ltd., Hong Kong.

9 8 7 6 5 4 3 2 1

ISBN-13:978-1-4613-9182-1   e-ISBN-13:978-1-4613-9180-7
DOI: 10.1007/978-1-4613-9180-7

Preface

This book had its origins in conversations held at various meetings of the International Society of Political Psychology. The editors and contributors are grateful for the forum that has given us the opportunity to discuss these topics over the last 10 years. We are most grateful to our contributors both for their chapters and for the intellectual stimulation they have given us. Jos Meloen in particular has been free with his time, advice, and enthusiasm. Although he declined to contribute a chapter, Bob Altemeyer has been a source of encouragement and a ready adviser on any question we have asked.

The staff of Springer-Verlag has been most patient in adapting to our schedule. We are indebted to the secretarial staff at the University of Maine, and especially to Kathy McAuliffe, who has put in many extra hours above and beyond the call of duty. Finally, we dedicate this book to our departed friend and colleague, Silvan Tomkins, with whom we conversed at length about these and other topics, and from whom we received inspiration and diversion.

William F. Stone
Gerda Lederer
Richard Christie

Contents

Contributors

MARINA ABALAKINA, PhD
Department of Psychology, New Mexico State University,
Las Cruces, NM 88003, USA

VLADIMIR AGEYEV, PhD
Department of Psychology, Moscow State University,
Moscow, Russian Federated Republic

RICHARD CHRISTIE, PhD
Department of Psychology, Columbia University, New York,
NY 10027, USA

CHRISTEL HOPF, PhD
Institute for Psychology and Sociology, University of
Hildesheim, Marienburger Platz 22, 3200 Hildesheim, Germany

GERDA LEDERER, PhD
Currently doing research with Justus Liebig University, Giessen;
the University of Hamburg, Germany; and the University of Vienna,
Austria

SAM MCFARLAND, PhD
Department of Psychology, Western Kentucky University,
Bowling Green, KY 42101, USA

JOS D. MELOEN, PhD
Institute for Social Science Research, University of Leiden,
Leiden, The Netherlands

FRANZ SAMELSON, PhD
Psychology Department, Kansas State University, Manhattan, KS
66506, USA

LAURENCE D. SMITH, PhD
Department of Psychology, University of Maine, Orono, ME
04469-5742, USA

WILLIAM F. STONE, PhD
Department of Psychology, University of Maine, Orono, ME
04469-5742, USA

Part I
Overview

1
Introduction: Strength and Weakness

WILLIAM F. STONE, GERDA LEDERER, AND RICHARD CHRISTIE

Dispirited and shamed by the low estate to which Germany had fallen with its defeat in the First World War, German citizens were ready for strong leadership. They were alert for a leader who promised to restore national pride and rebuild the German economy. Hitler promised such leadership; his anti-Semitic harangues also struck a chord with many Germans. Both Jews and communists served as handy scapegoats, the former because of historic German prejudices, the latter as challengers of traditional authority.

In his preface to *The Authoritarian Personality* (Adorno, Frenkel-Brunswik, Levinson, & Sanford, 1950; referred to as *TAP* in the following pages), Max Horkheimer noted that the purpose of *TAP* was to describe "an 'anthropological' species we call the authoritarian type of man" (p. ix). A major goal of describing such individuals was to suggest origins, in the psychology of the German people, of the mass support for the Nazis. However, there were many sources of Adolf Hitler's allure. The German people's insecurity, both physical and economic, might explain some of their need for strong leadership. Germanic culture stressed obedience to authority, discipline, and nationalism. Thus, without considering personality at all, these factors go a long way toward explaining Hitler's appeal. Even in countries that do not go to the Fascist extreme, environmental threats do lead to authority-seeking behaviors. In their foreword to an abridged edition of *TAP*, Daniel Levinson and Nevitt Sanford (1982) noted that they had come to recognize "the need for a broader approach . . . [taking] sociocultural forces more into account" (p. vi). A notable attempt to present a broader account of the psychological and social forces responsible for the Holocaust and other instances of mass killing is to be found in Erwin Staub's (1989) *The Roots of Evil*, an attempt to construct a comprehensive theory of the causes of genocide. Focusing on the Holocaust, Staub also examines the "disappearances" during the reign of military terror in Argentina and other instances of group violence.

Our purpose is to assess the current status of *TAP*. One difficulty is that *TAP* did not present a concise, coherent theory that can be presented in a logical, testable form. But there has developed a broad understanding of the "anthropological species." Briefly, the authoritarian individual is conventional; has aggressive feelings toward "legitimate" targets (e.g., homosexuals); and is submissive to authoritative or strong leadership. The personality makeup represents well-entrenched defenses against anxiety. The aggressive feelings are easily directed against outgroup members who are designated as being worthy of contempt by authority. This is the classic displacement mechanism described by Freud.

Authoritarians develop this personality, which has its basis in inborn drives that are socially unacceptable, notably sexual and aggressive ones. When the restraints against expression of these impulses are unusually harsh, the individual becomes anxious, insecure, and unusually attuned to external authority sources for behavioral guidance. Thus, harsh, punitive, and vindictive parents and rigid social codes help to shape the authoritarian syndrome. Duckitt (1989) summarizes the theory as follows:

Essentially, it relates together causally phenomena at four different levels. Thus, strict and punitive parental socialization sets up an enduring conflict within the individual between resentment and hostility toward parental authority, and by extension all authority, which is repressed and displaced because of a more powerful fear of and need to submit to that authority. These psychodynamics are given expression at the surface of personality in a syndrome of nine covarying traits. It is this constellation of traits which then constitutes the authoritarian personality per se. Finally, these traits in turn are expressed in certain social behaviors and beliefs. This is manifested most notably in those implicitly anti-democratic beliefs which are sampled by the F Scale in order to measure this authoritarian personality syndrome, as well as in phenomena such as intergroup and political attitudes and behaviors. (p. 64)

We believe that the evidence presented in this book supports this general approach. With modifications, of course, the theory still has relevance for the modern world. Our title, *Strength and Weakness*, reflects our conclusions in two respects. First, we think that the authoritarian personality syndrome's essential core is that the person fawns before admired authority (representing strength) and loathes weakness—in Jews, women, homosexuals, or other outgroups. The second meaning of our title has to do with the major strengths and weaknesses that exist in the study of the authoritarian personality as a whole. Viewed in a more balanced way than some of its past critics have viewed it, *TAP* seems to us to be strikingly relevant in today's world. The theory may no longer stand on its own as a personality explanation of attraction to current fascist movements in Eastern Europe, the United States, or elsewhere, but taken in a more relativistic and sociological context, *TAP* can help us to understand many of these phenomena in the modern world and can help us to construct explanations of the attractions of fascism in yesteryear as well as in the 1990s.

In this chapter, we begin our survey of the current status of authoritarianism with some comments by the editors of this volume. The following section represents a kind of retrospective by Richard Christie, whose interest in *TAP* began when, as a graduate student at Berkeley, he became acquainted with two authors of the work, Else Frenkel-Brunswik and Nevitt Sanford. His interest continued over the decades, from *Studies in the Scope and Method of "The Authoritarian Personality,"* edited with Marie Jahoda in 1954, to his 1991 chapter on authoritarianism scales in *Measures of Social Psychological Attitudes*.

Origins and Reactions to *The Authoritarian Personality*

The Authoritarian Personality was a product of its times—of the historical circumstances and the state of development of social psychological research and theory. Professional reactions to *TAP* were likewise conditioned by these factors. In the following discussion, we will try to recapture this ambience. As a guide, we have prepared a chronology of the scientific research that led to *TAP* (summarized in Table 1.1).

Origins

The publication of a book like *The Authoritarian Personality*, representing the synthesis of psychoanalytic concepts with empirical methodologies from such disparate fields as survey research and projective tests of personality, would create interest and controversy at any time. Whatever its content, the territorial prerogatives of related disciplines would be infringed upon; reactions could be expected to vary from admiration for a new synthesis to outrage at poaching on established fields. Because the topic was authoritarianism—a subject fraught with ideological, practical, and theoretical implications—one could have confidently predicted the subsequent elaborate praise and bitter criticism.

The dominant theme of *TAP*—that anti-Semitism is primarily the result of the repression of one's aggressive impulses, their projection upon not only Jews but members of other minority groups as well, and the greater occurrence of this pattern among individuals on the right of the political spectrum—had obvious political implications. Liberals were happy to see their suspicions confirmed, and conservatives were outraged that their convictions should be viewed as based on irrationality. The authors of *TAP* identified the right-wing or authoritarian personality syndrome underlying anti-Semitism and other forms of prejudice as prefascistic. (The paper-and-pencil scale designed to capture this syndrome was dubbed the F—for fascist—scale.)

TABLE 1.1. Brief chronology of events leading to *The Authoritarian Personality* (*TAP*).

Date	Event	Source
1929–1931 (?)	Questionnaire study of 3,000 German workers sponsored by Horkheimer and the the Frankfurt Institut with Erich Fromm's participation	Jay (1973); see also ch. 2
1933	Frankfurt Institut's members flee from Germany following Hitler's assumption of power	Jay (1973)
	Reich and Fenichel flee Berlin for Scandanavia	Jacoby (1983)
	Massenpsychologie des Faschismus (a Freudian-Marxist interpretation)	Reich (1933)
1936	*Studien uber Authoritaet und Familie* (chapters based in part on interpretations of the 1929–31 studies)	Horkheimer, M. (ed.).
	The first known scale to measure Fascistic attitudes (based on a content analysis of Fascist publications)	Stagner (1936)
1939	*Moses and Monotheism*. Freud's interpretation of Jewishness and anti-Semitism	Freud (1939)
1940	The first known published article on anti-Semitism from a psychoanalyic perspective	Fenichel (1940)[1]
1941	Research proposal for study of anti-Semitism by Horkheimer and Institute for Social Research	Institute for Social Research (1941)
	Scale for measurement of unlabeled fascist attitudes	Edwards (1941)
	Escape from Freedom. Fromm's revisions of his earlier position	Fromm (1941)
1942	The most succint known statement of anti-Semitism from a psychoanalytic viewpoint	Brown (1942)
1943	"The Authoritarian Character Structure." A provocative quasi-Freudian interpretation of fascist personality	Maslow (1943)
1943	Nevitt Sanford receives a $500 grant to study anti-Semitism and recruits Daniel Levinson to develop the first known anti-Semitism scale	Levinson & Sanford (1944)
May 1944	The American Jewish Committee decides to finance a collaborative research project on anti-Semitism and personality involving the participation of Horkheimer & Adorno, with Sanford and his collaborators.	*TAP*, p. v.
June 1944	Else Frenkel-Brunswik and Sanford present a pioneering report on an empirical pilot study of the relationship between anti-Semitism and personality measures at a meeting of the San Francisco Psychoanalytic Society.	Frenkel-Brunswik & Sanford (1945)
Spring 1945	First version of the F Scale (Form 78) administered; it includes a 10-item version of the Anti-Semitism Scale	*TAP*, p. 242; *TAP*, p. 83
Summer 1945	Second version of the F Scale (Form 60) administered	*TAP*, p. 123
Fall 1945, Spring 1946	Third version of the F Scale (Forms 40/45) administered	*TAP*, p. 130
1947	First known *experimental* study relating Berkeley scales to behavior	Rokeach (1948)
1950	Publication of *TAP*	

1. Jacoby (1983, p. 113) reports that Fenichel's "Psychoanalysis of Anti-Semitism," originally delivered before a Prague Zionist group, was later published in several versions. Fenichel was in Prague from 1935 to 1938. It was considered politically dangerous to publish such an article at that time.

The hypothesized causal influence of early exposure to the authoritarian patriarchial family raised problems for liberal and conservative alike, although for different reasons. If authoritarianism had deep-seated roots within the personality that led to prejudice, how then was it possible to enact legislation or implement social policies based upon the liberals' assumption that people were rational and acted in their own and others' best interests? Conservatives were put on the defensive; their observations that anyone could look "objectively" at the social scene and observe that Negroes were inferior and that Jews had obnoxious characteristics were challenged by the assertion that they were projecting their own deep-seated hostility onto members of outgroups.

Crosscutting (and sometimes related to) these personal reactions to *TAP* was membership in or identification with a particular scholarly approach to the roots of anti-Semitism. There have been explanations of the problem from economics, history, political science, social psychology, sociology, theology, and myriad combinations of these and other disciplines. Any attempt, as in *TAP*, to focus primarily on the psychodynamics of the authoritarian meant that contributions from other fields must of necessity be neglected, ignored, or slighted, thus leaving the work open to being criticized as one-sided.

Fascism as a descriptive phrase became popular in the 1920s when Mussolini utilized the Roman symbols of fasces as emblematic of his dictatorial regime. When Hitler came to power in 1933, his dictatorship was given the same appellation, and the term came to be ascribed to any right-wing dictatorship, at least among Americans. The term was subsequently generalized even further to apply to any individual to the right of the political spectrum from the person making the judgment.

Sir Isaiah Berlin (1990), in a provocative essay, proposed that the basic fascist view of human nature and government can be traced back to Joseph de Maistre, a minor nobleman from Savoy who was appalled by the consequences of the French Revolution, which threatened the end of the royalist world in which all authority came from crown and church. Berlin notes, "Maistre may have spoken the language of the past, but the content of what he had to say presaged the future" (p. 96). Further, "He dwelt on the incurably bad and corrupt nature of man, and consequently the unavoidable need for authority, hierarchy, obedience and subjection" (p. 108). And, "He emerged a ferocious critic of every form of constitutionalism and liberalism, an ultramontane legitimist, a believer in the divinity of authority and power, and of course an unyielding adversary of all that the lumieres of the eighteenth century had stood for—rationalism, individualism, liberal compromise, and secular enlightenment" (p. 105).

The novelty of *TAP* was not that its implicit definition of authoritarianism was original; the themes struck by Maistre a century and a half before are still present in the F Scale items, although in more guarded language. Nor was the linkage between authoritarianism and ethnocentrism (*TAP*'s term for ethnic prejudice) original; as Samelson points out in chapter 2 of this volume, Wilhelm Reich had at least by 1932 linked the patriarchial authoritarian family system with Nazi race theory in German fascism. What was novel was that the authors of *TAP* attempted an empirical demonstration of a relationship between the authoritarian character and ethnocentrism.

The linkage was not made by members of the Frankfurt Institute in their pioneering questionnaire study of German workers in 1929–31. Their 271 questions, although covering almost everything except the proverbial kitchen sink, did not ask direct questions about Jews or other members of minority groups. A few questions did elicit comments that mentioned Jews (e.g., "Who, in your opinion, has the real power in the State today?"). Only 3% of the 584 protocols that constituted the final sample mentioned "Jews alone or with Freemasons and Jesuits" (Fromm, 1984, Table 3.1, p. 84). (Of the 3,000 protocols originally distributed to the workers, 1,100 were returned completed, and of those almost half disappeared during the Institute's escape from Germany.) It is of passing interest to note that of the 27 self-identified Nazis in the sample, 50% responded in that way.

Levinson and Sanford (1944) published the first known scale of anti-Semitism (Christie, 1991). It was constructed partly on the basis of psychoanalytic theories about the irrationality of prejudice; respondents were given, among other items, two subscales containing apparently contradictory assertions about Jews, one asserting that Jews try too hard to assimilate and the other that Jews tend to be socially too seclusive. The high correlation between the two subscales was interpreted as evidence of the irrationality of prejudice. As a follow-up, Frenkel-Brunswik and Sanford (1945) conducted a pilot study of 20 female college students. Sixteen had been selected on the basis of having obtained extreme scores on the anti-Semitism scale; the other four were selected from the middle of the range. The women were assessed on a variety of personality devices including clinical interviews, Thematic Apperception Tests, and Rorschachs. The conclusions drawn, not surprisingly, forecast those subsequently reached in *TAP*. This study was conducted after Else Frenkel-Brunswik joined Sanford and Levinson in the fall of 1943 but before Adorno became a member of the group (Levinson & Sanford, 1982). In a footnote to the article about their study, Frenkel-Brunswik and Sanford (1945) state that an initial presentation was given to the San Francisco Psychoanalytic Society in June 1944. By the time the article was prepared for publication a year later, the association with the Horkheimer group (the Institute of Social Research) had been made, and the study is referred to as part of a joint study with them (Frenkel-Brunswik & Sanford, 1945, p. 271, footnote 1).

How did the Berkeley investigators get the idea of linking anti-Semitism to authoritarianism? Sanford had taken his doctorate with

Henry Murray in 1934. At that time, the Harvard Psychological Clinic was very concerned with both Freudian and Jungian psychoanalytic theory and attempts to test their implications. Sanford reported never having heard of any speculation about the relationship between psychoanalysis and anti-Semitism at the clinic and couldn't remember when he first met or had the association—although he did say, "That's an interesting question" (personal communication, 1987). Frenkel-Brunswik had taken her doctorate in psychology with Karl and Charlotte Buhler at the University of Vienna, where the graduate students were forbidden to have anything to do with psychoanalysis (but of course many of them did). In any event, Frenkel-Brunswik was a lay analyst by the time she joined the study and, like Sanford, was psychoanalytically oriented as well as committed to research. Levinson was a 23-year-old graduate student at the time the study began and thus unlikely to have been the initial source of the linkage.

Present speculations are based on a comment by J.F. Brown (1942), who, in a chapter on the psychology of anti-Semitism, noted that "this process makes use of three psychological mechanisms which are by now well understood by psychologists. . . . Viewed psychologically, anti-Semitism represents a displacement of aggression with a projection of guilt and a rationalization of motives" (pp. 136–137). The question is, Who were the psychologists who shared this knowledge? Brown (1942) lists Freud, Karl Menninger, and Otto Fenichel among his references. Brown (1940) had been senior author on a book on abnormal psychology with Menninger, but neither in his discussion of defense mechanisms nor in the book he refers to by Menninger (*Man Against Himself*, 1938) is there mention of anti-Semitism. He makes reference to Fenichel's (1940) article on anti-Semitism, which contains a reference to projection but is not as explicit as the definition that Brown gives in his 1942 chapter.

Brown (1940) noted in a foreword to his book with Menninger that he had taken a didactic analysis with Otto Fenichel in 1938–39. Fenichel had been a close friend of Wilhelm Reich when they both were rising young stars of the Viennese psychoanalytic circle in the late 1920s, although this friendship was bitterly broken later. Also a friend of Anna Freud, Fenichel (1940) wrote an essay on her highly influential 1936 book, *The Ego and the Mechanisms of Defense* (A. Freud, 1936/1946; see Young-Bruhl, 1988, p. 217). Frenkel-Brunswik and Sanford's (1945) treatment of projection appears much closer to that of Anna Freud than to that of Reich (1933) or to the dialectical materialism of the Frankfurt Institute. Fenichel was in Los Angeles at the time *TAP* was in gestation, as was J.F. Brown, who is listed as being in charge of data collection for *TAP* in the Los Angeles area and "who also contributed important theoretical concepts" (Adorno et al., 1950, p. xiv).

Thus, a case might be made for Fenichel's being an indirect link between Reich and the Berkeley investigators. An equally tempting possibility is Robert Merton's (1973) intriguing chronicle of independent simultaneous discoveries in science, in which a number of investigators, unknown to one another, come up with similar inventions or discoveries. Given a common acceptance of psychoanalytic mechanisms, it seems quite plausible that once one thinks about prejudice in these terms, the light should flicker and an "aha" experience occur. For example, the English psychiatrist, H.V. Dicks (1950) reported a psychoanalytically oriented study of captured German prisoners during World War II. Out of 1,000 prisoners, he found about 11% to be fanatical hard-core Nazis; another 25% ("near Nazis") were Nazis with some reservations. The findings from Dicks's interviews revealed a clinical picture of fascists with surprising similarities to the authoritarian described in *TAP*. Part of the sample consisted of airmen shot down in the Battle of Britain, so at least those subjects would appear to be randomly selected. Dicks reported in a footnote that he was not familiar with Fromm's (1943) *Fear of Freedom*: "This book and Fromm's views were not at that period known to the author" (Dicks, p. 113). In another footnote (p. 153), appended at the last moment, Dicks noted he had just become aware of the data published in *TAP* in the same year and viewed the similarity of conclusions as unexpectedly confirming his own findings. Were Dicks's conclusions an example of an independent discovery of a phenomenon that logically followed from psychoanalytic assumptions applied to political ideology? Or was Stanley Milgram's (1967) "small world" principle—in which everyone is linked to everyone else through intermediaries—operating? Could someone with Samelson's historiographic skills (e.g., chap. 2, this volume) uncover an intellectual chain between Reich and Dicks?

The question that is even more puzzling, however, is that we are unaware of any published statement (although some undoubtedly exist) about the relationship between psychodynamics and anti-Semitism in the years between the irrepressible Reich's first publication of *Massenpsychologie des Faschismus* in 1933 and Fenichel's 1940 article. One possibility might be that since most of the psychoanalysts were Jewish, they did not want to roil troubled waters until after the war broke out. A more subversive hypothesis might be to psychoanalyze the psychoanalysts, as it were: Freud's own book on anti-Semitism, *Moses and Monotheism*, did not appear until 1939, the year of his death. Were all the "psychologists" to whom Brown (1942) alluded as knowing the relationship holding their pens until after the death of the father figure?

Reactions

To return to more mundane matters: The publication of *TAP* in 1950 came at a critical time in the development of the social sciences. Psychoanalysis was at the peak of its popularity in academia, so a large audience welcomed the news that psychoanalytic hypotheses could be supported by scientific study. On the other hand, the rapid development of new methodologies in survey research, attitude measurement, and experimental design after World War II increased sophistication, soon making some of the techniques employed by the authors of *TAP* appear crude and inadequate. Another aspect of the reaction to *TAP* was the shift from a preoccupation with the threat of fascism to a resurgence of the fears of communism, which had been put on the back burner during World War II. The cold war revived communism as the enemy and *TAP*, it was argued, was irrelevant because it dealt only with authoritarianism of the right and not the left.

The increase in methodological sophistication in social science, together with political concerns during the McCarthy period, had profound implications for research on authoritarianism. There had been little financial support for the social sciences before World War II, but during the war social scientists had been active, and often even productive, in a variety of military and civilian roles related to the war effort. Thus, postwar support for social science research became available through such organizations as the Office of Naval Research, the National Science Foundation, the National Institute of Mental Health, and others. Academic prestige and promotion became increasingly dependent upon an individual's ability to obtain such funding for his or her research. Older investigators returning from duty in the services and the hordes of eager new graduate students quickly learned to use the arts of grantsmanship as an aid to the conduct of research and to publish their findings to complete in the race to "publish or perish."

New funding possibilities had few beneficial consequences for the study of authoritarianism. The funding agencies were interested in sponsoring research that met high standards of scientific rigor, and it was easier to justify laboratory research in which situational parameters could be manipulated. There was also an interest in sponsoring research that had practical applications. If behavior results from deep-seated personality constellations (à la *TAP*) that are difficult to manipulate or change, why spend money on research without practical applications? Also, lurking in the background was the specter of repression. Aides for conservative congressmen routinely scanned titles of research proposals for politically suspect research. In some instances it was possible to circumvent this: One investigator interested in promoting racial tolerance by experimentally manipulating interracial contact under favorable circumstances disguised his study as a methodological study of attitude change; a study of Machiavellianism bore the innocuous, if ponderous, title, "Impersonal Interpersonal Orientations and Behavior." It was also possible to slip relevant material on authoritarianism into larger, more complex research projects that dealt with more fundable topics. But all in all it was difficult to obtain direct support for research on authoritarianism.

Major contributions to *TAP*, directly and indirectly, were made by Germans and Austrians. Prominent among the contributors were Frenkel-Brunswik, who had fled Austria in 1938; Reich, who had been born in Austria and had also lived and worked in Berlin; and Horkheimer, Adorno, and Fromm, who had come to the United States as refugees from Nazi Germany. Not surprisingly, the reaction to *TAP* in post–World War II Germany was muted. The following section, by Gerda Lederer, discusses the German-American axis.

Postwar Germany and *The Authoritarian Personality*

Fourteen years after World War II, Heintz (1957), in the first article published on the subject in Germany, wrote that it can be assumed that reflections about authoritarianism and its causes, and in particular the specific analysis of the authoritarian attitude, were so affect-laden for a long time after 1945 that there was reluctance to deal with the subject. Metz (1971) hypothesized that the German failure to produce a body of work comparable to *TAP* was due to both a reluctance to accept empirical methods of research and a widespread feeling that interviews and questionnaires constituted an invasion of privacy.

The Authoritarian Personality in Germany

As a point of fact, the original, unabridged text of *TAP* has not been translated into German to this day. The abridged German translation (Adorno, 1973) that was finally published in 1973, 23 years after *TAP* was published in the United States, contained only 6 of the original 23 chapters, namely, those authored, or at least co-authored, by Adorno. No summaries or transitional passages clarify the gaps resulting from this abridgment. Among the material that was not included are the 200 pages of analysis of clinical interviews by Else Frenkel-Brunswik and the 100 pages of analysis of projective test material by Aron and Levinson.

When German scholars and students refer to the work on the authoritarian personality, they generally mean this abbreviated version. Few have ever read—or even seen—the original text. On its back cover, the abbreviated German edition (Suhrkamp Taschenbuch 107) is presented as "the first edition of Theodor W. Adorno's famous work, originating in the USA, 'The Authoritarian Personality'" (my translation). In the preface, Ludwig von Friedeburg states that this volume is being published to grant the late Adorno's special wish that his contributions be made available to the German public (Adorno, 1973, p. ix). Though Sanford, Frenkel-Brunswik, and Levinson are mentioned as co-authors of chapters

1 and 2, one cannot escape the impression that their contributions were minor.[1]

When Nevitt Sanford (1973) tells his story of the origins of *TAP* in his contribution to *The Handbook of Political Psychology*, Adorno's role rates hardly more than a footnote (p. 141). Others connected with the project at the time also attribute to Adorno and Horkheimer less than a leading role. It is almost an irony of fate that the authors of *TAP* are always cited in the customary alphabetical order as "Adorno et al." Had Theodor Wiesengrund-Adorno not officially changed his name in 1943, the authors of *TAP* would have been cited as "Frenkel-Brunswik et al." and Adorno would have remained relatively unknown in the United States—as Sanford and Levinson are in Germany. In Germany, Adorno is well-known and highly regarded even today, but not for *TAP*. It is his theoretical work that is widely studied and cited.

These differences are important to the extent that they reflect differences in tradition and outlook. Thus, it was one of the tenets of Critical Theory, a major theoretical pursuit of Horkheimer and Adorno, that theory could not be proved or disproved by empirical verification and, though they affirmed the value of empirical work, they attributed to it a different and more limited role. When the Institute for Social Research returned to Germany in the early 1950s, its members brought with them the social science techniques acquired in the United States and tried to introduce these techniques in Germany. According to Jay (1973, p. 251) and Gmünder (1985, p. 93), Horkheimer and Adorno felt that they had succeeded too well. By the end of the 1950s, they feared "the reductionist abuse of an empirical methodology," and in consequence their work underwent a reversal of emphasis. These differences in position led in 1961 to the great German controversy between dialectical and empirical methodologists.

German Research

As indicated earlier, authoritarianism research was off to a slow start in West Germany (and, incidentally, unknown in East Germany, where authoritarianism was officially associated only with the capitalist camp). Beginning in the early 1970s, an increasing number of German scholars included this variable as a focus of their research, and the political developments in Eastern Europe in the late 1980s have helped authoritarianism research to gather momentum in Europe.

---

[1] As this book is going to press, a serious effort is underway to prepare a German translation of the classical original and unabridged version of *TAP* for publication in Germany, no doubt testimony to the renewed interest in the subject in a time of political upheaval and reappraisal.

One of the first books (von Freyhold, 1971) dealing with authoritarianism in Germany was published by the Institute for Social Research after its return to Frankfurt; it is called *Autoritarismus und politische Apatie* (*Authoritarianism and Political Apathy*). It describes the development of the A Scale, a German version of the F Scale developed by Adorno together with assistants and students at the University of Frankfurt in the winter semester of 1959–60. They attempted to incorporate improvements based on methodological criticisms leveled against *TAP* (Christie & Jahoda, 1954). Von Freyhold (1971) reported the results of surveys using the A Scale on a representative sample of the German population in 1961 and a representative sample of 16- to 24-year-olds in 1964. She found that authoritarian aggression and authoritarian submissiveness, more than any other dimension, are central to the authoritarian character structure and inseparably linked like opposite sides of the coin (pp. 26, 33). Her findings are discussed further in chapter 8 of this volume.

Criticism of the theoretical underpinnings of authoritarianism and dogmatism were presented by Roghmann (1966). In addition, Roghmann undertook secondary analyses of two data sets and a small original empirical study to test the usefulness of reversed items in reducing response set. Like von Freyhold (1971), Roghmann found reversed items to be less effective discriminators than the original formulations; but whereas Roghmann opted for the retention of some reversed items in the scales, von Freyhold returned to the use of positively worded formulations for all items.

A particularly valuable little book is Zangle's (1978) *Einfuhrung in die politische Sozialisationsforschung* (*Introduction to Research in Political Socialization*). Zangle presented a critical analysis of theories and research concerning the genesis of the political personality and managed to integrate and compare German and American findings. His bibliography lists 86 English-language and 49 German-language references.

The intercultural approach is more common in Germany than in the United States. Neither Robert Altemeyer (1981, 1988a) nor American proponents and critics of Adorno and the F Scale have reflected the important German works on authoritarianism by Roghmann and von Freyhold, or those by Jarisch (1975) and Oesterreich (1974), who examined authoritarianism with reference to social class and political attitudes. The loss resulting from the failure of American research to reflect the considerable body of work carried out and published only in German is unknown. Certainly the interaction resulting from Roghmann's (1966) criticism of the theory of authoritarianism and Zangle's (1978) theory of early childhood socialization, as well as Metz's (1971) findings relative to authoritarianism among teachers, would have been fruitful. Beyond the simple neglect of a large body of theory and data are questions concerning the social and political bases for this apparent lack of interest.

At the same time, comparative international studies involving authoritarianism among the pertinent variables have stimulated thought and research in the years since the publication of *TAP* (e.g., Barnes & Kaase, 1979; Devereux, Bronfenbrenner, & Suci, 1962; Hepburn, Napier, & Krieger, 1987; Lederer, 1983; Oppenheim, 1975; Torney, Oppenheim, & Farnen, 1975; Zinnecker, 1985). Cooperative efforts in the 1970s and 1980s have established multilingual item and data pools that promise to broaden the concept beyond national and language boundaries (e.g., *ZUMA-Nachrichten*; see also *ZUMA Handbuch Sozialwissenschaftlicher Skalen*, 1983).

If we devote some attention to the history of the Institute for Social Research here, it is not only because of the influence the philosophy of Adorno and Horkheimer may have had on *TAP* from the time that they joined the Berkeley group in 1944 until the publication of *TAP* in 1950, but because of the role the work of members of the Institute played as predecessors of *TAP* [e.g., *Studien über Autoritat und Familie* (*Studies Concerning Authority and the Family*) (Horkheimer, 1936)].

The Frankfurt School

Jay (1973, p. 3 ff.) traced the beginning of the Institute for Social Research (Institut für Sozialforschung) back to the unexpected success of the Bolshevik revolution, which shifted the socialist center of gravity eastward, away from the left-wing intellectuals of Germany. When the Soviet leadership saw its task more in survival than in the realization of socialist aims, some of these intellectuals felt a need for an independent reexamination of the foundations of Marxist theory, with the dual hope of explaining past errors and preparing for future action. From the beginning, intellectual independence was understood as a necessary prerequisite for the task of theoretical innovation and unrestrained social research.

With Horkheimer's ascension to the chair for social philosophy at the University of Frankfurt and the directorship of the Institute for Social Research in 1931, a new focus and a new set of associates came to the fore. The Institute was now committed to a dialectical rather than a mechanical understanding of Marxism, and among the collaborators of the Institute were not only Henryk Grossman and Fritz Pollock but also Erich Fromm, Leo Lowenthal, Herbert Marcuse, and eventually Walter Benjamin. Close to the Institute and an important contributor to the Institute's journal, *Zeitschrift für Sozialforschung*, from the outset was the music critic Theodor Wiesengrund-Adorno.

With the Nazi assumption of power in January 1933, the future of the avowedly Marxist Institute, staffed almost exclusively by males of Jewish descent, was coming to an end in Germany. In March 1933, the Institute was closed by the Nazis and the library, containing over 60,000 volumes, was seized. The members of the Institute escaped to various countries such as Switzerland, France, England, and the United States. The future of the Institute had been assured by the fortunate and prudent transfer of the Institute's endowment to Holland in 1931.

The search for a new home for the Institute came to its successful conclusion when Horkheimer made his first trip to the United States in May 1934 and gained an interview with Nicholas Murray Butler, president of Columbia University. When Butler offered the Institute affiliation with Columbia University and a home in one of its buildings, Horkheimer could hardly believe his good fortune. Jay (1973) writes: "And so the International Institute for Social Research, as revolutionary and Marxist as it had appeared in the twenties, came to settle in the center of the capitalist world, New York City" (p. 39).

As new social realities emerged, Horkeimer and Adorno, the theorists of the Institute now in America, were most anxious to advance their theoretical work. *Dialectic of Enlightenment* (Horkheimer & Adorno, 1947) was written under both their names during the war, while work on *TAP* was also in progress, and was finally published in 1947 in German by a Dutch publishing house. Horkheimer's *Eclipse of Reason* (1947), published the same year in English, received very little notice. Adorno's most personal and idiosyncratic book, *Minima Moralia*, was published in German in 1961 and never translated.

In fact, there was almost no interest or understanding, let alone sympathy, among American social scientists for the theoretical work of the Frankfurt School, and Horkheimer and Adorno shared a critical disdain for the sociology being practiced by their American colleagues and by the emigrant scholars not affiliated with the Institute and its way of thinking. To cope with this dissonance, they tried to introduce as many of their ideas into *TAP* as seemed possible and prudent, but Critical Theory was never even mentioned. At all times, they seemed to be operating on at least two levels, adapting their language to what seemed acceptable to the American environment.

Illustrations can be found in the transposition of their ideas, not only from German into English but also from the climate of the friends of the Institute to the climate of American social science, a "practice of self-censorship considered strategic at the Institute," as Wiggershaus (1986, p. 408) formulates in his extensive work about the Frankfurt School. In *Studien über Autoritat und Familie* (Horkheimer, 1936), the opposite of the "authoritarian character" was the "revolutionary." In the series of volumes edited by Horkheimer called *Studies in Prejudice* (including *TAP*) (see Adorno et al., 1968), it became the "democrat." This fit better with the values expressed by the American and other European authors connected with the *Studies in Prejudice* who were outsiders to the Institute's ways of thinking and whose ideologies were liberal and New Deal rather than Marxist or radical. In preparing a paper for the American

Jewish Committee, references to *Marxism, socialization*, and *means of production* were replaced by *socialism, nationalization*, and *industrial apparatus*, respectively.

The discrepancy between the ideas expressed by Horkheimer and Adorno within the Institute and outside it is evident also in the Institute's theory on anti-Semitism. In September 1939, in the last German-language issue of the Institute's journal, Horkheimer published an article he had written a year earlier entitled "Die Juden und Europa" ("The Jews and Europe"). Thus, this piece was written before but published after the Hitler-Stalin pact. It had been watered down and carefully edited by the inner circle of the Institute, and according to Wiggershaus (1986, p. 288), it represented the only comprehensive political statement by the Institute. Whereas the work seemed to support the communist theory concerning fascism, it was actually critical of the Soviet Union, of its centralism and its planned economy. Horkheimer viewed fascism as an authoritarian state that is not simply a consequence of capitalism but can be diagnosed wherever the minority hold power due to having possession of the material means of production. In addition, fascism was seen as having a good chance for long-term survival.

Accordingly, it was feared that a careful reading of this piece would offend nearly all of its readers: the orthodox Marxists, the democrats supporting capitalism, the antifascists, and the emigrants who feared that the prognosis of the long-term survival of fascism would encourage American isolationism. The article was one of the last predominantly Marxist pieces Horkheimer wrote, and it was excluded from the collection of Horkheimer's (1972b) work published in 1968. Readers who find this line of theory of interest should peruse Rubenstein's (1975) discussion of the fate of capitalists in Germany during and after the Holocaust, in his book *The Cunning of History*.

A section of *Dialectic of Enlightenment* (Horkheimer & Adorno, 1944) was entitled "Elements of Anti-Semitism." It included a discussion of the Jew in western civilization and, as with Marx, it held that Jewishness was not only a matter of religion but that it was also a socioeconomic category, although one that had been forced on the Jews in the past and perpetuated largely out of irrational needs. Because of the continuation of the contradictions of capitalism, the Jews, or a group like them, were a necessary outlet for repressed frustrations and aggressions. The Jews were hated, Adorno and Horkheimer (1944, p. 234) argued, because they were secretly envied. Having lost even their economic function as middlemen, they seemed to embody such enviable qualities as wealth without work, luck without power, a home without boundaries, a religion without a myth. Such ideas were rarely expressed by the authors in English, but were referred to in some lectures and in private correspondence; and there is evidence of the effect these theories must have had on their work. Wiggershaus (1986, p. 406) reports that Horkheimer said in the course of a lecture held at the Psychiatric Symposium on anti-Semitism in San Francisco that social anti-Semitism in the United States was far worse than in Europe and suggested that, regardless of the differences between the United States and Hitler's Third Reich, the differences in their psychological bases were dangerously small.

From 1943 to 1945, the Institute for Social Research was engaged in a large-scale study of anti-Semitism within American labor. Funded by the American Jewish Committee and the Jewish Labor Committee, the Institute accumulated vast amounts of data and prepared a four-volume, 1,400-page, predominantly qualitative report whose focus was "the nature, not the extent of anti-Semitism among the masses of American workers." The text was prepared by Gurland, Massing, Lowenthal, and Pollock. The quantitative analysis was performed by Paul Lazarsfeld and his Bureau of Applied Social Research and Herta Herzog. The results indicated that anti-Semitism was widespread among American workers and that the customary stereotypes abounded. Wiggershaus (1986) writes that the members of the Institute agreed not to publish the report because its final form emphasized the quantitative and neglected the qualitative parts of the study while failing adequately to integrate the two (p. 410 ff.). Jay (1973) writes "that the conclusions of the study were so damaging to American labor that the Institute, with its characteristic caution, was hesitant about broadcasting its findings" (p. 225).

Overview

Our historical discussion of *TAP* continues in chapter 2 of this volume, in which Franz Samelson traces *TAP*'s roots to the efforts of Wilhelm Reich and Erich Fromm to explain the mass appeal of fascism in the 1930s. He discusses the chilling effect of anticommunism on their writing, and on the reception of *TAP*. Technical criticisms of *TAP* also diminished the book's impact. Samelson's conclusions are buttressed by careful historical scholarship.

Much of the research that followed publication of *TAP* was, as Samelson recounts, concerned with measurement issues. In many studies, the personality type distinguished by high scores on the F Scale does behave differently from those low on the scale. However, questions continually are raised as to what this "type" denotes. Is the "authoritarian" simply a person of poor education who easily finds agreement with F-Scale items?

Meloen's (chapter 3, this volume) count of studies of "authoritarianism" since 1950 numbers 2,341. Many of the empirical studies have yielded trivial, even if statistically significant, results. In-depth theoretical discussion of the underlying issues has been sparse. Because of the failure of inductive methods to follow up decisively on the initial insights of *TAP*, authoritarianism research declined in the 1960s and languished for many years. There have been advances, however, both theoretical and empirical. Chapter 3 is devoted to Meloen's diligent survey of empirical studies to evaluate the validity of the F Scale as a measure of fascism-proneness.

In chapter 4 of this volume, Richard Christie addresses a question that has been raised about the experimental validity of research on authoritarianism. He takes the position that much of the disillusionment with the F Scale as a predictor of experimental behavior was based on the optimistic assumption by the early experimenters that the authoritarian syndrome would manifest itself indiscriminantly in almost any situation. Many of these early experiments were also characterized by the methodological naïveté characteristic of the period and inadequate reporting of procedures. It is argued that the person–situation interaction is crucial—Under what conditions should authoritarian persons behave rigidly or punitively?—and that a reanalysis of the material suggests the picture was not as bleak as portrayed.

Christie's examination of experimental studies on punitiveness as reflected in assigning punishment to crimes (chapter 5, this volume) indicates that authoritarianism is strongly related to authoritarian aggression. The high F-Scale scorer's aggressiveness is not random, however; the differences between high and low scorers are most marked when low-status individuals commit serious crimes in which there are mitigating circumstances. Again, the importance of interactions is stressed.

There has been empirical support for the hypothesis that punitive methods of child training produce fascism-prone individuals. Christie and Cook (1958) summarized the results of their review of the early literature as follows: "The bulk of the evidence supports the hypothesized relationship between strict practices in childrearing and intolerant beliefs" (p. 180). They observed further that the Freudian scenario that purports to account for these relationships has not been tested: "The actual specification of what parent behaviors or combinations of them led to a higher probability of authoritarianism in children is little advanced beyond the factors noted in *The Authoritarian Personality*" (p. 180).

Christel Hopf, in chapter 6 of this volume, takes this discussion of the familial origins of authoritarian character further. She focuses on the clinical interviews reported in *TAP*, and those by Ackerman and Jahoda (1950), which have received little examination by critics. Referring to advances in psychoanalytic theory since *TAP*, Hopf suggests that some of the new approaches such as object relations and attachment may be useful in the understanding of the genesis of authoritarianism.

Next to the response-style controversy over the wording of the F Scale, the greatest heat has been generated over the question of left- versus right-wing authoritarianism. *TAP* differentiated several varieties of high scorer, including the "pseudoconservative." Low scorers included the genuine liberal and some less healthy alternatives (Sanford, 1973).

Despite this differentiation, *TAP* was attacked for its stress on authoritarianism's association with conservative political belief. Prominent among the critics were Edward Shils (1954) and Hans Eysenck (1954). These critics seemed to have an axe to grind, but the liberal social psychologist Milton Rokeach (1960) lent weight to their concerns in his search for "general authoritarianism," an authoritarianism that had no political attachments. Stone (1980) weighed these criticisms, concluding that authoritarianism is by nature much more closely affiliated with right- than with left-wing views. In chapter 7 of this volume, Stone is joined by the philosopher of social science Laurence Smith in examining these issues.

Although the sheer volume of literature prevents this volume from reviewing the research that has been amassed over the years, in chapter 8 we will focus on some significant contributions made during the decade of the 1980s. In particular, we will review the work of Bob Altemeyer, whose work is the focus of much current discussion and debate.

Because of the interest in the implications of *TAP* for Holocaust studies, the research on authoritarian attitudes of German and American adolescents by Gerda Lederer (1981, 1982) was greeted with enthusiasm. The 1945 data that she reported confirmed the hypothesis of high authoritarianism of German adolescents, as compared with U.S. adolescents. Trends since that time also tended to support German efforts to teach children to defy authority. The question is left open whether the effects Lederer has documented represent personality change or simply attitude change. Her discussion of her findings, together with newer results, constitute chapter 9.

The Authoritarian Personality had little impact on social science in the Soviet Union. *Authoritarianism* was used as a disparaging term for the attitudes of the decadent members of Western bourgeois societies (Ageyev, 1990). The term did not apply in the USSR where, allegedly, truly novel human beings were being created by communist society. Discussions of the authoritarian personality were not to be found in the Soviet literature, although in recent years the concept of authoritarian leadership styles has had some currency. With the beginning of *perestroika* about 1985, however, social science has been opening to the West. An exciting recent collaboration, between a professor from Western Kentucky University and two professors from Moscow State University, is reported in chapter 10: McFarland, Ageyev, and Abalakina translated Altemeyer's (1981) RWA scale into Russian and administered it to samples in Moscow and Tallin, Estonia. The mean RWA scores for these samples were significantly lower than those in American samples. Thus, there is some evidence that authoritarianism is lower in these cities in the former Soviet Union than in the United States or Canada. Overall, it seems, authoritarian individuals support the status quo, existing institutions, and the strong over the weak.

It is, at the very least, prudent to conclude that the initial wave of enthusiasm for *TAP* withered in the two decades after its publication. As chapters 3 to 7 of this volume indicate, the reasons for this neglect may be questionable; despite the general negativism, the concept survived. As Roger Brown (1965) observed in his beautifully written chapter on the authoritarian personality,

Do you know him—the Authoritarian, the Antidemocrat, the Pre-Fascist? It seems to me that I do. Item after item in the F Scale is something I have heard or very like something I have heard. Furthermore the people I know who have made one of these statements have usually gone on to make others of them. (p. 489)

2
The Authoritarian Character from Berlin to Berkeley and Beyond: The Odyssey of a Problem

FRANZ SAMELSON

Enemies of Freedom, Bob Altemeyer's (1988a) latest entry in the attempts to clarify the issue of authoritarianism, recently described 15 years of empirical research by a lonely but tenacious investigator. According to his summary, the effort "confirms much that was first published in 1950. . . . [Especially] Nevitt Sanford's theory has been stunningly supported . . . [: The] three traits . . . conventionalism, authoritarian submission, and authoritarian aggression . . . turn out to be [the authoritarian personality's] most enduring and distinctive characteristics" (p. 330).

Return to the Beginnings

Altemeyer's (1988a) reference to 1950 implies, of course, the book *The Authoritarian Personality* (*TAP*) by the "Berkeley group": Theodor Adorno, Else Frenkel-Brunswik, Daniel Levinson, and Nevitt Sanford. Over 5 years in the making, the 1,000-page volume had attempted to describe, according to Max Horkheimer's preface (p. ix), a new "anthropological" species: the potential fascist who, in contrast to the old-style bigot, combined the skills of industrial man with irrational or antirational beliefs. Implicit in the argument, and heightening its relevance, had been the question of whether "it could happen here, too." At the time of its publication, the work was considered a milestone in the history of American social psychology. It also may have marked a turning point.

Reactions to the book were quick, strong, and numerous. Soon they included a veritable flood of empirical follow-up studies lasting through the 1960s (Christie & Jahoda, 1954; Kirscht & Dillehay, 1967). But by the early 1970s the stream had become a trickle. More recently, social psychology texts seem to either ignore *TAP* altogether (e.g., Tedeschi, Lindskold, & Rosenfeld, 1985) or mention it only in passing (e.g., Brehm & Kassin, 1990; cf. also Seeman, 1983, p. 172; Smith, 1983, p. 173), in spite of occasional attempts at revival (Altemeyer, 1981; Gieser, 1980;

22

FIGURE 2.1. Seid untertan der Obrigkeit. (Be submissive to the authorities.) ©
1992 the estate of George Grosz/VAGA, NY.

Meloen, 1983). It may have been an instant "classic of social science" in
1950, as Jay (1973, p. 224) described it. But soon thereafter, the interests
of American social psychologists had turned elsewhere. Altemeyer's
struggle to pin down the empirical substrate of authoritarianism in the
Canadian outback was a lonely battle, indeed, as his plaintive acknowledgments (1988a, pp. xxiii–xxvii) suggest.

However, before exploring in greater detail the Berkeley volume's
sudden rise to prominence and subsequent decline to oblivion, we need to
look first in the opposite direction: to its prehistory. This earlier phase,
which had given rise to the problem in the first place, was totally ignored
in Altemeyer's (1988a) book. The reason for this omission was apparently
not a complete lack of awareness (cf. Altemeyer, 1981, p. 13), but rather
the—for him—obvious irrelevance of this "prescientific" phase to his
self-appointed task: the presentation of hard empirical data for the
purpose of separating scientific wheat from speculative chaff. Yet the
narrow, ahistorical focus and selective memory of recent works may be
the real culprits in the fate of *TAP* and of "empirical" social psychology
more generally. (For an example of the opposite, conceptual approach by
a European scholar, see Kramer, 1990.) Let us look back, then, to the
beginnings of the idea in Weimar Germany of the late 1920s.

Collaborating, in 1928, with the revolutionary director Erwin Piscator
in the production of the antimilitarist play *The Good Soldier Schwejk*
in a Berlin theater, the graphic artist George Grosz created a series of
sketches to serve as stage backdrops. One of these, entitled *Seid untertan
der Obrigkeit (Be Submissive to the Authorities)* is reproduced in Figure
2.1.

Other Grosz drawings presented, in fierce expressiveness, images of authoritarian aggression and of conventionalism, in addition to this biting depiction of authoritarian submission. They show us the artist's awareness of these three core "traits" some 60 years before empirical research "stunningly confirmed" their existence, or even decades before the Berkeley group had begun to theorize about them. It is not that Grosz was the inventor of authoritarian theory, or even of the term *authoritarian*, which had existed in English and French for half a century (*Oxford English Dictionary*, 2nd ed.; *Le Grand Robert*, 2nd ed.) but apparently did not enter German until this time. Rather, the phenomena he portrayed in his acerbic drawings were visible, and becoming more threateningly visible, to keen observers of the contemporary scene. One of them, the psychoanalyst and political activist Wilhelm Reich, proceeded to translate them into more abstract concepts over the next few years, in order to explain if not to prevent the approaching political catastrophe.

In the 1920s, the young Reich had been one of the rising stars of Freud's psychoanalytic circle in Vienna. Taking libido theory a step or two beyond Freud while rejecting, especially in his formulation of the masochistic character, Freud's new "death instinct" theory, the impetuous Reich got himself into difficulties with the psychoanalytic establishment. It did not help matters that by 1927 he had also become a Marxian and a political activist. A member of the Social Democratic Party and affiliated with a medical group of the Austrian Communists, Reich spearheaded efforts to provide health care as well as political and sexual enlightenment to the workers of Vienna and their children. Struggling to unite these two revolutionary doctrines, Reich (1929) became one of the pioneers in what soon was to turn into a cottage industry in the United States: attempts to integrate psychoanalysis and Marxian theory.

Patriarchy, Sexual Repression, and the Roots of Fascism

The core problem for leftist politicians and intellectuals was the failure of the proletarian revolution to establish socialism in the industrial countries. Why had the working class not risen to its historic role when the appropriate "objective conditions" had been created after the Great War? This failure of class consciousness, and with it the apparent failure or at least insufficiency of Marx's theory, was the backdrop for several of Reich's writings between 1929 and 1934. In the beginning, he hardly mentioned the threat of fascism; in its stead, he developed psychological ideas intended to explain the cleavage between the economic situation and the workers' false consciousness that prevented the overthrow of capitalism. Although Reich conceded that the state's welfare measures might have bought off part of the population, he nonetheless insisted that the major contributor to political passivity was *sexual repression by society*—repression that instilled in the child a deep anxiety, insecurity, and the need to internalize society's prescriptions. In the course of his arguments, he began to develop several additional themes: a conceptual shift from capitalism to patriarchy as the essential structural factor; the crucial role of the family as the "factory of bourgeois ideologies" (Reich, 1930, p. 50; cf. Fenichel, 1931, p. 405); an awareness of women and their doubly oppressed situation; and some marginal attention to the lower middle class as the politically most problematic sector of society. Although Reich made important contributions to psychoanalytic characterology, and although he had begun to talk about *autoritäre Unterjochung* (Reich, 1930, p. 21), he apparently did not combine the two into the term *autoritäre Character*. In its place he used the image of the *Feldwebelnatur* (top sergeant nature), which *duckt sich nach oben . . . und herrscht nach unten* (cringes upward and dominates downward) (Reich, 1930, p. 51). And finally, lecturing before the Berlin Psychoanalytic Society on "mass psychology and economic crisis" in June 1932 (*Korrespondenzblatt*, 1932, pp. 559–560), he discussed the psychology of the Nazi movement and its race theory, shouting, according to Karen Horney's recollections of the meeting, that German fascism was the inevitable outcome of the patriarchal authoritarian family system (Rubins, 1978, p. 196). Adding all these ideas together, it appears that by this time Reich had assembled most of the elements that eventually made up the theory of the authoritarian character, together with some idiosyncratic notions (and, as yet, without any systematic empirical data).

Having joined the KPD (German Communist Party) after his move to Berlin in 1930, Reich soon found himself in trouble with the communists as well as with the psychoanalysts over his lack of respect for orthodoxy. What was infinitely worse, his prediction came true with Hitler's rise to power in January 1933. Escaping first to Vienna, he began the hard life of an émigré, moving from country to country until finally settling in the United States. He also finished, in the months after the *Machtergreifung*, his *Massenpsychologie des Faschismus*, elaborating his earlier ideas into a (nontechnical) account of the appeals of National Socialism (Reich, 1933). Rejecting shallow explanations that invoked either the magic of Hitler's personality or a simple "befogging" of the masses by propaganda, Reich found the deeper roots of the catastrophe in the character structure of lower-middle-class and "integrated" working-class Germans. In patriarchal society, the family became the place where the state's structure and ideology were molded. By embedding sexual inhibition and fear in the child, the family produced identification with the authoritarian imperialism of the state. Although one might expect the largest amount of rebellion in the most oppressed group, working-class women, in fact sexual repression on top of economic exploitation produced conservatism, fear of freedom, and not only passive submission but also active support for the authoritarian order. The repressed sexuality turned into powerful yearnings after vague, mystical ideals of nation, duty, honor, religion, and motherhood—symbols the Nazi propaganda exploited to the fullest. Race theory was the theoretical axis, militarism and antibolshevism were allied themes, sadistic aggression their derivative. *Sexual politics*—a term apparently coined by Reich—was for him the key to understanding as well as combating fascism.

The impact of Reich's (1933) book is difficult to determine, but it appears to have been minimal. Published on the run and, together with Reich's other works, promptly banned in Germany, *The Mass Psychology of Fascism* did not appear in English until 1946. By that time, Reich had revised it (as well as other writings) extensively, using the term *authoritarian* much more frequently than in the original and totally elimating the originally Marxist language (Reich, 1970, p. xxiii ff.; cf. Ginneken, 1984)—drastic changes that raise problems, not only for the unwary, in the analysis of his early writings. The 1946 English edition produced few comments; by then, Nazism had been defeated and Reich's recent preoccupation with the "orgone" theory had pushed his reputation beyond the pale. But a decade earlier, the original 1933 *Massenpsychologie des Faschismus* had been reviewed briefly by Karl Landauer (1934), Erich Fromm's (training) analyst as well as Max Horkheimer's, in the *Zeitschrift für Sozialforschung*, the house organ of the Institut für Sozialforschung (Institute for Social Research) at the University of Frankfurt. Summarizing Reich's arguments, Landauer had commented approvingly on the broad and acute vision of this "loner" and "fighter," though he had ended with an objection to Reich's overemphasis on genital sexuality. A similar criticism of Reich's theories appeared 2 years later in Erich Fromm's (1936) social psychological essay in the Institut's volume entitled *Studien über Autorität und Familie* (Horkheimer, 1936), the next stage in the development of the idea.

Ambivalence and Authoritarian Character at the Frankfurt Institute

Like Reich, Erich Fromm was a young Freudian analyst. But like his friend Leo Lowenthal and unlike Reich, Fromm had been concerned with religious issues, at the Jewish *Lehrhaus* in Frankfurt, before turning to Marx. In February of 1929, Fromm was one of the speakers at the opening ceremony of the new Frankfurt Psychoanalytic Institute, directed by Karl Landauer and Heinrich Meng and given some space in the building of the *Institut für Sozialforschung*. Fromm's address dealt with the mutual contributions of psychoanalysis and sociology; it showed as yet little Marxian influence beyond a final quote, which in fact came from

Marx but was attributed only to a "most brilliant sociologist" (Fromm, 1929).

From here on, the story becomes a bit murky due to the gaps in surviving contemporary records, complicated by discrepancies among various retrospective comments by Fromm, other participants, and the historical–biographical summaries provided by Fromm's at times hero-worshipping editors, translators, and commentators. At issue are the trajectory of Fromm's developing ideas in relation to Reich's work, on the one hand, and his role in the empirical survey carried out by the Institute, on the other. Given the existence of different versions, it regrettably becomes necessary to deal with some confusing and tedious details.

Although Fromm was supposedly a lecturer at the new Frankfurt Psychoanalytic Institute, his name did not appear in its course offerings prior to the winter of 1930, when he lectured on the *Psychology of the Criminal* (Psychoanalytische Kurse, 1930, pp. 302, 605). Actually, he moved to Berlin in 1929, in order to continue his own training at the Berlin Psychoanalytic Institute (Hausdorff, 1972, p. 20; Mitgliederverzeichnis, 1930, p. 553). Sometime in 1930, Fromm was invited to become a member of the *Institut für Sozialforschung* in Frankfurt. Presumably he was to contribute expertise in analytic social psychology to what was called informally the Café Marx (Lowenthal, 1980, p. 47), about to embark on the creation of its historical-materialist *Gesellschaftstheorie*. Two years later, Fromm (1932a, 1932b) published two important articles on the tasks of social psychology in the first volume of the Institute's *Zeitschrift für Sozialforschung*. Like Reich's essays, Fromm's tried to integrate Freudian theory and Marxist ideas. A fairly orthodox exposition of Freud's libido theory was linked to Marxist concepts by the claim that socioeconomic structure shaped the *Triebstruktur* (drive structure) of society's constituent groups. The arguments were programmatic and mostly abstract, with no mention of an "authoritarian character" and with no references to the threat of fascism, as late as in the fall of 1932—years after the Institut allegedly had made preparations for its escape to Geneva.[1] Instead, the specific issue discussed in the second article (1932b) dealt with the character and "spirit" of capitalism and the bourgeoisie, exemplified by quotes from none other than Benjamin Franklin. Only in two final footnotes did Fromm mention fascism and the "anal" characteristics of the petit bourgeois, who displayed "reverence for paternal authority and longing for discipline in a strange union with rebellion" (Fromm, 1932b, p. 275, my translation). Here we have the

---

[1] It is not clear whether Fromm failed to see the coming storm, or whether he did not want to mix science with (dangerous) politics in public.

casual introduction of a new formulation—ambivalence producing an "object split" (ibid.)—that was to become, in Berkeley, the core idea of authoritarian personality dynamics (Frenkel-Brunswik & Sanford, 1945, p. 282). Except for this afterthought, Fromm's emphasis on the mediating role of the family as the psychological agent of an authoritarian society in the formation of character, and his references to patriarchy, sex morality, and the role of women, were similar to Reich's. Also similar to Reich is the absence of any references to empirical data or even to the need for such data.

Though Fromm acknowledged no influence, he mentioned approvingly some of Reich's contributions while criticizing others in his part of a few footnote exchanges between the two (Fromm, 1932a, pp. 32, 35; 1932b, p. 266). It is difficult to tell from these and other available sources how much Fromm took from Reich (and perhaps vice versa) or how much their ideas developed independently. Reich appears to have been a step or two ahead chronologically. In his own recollections, Reich (1976) claimed to have discussed his thoughts on masochism, sexual politics, and related topics after his arrival in Berlin, late in 1930, within a circle of friends. This group included Otto Fenichel and Erich Fromm (Reich, 1976, p. 136; cf. I.O. Reich, 1969, p. 43), who was just then publishing his first attempt to combine Freud and Marx in his analysis of the historical changes in the "Dogma of Christ" (Fromm, 1930). Contact between the two is corroborated by the published minutes of the Berlin Psychoanalytic Society, which listed Fromm's and Reich's presence at several meetings in 1931. One of these items noted Fromm's participation in the discussion of Reich's March 1931 lecture, entitled "Der Einbruch der Sexualmoral" (Korrespondenzblatt, 1931, pp. 292–293).

Five years later, the Frankfurter Institut had become the International Institute of Social Research, which had been exiled, after Hitler's victory, first to Geneva and then, in 1934, to New York, with a colony in California. The group put together an avowedly fragmentary progress report on its investigation of modern society in a book entitled Studien über Autorität und Familie (Horkheimer, 1936). At least in part intended to "legitimize [their] scholarly endeavors" in the new country (Lowenthal, 1989, p. 155), the hefty volume never appeared in English translation and was not much of a success (Lowenthal, 1980, p. 98). Horkheimer contributed the lead theoretical–historical essay, which dealt with freedom, reason, authority, and the family's role in modern society. Having defined autoritär as autoritätsbejahend (authority-affirming) in the foreword (1936, p. ix), Horkheimer discussed the "authoritarian character"—here making its first appearance in print—primarily as a submissive, masochistic type. He also pointed out that the family need not always serve as indoctrinating agent for state authority, but on the contrary might function as the latter's antagonist—an idea he attributed to Hegel, whose name he invoked much more often than Marx's. Having found refuge in capitalist America, the Institute of Social Research was moving away from historical materialism and toward Critical Theory.

Fromm's (1936) chapter in *Studien über Autorität und Familie* expanded his earlier ideas into a long social psychological treatise analyzing "the psychological impulses which cause people to submit to authority" (p. 908). An as yet quite orthodox outline of Freud's system led into a description of the anal character, which in authoritarian society metamorphosed into the *autoritär–masochistische* character, discussed with passing references to Reich's, and more detailed exposition of Karen Horney's, formulations of masochism. Only in two brief passages did Fromm return to the notion of ambivalence (introduced briefly in his 1932 article), mainly in the context of "rebellion" as a pattern of overthrowing one particular authority while longing for another one. Fromm contrasted this rebellion to genuine revolution, which involved abandoning the need for a strong authority altogether. This passing comment on revolution constituted the—surprisingly abstract and cursory—presentation of what supposedly had been one of the two main character types (revolutionary and authoritarian) underlying the empirical survey reported in the second part of the book. But then, Fromm's (1936) essay did not even so much as mention this survey which, according to Bonss's (1983) later claim, Fromm had designed and directed himself 6 years earlier. Also absent were any references to anti-Semitism or to the generalized prejudice so central to the later Berkeley work. Finally, there was no citation of Reich's *Massenpsychologie des Faschismus*, though it is hard to imagine that Fromm, who had reviewed approvingly Reich's earlier *Der Einbruch der Sexualmoral* (Fromm, 1933), would not have seen at least Landauer's (1934) review of Reich's book in the *Zeitschrift für Sozialforschung*.

From Survey Data to *Escape from Freedom*

The second, empirical part of *Studien über Autorität und Familie* (Horkheimer, 1936) reported on the several surveys carried out by the Institute of Social Research or its collaborators. A brief introduction by Fromm summarized these surveys and commented on their novel methods of interpreting the responses obtained. The next section presented a compact summary of what is considered the Institute's first major empirical study: an exploratory questionnaire survey of German *qualifizierte Arbeiter und Angestellte* (skilled workers and employees, which included civil service officials). The preliminary report listed some 270 factual, behavioral, and attitudinal-projective questions asked in order to ascertain the respondents' situation as well as mentality and to permit inferences about their "psychic structure." But no summary of the data was given. The only presentation of results was in the form of the actual answers from 15 questionnaires, selected to represent three types:

the *revolutionary*, the *authoritarian*, and an in-between character labeled the *ambivalent* (obviously used in a different sense than in Fromm's essays), each diagnosed through an intuitive interpretation of the answer patterns. (Such intuition was not really needed, because Question IV, 36, on party membership, already separated respondents into three groups: Communists, Deutsch-Nationale (not Nazis) or apoliticals, and Social Democrats.)

Although Fromm was named, in 1936, as the editor of the book's empirical Part 2 and author of its introduction, it is not at all clear who had constructed the original questionnaire or what the initial objectives of the survey had been. No contemporary documents seem to exist, and later accounts are confusing, to say the least. According to the best, though not all sources, the survey was designed and begun during the Grünberg era of the Institute, most likely in 1929, as shown by a refer-ence to it in Felix Weil's long 1929 memorandum concerning a possible successor for retiring director Grünberg (Migdal, 1981, p. 111; cf. Kluke, 1972, p. 503, and Fromm, 1983, pp. 7, 60). Yet Fromm did not formally become a member of the *Institut für Sozialforschung* until Horkheimer had taken over in the summer of 1930 (Fromm, 1980, p. xix). Even afterward Fromm is said to have worked at the Institut only rarely (Bonss, 1983, p. 41, footnote 42; Lowenthal, 1980, p. 51), presumably commuting by overnight train from Berlin, where he had moved to from Heidelberg in 1929 (see above, p. 27). In the absence of any contem-porary clues, it appears highly unlikely, though not totally impossible,[2] that Fromm had contributed to the survey design in 1929. Unfortunately, the earliest *published* reference to empirical surveys by the Institute was a very general one, listing such methods among others to be used in the Institute's work, without mentioning any specific study or naming its personnel. The comment appeared in the final part of Horkheimer's (1972a) January 1931 Inaugural Lecture at the Institut, where he de-scribed as the Institut's major theoretical focus the relation between economic conditions, cultural products, and changes in the "psychic structure" of social groups; the skilled workers and employees in Germany were selected as the first target of this effort (p. 43).

The first time Fromm was linked explicitly to the survey, by himself or others, did not occur until 1936, in *Studien über Autorität und Familie*. Even then it was Hilde Weiss, not Fromm, who was named as the person responsible for conducting the survey and its initial analysis (Horkheimer, 1936, p. 239, footnote 1, and p. 240), and the nature of Fromm's in-volvement was not spelled out. In his 1941 book, Fromm made no

---

[2] Fromm had been acquainted with Lowenthal for some years and had given at least one lecture at the Frankfurt Psychoanalytic Institute, housed in the building of the Institut fur Sozialforschung (Schivelbusch, 1983).

mention of Weiss[3] and named Hartoch, Herzog, and Schachtel as his collaborators in the 1929–30 study (p. 212, footnote 2). Thirty years later, Fromm wrote that the study was begun in 1931 and "planned and directed by Fromm in collaboration with Ernest Schachtel, Anna Hartoch, and the counsel of Paul Lazarsfeld," with whom he had indeed collaborated, but in New York, not earlier in Frankfurt. He also claimed that "the immediate reason for the study was the interest in knowing how many of the German workers and employees were reliable fighters against Nazism" (Fromm & Maccoby, 1970, p. 24). If this had indeed been the original reason for the survey, it had long remained a well-kept secret (cf. Fromm, 1963, pp. 147–148).

Trying to piece all of this together, I have come to believe that the 1936 analysis of the survey responses in terms of authoritarianism, together with later retrospective reference to its focus on anti-Nazi resistance, was an afterthought rather than the initial objective of the *enquete*. A similar conclusion was reached independently by H. Kramer, working on the original questionnaires at the reestablished *Institut für Sozialforschung* in Frankfurt (personal communication, 27 August, 1991). After all, the survey questions had been constructed years before anyone in the Institut had begun to formulate, at least in print, the notion of such a character (or of a Nazi takeover). This guess, that the interpretation of the responses in terms of authoritarian and revolutionary character types had been superimposed on the data later, is given indirect contemporary support by Fromm's 1932 articles on the problems for a new *Sozialpsychologie*. They show Fromm still talking about either libidinal structure or psychosexual character types, and any mention of empirical research is conspicuously absent. This hypothesis on origins is made more plausible by the extraordinarily diffuse contents of the questionnaire aimed largely at descriptive information. Less than 15% of the questions asked were eventually judged relevant to the alleged theoretical focus of the study by its analysts, and this number was reduced to fewer than 10 questions in the final determination of character syndromes (Fromm, 1983, pp. 41–2, footnote 49, and pp. 314–315). Not surprisingly, the results were judged to be "meagre" (Speier, 1936), if perhaps not any more so than other first attempts at empirical research.

In any case, a more complete report of the results, promised for a future issue of the *Zeitschrift für Sozialforschung*, was delayed—by 45 years, as it turned out. Different reasons for the initial delay have been cited by Jay (1973, p. 117) and Bonss (1983, p. 42); one was the loss of too many of the original questionnaires in the escape from Europe, another the negative political connotations of the findings showing the

---

[3] I have so far been unable to trace Weiss beyond 1936 in Paris (Rigaudias-Weiss, 1936) and would be grateful for any relevant information on her fate.

weakness of socialist resistance to Hitler. A third reason cited a quarrel between Horkheimer and Fromm about the scientific value of the study, a quarrel that became one of the issues leading to the latter's departure from the Institute in 1939. Indeed, Fromm left the Institute in what appears to have been an atmosphere of ill feeling, as indicated by some fairly hostile comments in a letter from Lowenthal to Horkheimer in 1941 (Lowenthal, 1989, p. 186). Closed collections may hold other letters containing more details about the survey's fate. But as long as such letters are inaccessible, we have to work with the retrospective accounts, though judiciously interpreted rather than taken at face value.

On that basis, I find it plausible that the study's scientific weaknesses were sufficient reason for the failure to publish it at a time when the American social science community was getting progressively more rigid about methodological purity. The justification for the posthumous publication of Fromm's old unfinished manuscript (in Bonss's 1980 translation, and its 1984 retranslation back into English—which did not improve matters) as an important scientific contribution is not supported by critical reading of the text and contains some elements of an "origin myth" creation (Samelson, 1974). For instance, what in 1936 had been called the *Mittelstandsenquete* by Horkheimer (p. x) and Fromm (p. 235) was introduced in Bonss's foreword (Fromm, 1983, p. 22) as a "step in the rediscovery of the *Proletariat*," even though less than 10% of the subjects had been unskilled workers (Table 2.3, p. 83). The book became *The Working Class in Weimar Germany* in the title of the 1984 retranslation, and—to move from the sublime to the comic—eventually wound up being cited as "*Revolt* [italics added] of the . . . Workers" (instead of *survey* as the proper translation of *Erhebung*) in the English version of a book on Critical Theory (Dubiel, 1985, p. 11, all emphasis added). More seriously, the crucial Tables 4.14 and 4.15 (Fromm, 1983, pp. 246 and 251) contain some sizable errors and/or unexplained omissions—in plain language, the numbers and percentages simply don't add up. Nor do they match the numbers in the text (p. 245) and in other tables, such as Table 4.10 and Table 4.13. Yet these and other fairly obvious errors, which make it impossible to evaluate Fromm's conclusions, were retained in the translation. Had nobody given the book a close reading in the intervening 5 years?

At issue here are neither trivial slips in proofreading nor the status of Fromm's unfinished manuscript as an interesting historical document about the Frankfurt School and the developing concept of authoritarianism, which it certainly is. The relevant question is whether or not it does in fact constitute a substantial analysis of the character structure of pre-Nazi Germans, as such providing information of lasting value. Apart from showing technical shortcomings with sampling, coding, and so forth, likely to occur in a pioneering attempt, a close examination of the data raises some major questions about Fromm's interpretations. His inferential jump from the manifest level of questionnaire responses to the presence or absence of unobservable character traits seems untenable. On this basic theoretical issue, Fromm ran into similar but even worse difficulties than would the Berkeley group's F scale later. *Worse* difficulties, because Fromm's inferences to the latent level were based on answers to some half-dozen-plus miscellaneous questions (one of them, 424, used twice!) simply *postulated* to be valid indicators of his theoretical types. Thus, the failure to reply in what the theorists' freewheeling interpretations had defined as a "consistent" manner was taken as reflecting the respondents' confused, "ambivalent" character. But it may instead have been a problem of the odd assemblage of questions, apparently never pretested for anything, certainly not for unidimensionality. To put it differently, it appears that the researchers did not *listen* to what the respondents were telling them. Having escaped to safety, they sat instead in judgment over their respondents, failing most of them on this test of freedom-loving revolutionary character—as judged on the basis of some doctrinaire, untested criteria assembled a priori, or rather a posteriori because by that time the German debacle of 1933 was already history.

This evaluation of the survey is supported by Fromm's neglect of the empirical results when he published a reformulation of his theories in *Escape from Freedom* (1941), two years after he had left the Institute. As he argued then, modern man (*sic*) had acquired more and more freedom from constraints since the Reformation and, at the same time, had become increasingly isolated and lonely. Several mechanisms of escape from this isolation had developed over time: (a) the authoritarianism of the ("symbiotically") sadomasochistic character; (b) destructiveness; and (c) automaton conformity, the solution adopted by the majority in modern democratic society. In this analysis, Fromm introduced the new concept of "social character," which he had been groping toward earlier. It developed his "neo-Freudian" ego psychology, coupled with a deemphasis of sexuality that had—notwithstanding his criticism of Reich and mild questioning of Freud's libido theory—still played a major role in 1936 (e.g., pp. 96–97 and 104–105). Responding to his new American environment as well as returning to his initial concern with capitalist society, Fromm now saw the greater challenge not in the threat of fascism but in the transformation of democracy's lonely citizens into more spontaneous, loving, and creative personalities. Fromm had drifted away from the negations of the Institute's Critical Theorists toward positivity, toward a more optimistic, transcendentalist orientation. Indeed, by 1963, he defined the "revolutionary character" not as one who participated in political revolutions (or fought fascism), but as "the sane, alive, mentally healthy person" (Fromm, 1963, p. 165). Although Fromm personally took some unpopular political stands in the 1950s, his more popular social psychology was moving, like the field as a whole during this time, in the direction of apolitical "interpersonal relations."

The Fascist Character in Berkeley

Meanwhile, the Critical Theorists, headed by Horkheimer and later joined by Adorno, had outlined a research project on anti-Semitism (International Institute of Social Research, 1939; Institute of Social Research, 1941), a topic conspicuously absent from the 1936 volume on authority and family (Horkheimer, 1936). In contrast to Reich's discussions, Fromm's (1936) essay had contained only one oblique reference to race (p. 115). Essentially none are found in the Institute's earlier work (cf. Jahoda, 1954, p. 14; Jay, 1980), notwithstanding the fact that Felix Weil's 1922 memorandum on the founding of the Frankfurt Institute had explicitly included "anti-Semitism as sociological problem" among the tasks for the new organization (Migdal, 1981, p. 42). This lack of interest most likely reflected in part the personal, assimilationist attitudes of the Institute members, in part their historical materialist theory that took fascism to be only a late variant of capitalism rather than a development sui generis, and class rather than race as the important analytic category. The course of events taught them otherwise.

Having discovered the need to develop empirical methods for their undertakings, in order to reach an American audience as well as receive financial support (American Jewish Committee Archives, 1939–1955: Frank N. Trager, memorandum, October 9, 1942; cf. Adorno, 1969, pp. 113–148), the Critical Theorists reformulated the project several times and succeeded eventually in obtaining a research grant from the American Jewish Committee (AJC) (American Jewish Committee Archives 1939–1955: Institute of Social Research). Work on the project began in Los Angeles, in cooperation with J.F. Brown, F. Hacker, and others (Adorno, 1969, p. 136). In 1943, Horkheimer was brought into contact with Nevitt Sanford, a young psychology professor at Berkeley who had been interested in the problems of personality structure and ideology for some time. Sanford was then involved in the construction of the anti-Semitism scale (Levinson & Sanford, 1944). The seminal work was carried out by Daniel Levinson, a Berkeley graduate student, after his professor had been offered $500 by an anonymous donor for activities aimed at combating anti-Semitism. They had decided to try instead, successfully as it turned out, to *measure* anti-Semitism with a new instrument (Sanford, 1956). Now the expanding project (Frenkel-Brunswik & Sanford, 1945) was linking up with a new set of persons, with different traditions, and with ideas that had been formulated in Frankfurt more than a decade earlier and had—at least in explicit form—barely included race prejudice at all.

After some delays, a cooperative research plan was developed by the Berkeley group and the Institute, in the context of the project on social discrimination funded by the AJC and directed by Horkheimer. Adorno was the member of the Critical Theory group directly involved in the study of what was initially called the *fascist character*, then the *anti-democratic*, and finally *the authoritarian personality*, as the volume reporting the project in 1950 was titled.[4]

Initially, *The Authoritarian Personality* was praised as a model of imaginative and integrative social science research: It had brought together sophisticated attitude scaling, opinion research, projective testing, and clinical interviews; it combined hardheaded empirical methods, clinical sensitivity, and original theoretical insights; and it dealt with a problem of major social significance. Even before *TAP*'s publication, Shils (1948) had praised the work in progress as "conducted with originality and precision in technique" (p. 29). He saw *TAP* as one of the bright spots in an otherwise fairly dim sociological landscape, although he was to change his mind rather soon. The major thrust of the gradually emerging criticism, beginning with Cohn (1953),[5] was ostensibly aimed at various technical problems. The most sophisticated, detailed, and comprehensive analysis (Hyman & Sheatsley, 1954) arrived at a Scotch verdict of "not proven," after applying what seemed to be ideal standards of methodological perfection, not likely to be met by any existing piece of social science research other than exercises in Experimental Design texts. One of the aspects ignored by these and other critics, and *TAP*'s supporters as well, was the fact that the published work did not represent the implementation of a "grand design" well laid out in advance. Instead, it described research efforts that had grown over the years like Topsy, from a rather specific initial question to an enormously wider complex of problems with the addition of new personnel, new orientations, and new sponsors. Furthermore, critics seemed usually unaware that most of the issues they raised, including the most popular one, the so-called "response set" problem, had been recognized and discussed (though not always solved) by the original authors (Levinson & Sanford, 1944, pp. 341–342).

Denouement

Taking anti-Semitism as its starting point, the Berkeley approach had elaborated the notion of generalized prejudice and undergirded this elaboration with some intriguing and powerful theoretical ideas of

---

[4] Stagner (1936), Edwards (1941), and Maslow (1943) had, of course, published on this subject earlier.

[5] Although Smith (1950) had anticipated such criticism in an early review.

(Freudian) personality dynamics involving the ramifications of ambivalence into other areas of functioning. On the other hand, the psychological emphasis had more or less severed the dialectical bonds to the social–historical forces creating the phenomena. One of Adorno's main functions had been to teach the American academics some Marxist (or Critical) theory (personal communication with R.N. Sanford, August 18, 1972). But the end product did not show much of an overt impact from this effort.[6] The antitype to the prefascist personality had changed from the "revolutionary" to the "genuine liberal"; the historic social forces determining character and ideology had been reduced to amorphous "antecedent sociological and economic factors," passed over quickly in the Introduction to disappear from sight afterward; class and class consciousness had in effect vanished; and "ideology" had become anybody's "organization of opinions, attitudes, and values" (p. 2)—as long as the correlation coefficients were high enough. Reich's original problem of the interplay between societal organization and individual character mediated by the family had been transformed to make it fit into an American liberal, empiricist, individual-psychology framework; indeed, at one time it was in danger of being subsumed under the categories of psychopathology (American Jewish Committee Archives, 1939–1955: M. Horkheimer to T.W. Adorno, October 11, 1945; and Adorno's memo, n.d., p. 3).

Alas, even these adaptations soon turned out to be insufficient. For a while, the F scale became an extremely popular instrument among the liberal social psychologists, who expected it to predict just about everything undesirable in sight, including the personality structure of their political enemies. But a two-pronged counterattack on *TAP* developed within a few months of its publication. The first one involved politics more or less directly in a rather one-sided debate (Kecskemeti, 1951; Shils, 1954; Eysenck, 1954). Adapting the "Totalitarianism" theory of fascism then being developed by Arendt (1951) and others, the critics' basic charge was that the Berkeley group had concentrated exclusively on the "right-wing" authoritarians while ignoring the "authoritarians of the left": the communists. Although the two groups might differ (for doctrinal reasons) on surface attitudes such as anti-Semitism or ethnocentrism, the new theory declared them to be rather similar in the core characteristics of authoritarianism, power orientation, rigidity, and so forth. In this vein, Shils (1954, pp. 32–42), reversing his earlier glowing evaluation of the work, now made what he called the "reasonable interpretation" that the interview responses of some of the "deviant" Low Scorers (labeled "Rigid" Low scorers by Adorno) had been produced

---

[6]Buck-Morss (1977), however, sees many traces of Adorno's thinking in the book; perhaps it takes a specialist to find them.

by the five "Leftists" in the sample, even though he had no evidence whatsoever about the identity of the interviewees. Nor did Shils have any systematic data showing that in fact Communists possessed these psychological characteristics. His claim, which implies a remarkable uniformity of "Leftist" personality, certainly did not fit with the sample of ex-Communists studied by Almond (1952). Yet on the basis of such speculative inferences, Shils complained about the naive left–right scheme and other assumptions of the Berkeley group, which was "holding fast to a deformed intellectual tradition" (Shils, 1954, p. 31). Shils concluded his argument by rejecting any possibility of a real threat coming from American nativist-authoritarians; on the contrary, "even authoritarian personalities are especially useful in some roles in democratic societies and in many other roles . . . at least harmless" (p. 49). One might wonder whom he had in mind, and why only the leftist authoritarians appeared dangerous to him.

Eysenck (1954), going Shils one better, actually presented some data allegedly showing that both English communists and fascists scored high on his "tough-mindedness" factor. Thus he "proved" at least to his own satisfaction that the F Scale was "essentially a measure of tough-mindedness rather than of Fascism" (p. 132). The only existing data on the psychology of communists—Eysenck's own, which had to be imported from England—were soon controverted in an extended exchange in the *Psychological Bulletin* (Rokeach & Hanley, 1956, and sequelae), thus adding some opera buffa aspects to what was fast becoming a deadly serious issue. (For a revival of the argument, see Stone, 1980; and Stone & Smith, chap. 8, this volume.)

Although these charges were published in fairly polite language, some of them had been toned down only after creating considerable stir at the AJC, which led to prepublication negotiations (American Jewish Committee Archives, 1939–1955: correspondence 1950); they were not purely academic debates either. At the height of the cold war, with efforts to rearm the defeated Germans under way, the Berkeley group was at least implicitly accused of facing the wrong enemy (see American Jewish Committee Archives: S. Flowerman to E. Cohen, November 1, 1950). Allegedly, the Berkeley group had completely ignored the authoritarianism of the left (i.e., communism), even though it was the greater threat by far. Such naïveté or disloyalty could only play into Moscow's hands at a time when the (secretly CIA-supported) Congress for Cultural Freedom (Dittberner, 1979, p. 110) was trying to rally the intellectuals of the free world, and when various agencies of the U.S. government selected ex-Nazis and Nazi collaborators as their best allies in anti-Soviet activities (Loftus, 1982; see also "Ex–U.S. Agents," 1983; and Hoyas, 1985, on the notorious Klaus Barbie affair).

Apparently, these political innuendos evoked some protests made in private (Shils, 1980, pp. 408–409). The public record, on the other hand, shows only a rather limited reaction to these attacks on the Berkeley work and its authors. Usually, the response amounted to acceptance of what was becoming a truism, in the absence of any research evidence (Christie, 1954, p. 132), that communists were indeed authoritarians even though they might reject the right-authoritarian F-scale items for ideological reasons. As a minimum concession, a passing comment would establish one's anticommunist credentials (Frenkel-Brunswik, 1954, p. 254), a practice which had become obligatory by then. Only Sanford, who several years earlier had refused to sign the California Loyalty Oath, stood his ground, countering with a comment on the "similarities between the Communists and cultist anti-Communists . . . both . . . attacking liberals" (Sanford, 1956, pp. 264, 292–294).

Such political attacks occurred in a historical context that included difficulties for and dismissals of psychologists for alleged or demonstrated left-wing involvements (Finison, 1983; Sargent & Harris, 1986; see also Lazarsfeld & Thielens, 1958, for a more general description of these "difficult years"). Apparently such attacks put some chill on further discussion and research on authoritarianism and related issues—although it is, for obvious reasons, hard to find any clear-cut evidence in the journals (cf. Melby, 1953, p. 2; see also Gundlach & Riess, 1954). There were other constraints, of course. Given the reigning climate in America, just to track down members of the recently outlawed Communist party for an empirical study of their psychological makeup would have been impossible. Beyond this technical difficulty, the earlier involvement with left-wing causes or ideas, not unusual among social psychologists of the depression and antifascist years, had been followed by their disillusionment with Stalinism and their integration into the national war effort. Furthermore, some social scientists felt the need to distance themselves from their youthful political errors when the cold war started to produce heat (cf. Smith's, 1986, rare and remarkably courageous retrospective). One of the more visible consequences was that mention of Marx and Marxist ideas disappeared almost completely from the social psychological literature (cf. the editorial comment in Sargent & Bramelt, 1955, p. 54; see also Cook, 1986) until the upheavals of the late 1960s. This development is obliquely reflected in, for instance, the striking figures concerning "conformity pressures" and the "decline of left-wing ideology" among social psychologists belonging to the social activist SPSSI organization (Katz, 1958, Table 6, p. 19),[7] as well as in the two issues of the *Journal of Social Issues* addressing the problem under different labels:

---

[7] What is a bit surprising today is the absence of *any* commentary on the rather lopsided responses concerning the decline of left-wing ideology and its relation to SPSSI functioning. Perhaps it was not possible to do so in 1958, and may be problematical even today, as it may involve reopening some painful memories and distasteful issues.

"Academic Freedom" and "Anti-Intellectualism" (Smith, 1953; Sargent & Bramelt, 1955). Yet the repercussions of these developments on the general direction in which American social psychology moved during the 1950s and 1960s have not yet been explored in any systematic way.

Upon further reflection, one is also struck by the almost total absence from the social psychological literature (including *TAP* itself) of studies of anticommunist attitudes (for the exception to prove the rule, see the sociologist Stouffer, 1955), an absence all the more striking if one considers that anticommunism has played at least as important and enduring a role in American attitudes and politics as has anti-Semitism. Furthermore, it might be theoretically relevant to social psychology for a number of reasons (cf. Allport, 1958, pp. 179–182, 244–247; see also Smith, Bruner, & White, 1956, for work carried out in a less tense atmosphere of the early postwar years). But liberal, and by then staunchly anticommunist, social science had found it more appealing to attack, contrary to Horkheimer's claim, the dwindling number of *old-style* bigots from the moral high ground of antiracism. After all, the popular American notion of Hitler focuses much more on his anti-Semitism than on his antibolshevism, even though the latter theme had played, arguably (Gordon, 1984), a greater role in his rhetoric and his political appeal; indeed, he had often combined the two into one pungent phrase.

"The End of Ideology"

While this kind of attack on *TAP* sought, with some success, to mute or redirect the *political* impact of the research, the other line of criticism, more indigenous to psychology, took the opposite tack. It tried, in effect if perhaps not in a deliberate response to the ideological pressures, to drain the phenomenon of all political meaning. The dominant positivist–empiricist research style had already reduced the complex Berkeley project to the "California F Scale," a handy tool to generate reams of data, while ignoring the rest of the tome. Realizing that all of the F-scale items were worded in the same direction, researchers proceeded to "demonstrate" that the scale did not measure any ideological content but only a tendency to agree—with anything (e.g., Bass, 1955). This demonstration overlooked the original authors' treatment of the problem of item direction (Adorno et al., 1950, pp. 161, 280; Levinson & Sanford, 1944, pp. 341–343). It also disregarded the rather superficial nature of the arguments alleging the biasing effects. Not unlike Fromm's interpretations 20 years earlier, these conclusions were based on gratuitous assumptions about the questions, this time about the operating characteristics of the original Likert-type items and their attempted reversals, which did not withstand closer inspection (Christie, Havel, & Seidenberg, 1958; Samelson, 1964; Samelson & Yates, 1967). Nonetheless, while the outsiders had faulted the F scale for capturing only one kind of extremist, and the wrong one at that, the insiders' professional consensus declared the F scale invalid for the opposite reason: It had not identified any genuine protofascist authoritarians, but only singled out some very agreeable persons without strong opinions, or in one variant of this depoliticization process, only a deliberately formal and apolitical dogmatism (Rokeach, 1960).

Attempts to repair the allegedly flawed measuring tool provided remedies at least as problematical as the original. After all, if the new reversals were correlated with the old F scale, contaminated by acquiescence, they did not really improve anything but cosmetics. To the extent that they did *not* correlate with the original, what latent dimension were they measuring? Even Altemeyer's balanced Right-Wing Authoritarianism scale (1981), laboriously constructed long after the F scale had fallen out of favor, taps a much more restricted set of attitudes. Thus, it does not test the intimate relation between surface opinions and underlying personality dynamics, to say nothing about its determination by childhood experiences, as postulated by the theory of the authoritarian personality. Though not realized by everybody, it should be obvious by now that neither the F scale nor any of its descendants can settle this basic issue by itself. Furthermore, although it had been demonstrated that each individual F-scale item possessed its own (short-term) stable item properties (Peabody, 1961), most studies completely ignored such differences between items. Typically, result sections reported only pooled F-scale scores obtained with various combinations of original and substitute items, or even translated (Meloen, 1983; McFarland, Ageyev, & Abalakina, 1990) items, varying in number from 4 to the original 30 in Form 40/45. No wonder the empirical results turned out to be totally confusing, as one should expect simply on the basis of a strict operationism proclaimed in principle but ignored in practice. Thus, whatever interesting results may be produced by tracking F-scale means over time and space (Meloen, 1983, and chap. 4, this volume), they add little to our understanding of the theory. Without a detailed item-by-item analysis, the results may also provide even less information about general opinion shifts in various samples than the mean score comparisons claim.

The fixation of investigators on the paper-and-pencil F scale and its real and alleged flaws led to the gradual abandonment of this research, except by isolated individuals mostly on other continents. But nobody thought to take up afresh the original theoretical problem first raised in Berlin and Frankfurt in its social–political dimensions, and to push it toward a sounder solution. Instead, mainstream social psychologists let the problem disappear slowly from their field of view. As society changed, the predominant liberalism gave way to an apolitical scramble for practical applications capable of generating grants. The complexities of the real world and its political liabilities had turned out to be too much for professionals insisting on being legitimate scientists. Value-free empiricism had won the day—but only by reducing a genuine, important, and complex problem to a meaningless artifact, a "response set," drained of interest to anyone except methodologists. As it happened, the issue was left to the mass media, which skillfully and successfully personalized it in the stereotype figure of the bigoted but basically harmless Archie Bunker—an utterly different, American version of the young George Grosz's cutting and prophetic sketches. In the meantime, the "neoconservatives," who had insisted on the similarity of right- and left-wing authoritarianism in the 1950s, had begun to stress the differences between the authoritarian Right, with whom alliances were possible, and the totalitarian Marxist-Leninists, with whom one could not truck. The psychological argument had turned into polemic, and the label had become an epithet.

Epilogue: Authoritarianism and the Dialectics of History

Have we learned anything from this story of the metamorphoses of an idea? Do we know more today, after all the scientific labors, than what the artist George Grosz saw when he observed the scene in Weimarperiod Berlin?

What strikes me most is the transformation of the problem by different actors responding to different times and circumstances, as well as their varied fates in these settings: The movement of the nuclear idea proceeded through the political spectrum from the far left, in the revolutionary and "extreme" formulation by a communist Freudian activist, to the milder Marxist-socialist, and incipiently empirical, versions of Fromm and the Institute, on to the liberal American social scientists at Berkeley and their followers, to end up in the value-free empirical data-crunching of the late 1950s, eventually jumping tracks to the media and the neoconservative camp. Retreating from broad theory and increasingly encapsulated, research interests moved away from the events of the outside world toward laboratory-generated problems, a process legitimated as the way of true science. Yet although the approach became progressively less politically "engaged" as well as more "empirical," it would be hard to argue that this "improvement" in the objectivity of methods and quantity of data succeeded in solving the problem; instead it ended by defining the problem away. If the whole process taught us anything, it appears to confirm the Critical Theorists' allegations about the function of positivist–empiricist research: to take real and complex political issues and to reduce them to small fragments drained of meaning.

Behind the immense complexity of the conceptual and empirical task the theorists had somewhat naively set for themselves looms the seeming impossibility of evading political connotations and implications. Even an explicitly apolitical stance may only submerge its ideological assumptions. All of the authors believed in their own objectivity, yet looking back we can see the specific historical settings refracted in their work in substantial fashion. It is not just a simple "historical relativism," showing a difference in approaches as well as evaluative criteria in different contexts. We also get a glimpse of the dynamics of historical change in the phenomena themselves and in the perspectives of the researchers enmeshed in these changes and struggling to comprehend them.

Confronted by such complexities, should we drop such issues as the authoritarian character altogether in exchange for smaller, safer, and more salable topics, as social psychology by and large seems to have done? After all, the predictions, or fears, implicit in *The Authoritarian Personality* turned out to be unwarranted on the face of it: Automatic obedience corroded into the "crisis of authority," sexual repression turned into ubiquitous pornography, and anti-Semitism into broad-based support for a militant Israel; narrow ethnocentrism succumbed to the blandishments of ethnic foods; rigid sex roles were softening; and gays were allowed to come out of the closet. Corruption in high places became a daily news story, and prying into private affairs lucrative business; since 1950 nearly all of the F-scale items seem to have lost their original meaning, at least for a time. But has the underlying issue evaporated with them? The problem seen by Reich, Horkheimer, and Fromm concerned not only the still enigmatic question about the psychological underpinnings of a defunct tyranny, memory of which is receding into shibboleth. Behind it stands one of the basic problems at the core of the human sciences: how to understand and deal with the interdependencies between individual lives and their—our—societies, caught up in concrete historical developments that impinge not just on our "subjects" but on all of us, researchers included, if perhaps in different ways.

As this is written, momentous events are shaking Eastern Europe in dramatic ways. Without a shot fired, they swept away the Berlin wall and all it stood for. Yet there does not seem to be a social scientist, politician, or even military strategist in the West who predicted such an outcome. How does one explain this total failure of prevision on the part of experts and the rest of us alike? Perhaps all of us, notwithstanding our varied political persuasions, had basically accepted the authoritarians' fixed image of the "evil empire": monolithic, ruthless, implacable, and unchangeable except by the force of arms. As it turned out instead, the Kremlin was ruled no longer by Darth Vader, but by a rather impotent Wizard of Oz—though sadly with nuclear bombs in his arsenal. Apparently we had failed to learn the central lesson of the Frankfurt theorists, who believed in change and in the dialectical transformations of history. Similarly, to treat the phenomenon of authoritarianism as if frozen in time, implicit in the continued use of the F scale and its editorial variants, seems to contradict this historical conception. But the transhistorical validity of our knowledge (Schlenker, 1974) may be a noble ideal; in the real world it may be gratuitous assumption, directing attention away from historical processes as well as from critical self-examination.[8] Thus, the nature of authoritarianism itself and of its manifestations have likely changed. Though the F scale was an ingenious stab in the dark at the time, it is probably not worth reviving. It will take a new vision to bring the issue back to life. In the meantime, the history of the authoritarian character may have more to teach us about theorists and researchers themselves than about the targets of their research.

Acknowledgments. A shorter version of this chapter was presented at the Annual Meeting of the International Society for the History of Behavioral and Social Sciences (Cheiron) at York University, Toronto, Canada, in June 1983, and subsequently published (1986) in the *Journal of Social Issues*, *42*(1). I would like to acknowledge support from NSF Grant SOC78/12165, Program for History and Philosophy of Science, during the archival research stage, and my appreciation of the American Jewish Committee's willingness to grant access to relevant archival material. Thanks are also due to Ben Harris for various helpful hints, and to the Archives of the History of American Psychology at Akron, Ohio, the library of the Menniger Foundation in Topeka, Kansas, as well as the Max Horkheimer-Archiv in Frankfurt am Main.

---

[8] On the other hand, the discovery that social psychology was "history" (Gergen, 1973) did not produce much more than a slogan.

Part II
Perspectives on Continuing Questions About Authoritarianism

3
The F Scale as a Predictor of Fascism: An Overview of 40 Years of Authoritarianism Research

Jos D. Meloen

From 1950 through 1989, *Psychological Abstracts* listed 2,341 publications on authoritarianism and dogmatism. To make sense of the often contradictory results reported in this vast literature on authoritarianism, a search was initiated to discover whether there are systematic tendencies, focusing on F-scale levels across the many groups tested. The object was to assess the validity of the F scale. Are high scores associated with antidemocratic, profascist tendencies? This was one of the issues that the Berkeley group was unable to address. Surprisingly, such a systematic analysis of F-scale scores has never been conducted, either by follow-up investigators or by reviewers such as Wrightsman (1977), Brown (1965), Byrne (1974), Cherry and Byrne (1977), Dillehay (1978), Goldstein and Blackman (1978), or Altemeyer (1981). The present global meta-analysis, in the classic sense of a combinational approach, is an attempt to correct for this important omission. The present study was part of a wider survey into the validity of authoritarianism research. Only the initial global meta-analysis over the first three decade period will be presented here. For a more complete account see Meloen (1983). Later findings in the 1980s generally supported its conclusions, and some relevant ones have been included in this report.

To begin this task, working definitions of antidemocratic and profascist tendencies as well as of prodemocratic tendencies were developed, guided by the vast literature on authoritarianism.

Tendencies were considered to be *antidemocratic* if they advocated the reduction of existing levels of democracy in a given political system. The antidemocratic advocate will favor restricting existing forms of political representation and prevailing human rights. Carried to extremes, such tendencies will lead to the authoritarian one-man control of the state.

Fascist tendencies are characterized by the support of extreme forms of nationalism, ethnocentrism, or racism and verbal or physical combat against internal enemies (e.g., the democratic opposition, socialists, communists, minorities of all sorts or other scapegoats). The fascist intends to create a strong and unified state, with dominant centralist and/or militaristic aspects. The existing economic system is to be maintained, but major restrictions are to be imposed on democracy and human rights. Also included in fascist appeals is emphasis on the threat posed by external (international or secret) enemies, and consequently the need for fighting these enemies, whether or not territorial expansion is the goal. In the context of the liberalization and democratization that has marked development throughout much of the world during the past decades, such fascist tendencies are today associated only with extreme right-wing views and politics and not with those of genuine conservatives, who adhere to the principles of parliamentary democracy.

By contrast, *prodemocratic tendencies* are characterized by the advocacy of expanded political representation, the extension of human rights, and the rights of ethnic minorities. No prototype can be defined for this tendency, mainly because the content of this process of democratization, by its very nature, can develop in various ways. In the United States and Western Europe, advocates of antidemocratic tendencies would demand the restrictions mentioned above; advocates of democratic tendencies would be proponents of the opposite. Thus, the major criterion for validity of the F scale is that it measures antidemocratic and profascist tendencies as intended by Adorno, Frenkel-Brunswik, Levinson, and Sanford (1950).

Method

To operationalize this criterion, four "criteria for differentiation" were developed that would indicate whether the results of authoritarianism research could be interpreted as supporting the validity of the F scale. These criteria were as follows:

1. Groups that support antidemocratic and profascist principles will have high F-scale means.
2. Antidemocratic and profascist groups will have higher group means on the F scale (or related F scales) than the population as a whole.
3. Groups that explicitly support democratic and antifascist values will have mean F-scale scores below those of the general population.
4. Regional differences in authoritarianism in the United States as a consequence of the country's historical development are confirmed by regional scores on the F scale or similar scales.

---

[1] The United States was the only country in which regional differences could be examined in this analysis, because only from the United States were enough samples from different regions available. Later on, regional differences were also found in a small country like The Netherlands, the "orthodox" regions (in the Protestant north as well as in the Roman Catholic south, Meloen & Middendorp, 1991) showing higher levels.

Therefore, the main research question in this study was to determine how well the results of past F scale research met these criteria.

To begin, hundreds of studies carried out over a period of more than three decades using the F scale and related authoritarianism scales were taken from books and journals. Instead of taking a random sample of publications, the exhaustive method was used. Random sampling would not have been appropriate because many authors failed to report group mean F scale scores of their samples. About 125 research reports mentioning group mean scores on such scales were finally available for analysis. This constituted only about 10% of all the published reports on authoritarianism listed in *Psychological Abstracts*.[2] Nevertheless, these publications mentioned some 350 samples consisting of 29,000 persons in the United States and 17,000 in 23 countries outside the United States.[3]

Standardization

Although the original California F Scale (Form 40/45) consisted of 30 items with seven answer categories,[4] in the follow-up research many combinations of number of items and Likert points can be found: Investigations have used from as few as 3 to as many as 60 items and from two to eight answer categories. Most F scales, however, consist of 20 to 30 items and six or seven Likert points. Therefore, standardization was necessary to make comparisons possible. All of the group mean F-scale scores were recomputed to a 1.00 to 7.00 scale, as used by Adorno et al. (1950), 4.00 being the neutral, midpoint position. This scale will be referred to as the standard F scale (SF scale); high scores indicate authoritarianism.

Sample Selection

The studies included in the sample used original F scales or closely related scales developed according to Adorno et al.'s (1950) assumptions. No studies using Rokeach's (1960) Dogmatism scale; Wilson's Conservatism scale (Eysenck & Wilson, 1978); or Altemeyer's (1981, 1988a)

---

[2] This analysis concerned the 1950–1979 period with a total at that time of 1,224 authoritarianism (F scale) and 702 dogmatism publications reported in *Psychological Abstracts*. The total for the 1950–1989 period is 1,504 for authoritarianism (F scale) and 837 for dogmatism. Because not all publications on authoritarianism are included in *Psychological Abstracts* these numbers are the lower limits (Meloen, 1991a).
[3] A table of more than 20 pages showing all these samples and their characteristics appears in the appendix of the Meloen (1983) study.
[4] Some answering options, also called Likert points, included the "no answer" category.

RWA scale were sampled. Thus, the studies selected used scales containing Adorno et al. (1950) items or items meant to measure the same phenomenon. They all mentioned the use of an "F scale" or an "authoritarianism scale." Studies using other scales were accepted as "related F scales" if they were meant to measure authoritarianism or correlated highly with the F scale.

Extensive pretesting showed that levels of authoritarianism in studies using related scales did not differ much from those using the F scale when comparable groups were involved. Likewise, no substantial differences in level appeared between groups tested with the original F scale and so-called balanced F scales. In all, the studies selected used scales that appeared to satisfy the requirements mentioned. (A full list of included and excluded scales appears in Meloen, 1983).

Analysis

Most contributions originated in North America (United States, Canada), and it is mainly these data that are analyzed here. The data were partitioned in many ways, partly for reasons of exploration, partly to control results for expected but unrelated differences. In general, overlap of categories was avoided.

The analysis proceeded as follows: Two groups of samples were chosen for analytical reasons, for instance "student samples" versus "nonstudent samples." For each of these two groups of samples, the *group means* were computed. These means were compared with each other, or with those of control groups, in order to find out whether the differences supported theoretical expectations. The group means were always weighted by the number of subjects (not of samples) in the group reported by the original author.

Standard tests of significance for differences between such group means were not very helpful in this analysis. Due to the large numbers, running to thousands of subjects, small but irrelevant differences in the means would be significant. Such differences do not, therefore, clearly reflect the actual differences within the sampled population. For this reason, the conclusions were based on rather pronounced, or global, tendencies.

Results

Applying the criteria for differentiation, the following results can be reported.

The First Criterion

One of the problems with authoritarianism research is that although many different groups have been studied, antidemocratic and fascist groups have rarely been studied *with* the F scale. The few published F-scale studies of such right-wing extremist groups have rarely been cited. The results of the research on such groups using F scales are reported here.

If the first criterion for F-scale validity holds, then the individuals supporting right-wing extremist groups will tend to agree with the scale items and their scores will classify them as high Fs. The group means will be high.

The Coulter Study

In the early 1950s, Thelma Coulter infiltrated a group of Sir Oswald Mosley supporters and activists. This group, called fascist and anti-Semitic by Eysenck, had the highest mean score ever for right-wing extremist groups (Coulter, 1953; Eysenck, 1954; Eysenck & Coulter, 1972; Eysenck & Wilson, 1978). The 43 Fascist party members had a group mean of 5.30 on the full-length original California F Scale (see also Christie 1956a, 1956b). In general, the sample showed strong acceptance of the F-scale items.

The Hoogvelt Study

Hoogvelt (1969) sent out a 15-item F scale and an ethnocentrism scale to writers of letters-to-the-editor of an English newspaper. These letters related to a speech by the English member of parliament Enoch Powell in April 1968, a speech that was considered by many to have anti-immigrant and racist elements. The 60 Powell supporters had a group mean on the F scale of 5.17, indicating clear acceptance of F-scale items. Twenty-three anti-Powell letter-writers scored much lower, 3.06, indicating rejection. Those who reacted to Powell before his speech showed comparable group means: Fifteen pro-Powell subjects had a mean of 5.11; five anti-Powell writers, 2.84. For a group of 96 neutral students, the mean was in the neutral part of the scale, 4.16. Except for Hanson (1975, Eysenck & Wilson, 1978), who does not mention the high score of the pro-Powell groups, this report has not been cited by authoritarianism researchers.

The Sherwood Study

A study by Sherwood (1966a), similar to Hoogvelt's (1969), was conducted in the United States on members of a "super-patriot" organization, an ultraconservative and nationalistic movement comparable to the one investigated by participant observation by Chesler and Schmuck (1962). Using a balanced F scale, Sherwood's 49 respondents showed a group mean of 5.10. A group of 65 art students scored only 2.51 on the same scale. The extremely high score of these super-patriots has seldom been commented on by subsequent reviewers.

The Orpen Study

Orpen (1970) used a translated version of the original F scale with 100 white Afrikaner South African students at the University of Stellenbosch in South Africa. This university was considered by the author to be an important training center for future leaders and at the time a bulwark of apartheid supporters. Their group mean was 4.88; Orpen stressed that this was the highest score ever recorded for a student group. The present author knows of no student group of this size that has scored as high, before or since in western samples.

The Mynhardt Study

In Mynhardt's (1980) study, a sample of white psychology students in Johannesburg, South Africa, completed the California F Scale (Form 40/45) with 29 of the original items. White Afrikaans-speaking students ($N = 134$) produced a group mean of 4.72; English-speaking students ($N = 112$) had a mean of only 3.79. The group mean score of Afrikaner students suggests even more extreme scores among the general population of Afrikaners, since (a) psychology students in the United States or Western Europe have not scored this high on the accepting side of the F scale, (b) psychology students are usually among the lowest scoring groups, and (c) students in general have lower scores than the general population (as will be shown below). The differences in the mean scores of English-speaking and Afrikaans-speaking samples reflect differences between these cultural groups: more resistance to apartheid among English speakers, more acceptance of racial separation among the Afrikaans speakers. Mynhardt also reported significant and substantial correlations between the F scale and the anti-Semitism, antiblack, and patriotism subscales.

The Steiner and Fahrenberg Study

One of the most important investigations bearing on the validity of the F scale was conducted during the 1960s in Germany among former members of the SS and the Wehrmacht (the regular German army in the Nazi period). Steiner and Fahrenberg (1970a, 1970b) were inspired to study these groups by Else Frenkel-Brunswik, one of the original authors of *TAP*. They managed to secure cooperation from these groups with the help of a former SS general. F-scale items were carefully translated into German for the questionnaire. The group mean of 229 former SS men was 5.23; the comparable mean for 201 former Wehrmacht members was only 4.52. These scores can be considered as particularly high if one bears in mind that social desirability would tend to produce distortion in the democratic direction after more than 20 postwar years of democracy. In fact, the former SS men still advocated "dictatorship" instead of "monarchy" or "democracy." The higher ranks in the Wehrmacht advocated monarchy (traditionally), whereas support for democracy existed mainly in the lower ranks. All respondents had read Hitler's *Mein Kampf*. There is little doubt that SS members were anti-Semitic as well, but 20 years after World War II this was still too sensitive a topic to be included in the questionnaire. This report has received no comment in the literature, even though it was abstracted (*Psychological Abstracts* 1972: 2961) and was mentioned explicitly by Meloen (1983).

The Dutch Fascism Studies

In 1982, a new political party gained a seat in the Dutch parliament. This party, the Centrumpartij, was condemned by all other parties represented in parliament for its xenophobic and antiminority stands. The party was associated with racist and fascist tendencies. In three large surveys (Hagendoorn & Janssen, 1983; Raaijmakers, Meeus, & Vollebergh, 1985; Meloen, Hagendoorn, Raaijmakers, & Visser, 1988; Poppelaars & Visser, 1987) among thousands of Dutch high school students, a clear picture emerged: The potential support for the Centrumpartij was extremely ethnocentric. Somewhat surprisingly, since the party's propaganda hardly seemed to include this, supporters were highly authoritarian and also held antifeminist and extreme right-wing views. The authoritarianism group means (see Table 3.1) of Centrumpartij members in the three surveys were 4.71, 4.76, and 4.55, respectively. These averages were significantly higher than the total group means of the three samples (3.60, 4.20, and 2.98, respectively) and also higher than the group means of the supporters of the more conservative democratic parties combined. Since these young age groups scored lower than the older ones of the general population (Meloen & Middendorp, 1991), the adult supporters of the Centrumpartij in general may have had even

TABLE 3.1. Authoritarianism among Dutch high school students.

	Hagendoorn et al. 1982/83			Raaijmakers et al. 1983/84			Visser et al. 1984		
	N	SF mean	(SD)	N	SF mean	(SD)	N	SF mean	(SD)
Radical left	866	2.55	(0.91)	97	3.32	(1.17)	165	2.10	(0.87)
Left wing	864	3.37	(0.91)	469	4.25	(1.03)	223	2.76	(1.01)
Center	658	3.95	(0.84)	178	4.34	(0.95)	117	3.44	(0.88)
Right wing	1,520	4.13	(0.89)	361	4.51	(0.97)	242	3.46	(0.88)
Centrumpartij	57	4.71	(0.89)	90	4.76	(0.88)	16	4.55	(0.91)
Total	3,965	3.60	(0.91)	1,195	4.20	(1.05)	763	2.98	(1.09)

higher scores. Interviews demonstrated a broad and coherent pattern of related attitudes within the high scoring groups.

The Kohn Study

Some student groups have also showed high F scores, although the majority of students tend to score rather low. A small group of ultra-conservative members of the E. Burke Society in Canada were reported to have a mean score of 5.08 on a balanced F scale (Kohn, 1972).

The Billig Study

Finally, although no mean score was computed, Billig (1978) found acceptance of F-scale statements he used in interviewing a small group of extreme right-wing National Front members in Great Britain.

The Second Criterion

Antidemocratic and profascist groups are expected to score higher than the general population, possibly higher than the highest "normal" democratic groups. To show this, an estimate of the authoritarianism level of the general population should be available. Although it is hard to compare the different types of research on authoritarianism, an effort was made to estimate this level. The total mean of all the North American samples was 3.61 (see Table 3.2). If the few minority groups (blacks, Hispanics, Jews) were left out, this figure hardly changed (3.60). This mean, however, appears low, because random samples indicate an average much closer to the scale mean (which is 4.00 here): The computed random samples were 3.96, the estimated ones 3.88, which makes a weighted total of 3.92 for both groups together. The author's impression is that the low overall score (3.61) was due to rather low-scoring student groups that have been selected for investigation so often. The group means of the student and nonstudent groups support this impression (student, 3.43; nonstudent, 3.90). The student groups do indeed show much lower levels of authoritarianism. If those groups that consisted of ex-students (university educated persons, but not students) were left out of the nonstudent groups, the average was even closer to the scale mean: 3.98. This latter group then was comparable to the random samples.

The results described above are summarized in Table 3.2. Similar results were obtained with shortened versions of the F scale. Students showed lower levels than random samples (students, 3.18; nonstudent, 3.84). To find out whether the nonstudent group would have a different mean if the military groups were omitted from the calculations, new group means were computed. Though there was a slight difference (military, 4.00; civilians, 3.84) this difference almost disappeared when

TABLE 3.2. Estimates of authoritarianism levels: United States and Canada.

Group of samples	Number of samples	Years	Number of subjects	SF mean
1. U.S./Canada total	224	1945–80	30,567	3.61
2. U.S./Canada minus minorities	216	1945–80	29,824	3.60
3. Random samples computed	8	1953–80	2,729	3.96
4. Random samples estimated	5	1952–55	2,932	3.88
5. Random samples total	13	1952–80	5,661	3.92
6. Students[1] Adorno et al.	8	1945–46	581	3.66
7. Students follow-up	128	1951–79	17,580	3.42
8. Students total	136	1945–79	18,161	3.43
9. Non-students Adorno et al.	15	1945–46	1,518	3.85
10. Non-students follow-up	58	1950–80	6,517	3.92
11. Non-students total	73	1945–80	8,035	3.90
12. Non-students minus ex-students[2] Adorno	14	1945–46	1,455	3.87
13. Non-students minus ex-students follow-up	48	1950–80	5,730	4.00
14. Non-students minus ex-students total	62	1945–80	7,185	3.98
15. Students short version	1	1970	1,018	3.18
16. Non-students short version random	5	1953–72	2,262	3.84
17. Military	15	1953–73	3,268	4.00
18. Nonmilitary (civilians)	58	1945–80	4,767	3.84
19. Total non-students (military, nonmilitary)	73	1945–80	8,035	3.90
20. Nonmilitary minus ex-students	47	1945–80	3,917	3.96
21. 1945–60 Military	12	1953–58	3,132	4.01
22. 1945–60 Nonmilitary	26	1945–59	2,488	3.95

1. *Students* refers to college/university students.
2. *Ex-students* refers to nonstudents with college/university education.

the better educated groups (which were overrepresented) were left out (military, 4.00; nonmilitary without ex-students, 3.96). Also, when the time period was controlled, the difference was slight (1945–1960: military, 4.01; nonmilitary, 3.95).

The student levels of authoritarianism are lower than the nonstudent levels. The consistency of this trend has also been treated separately. The means of the student samples were compared with those of the nonstudent samples of Table 3.2. All 64 comparisons were as expected: There was no instance in which the means of student samples were equal to or higher than those of nonstudent samples. The trend of lower scores for student samples therefore appears to be extremely consistent over large groups.

Table 3.3 shows that these findings relating to the differences between student and nonstudent groups also hold for Western European countries such as (the former) West Germany and The Netherlands, where slightly higher means pertain than in the U.S. samples. Overall, the European

TABLE 3.3. Estimates of authoritarianism levels: Western Europe.

Region	Type	Number of samples	Period	Number of subjects	SF mean
Total Europe	Student	25	1959–75	3,330	3.03
Total Europe	Nonstudent	41	1953–77	10,581	4.43
Total Europe	All	66	1953–77	13,911	4.09

means are moderate, much lower than those of the high-scoring antidemocratic groups previously reviewed.

The results shown in Tables 3.2 and 3.3 suggest that there is a systematic difference between student authoritarianism and that of the general population. Students scored much lower, on average, both in North America and Western Europe. The general population, however, showed levels close to the scale mean of 4.00 in the 1945–1980 period in North America. U.S. estimates of population means here were between 3.80 and 4.05, whereas those in Europe were somewhat higher. Nevertheless, all these levels are much lower than those of the previously mentioned high-scoring antidemocratic groups, supporting the second criterion for differentiation.

The Third Criterion

The third source of evidence for validity of the F scale comes from the study of low-scoring groups associated with or sympathizing with explicitly antifascist and prodemocratic values, whatever their ideology. Quite a number of examples can be found in the empirical literature. Surprisingly, the lowest mean score on record was not reported in the late 1960s, as one might have expected, but at the beginning of the Cold War. Handlon and Squier (1955) tested a group of highly principled people who refused to sign an anticommunist loyalty oath, which meant the loss of their jobs at the University of California (mean: 1.88). The lowest means in the late 1960s were reported from a Berkeley counterculture group by Christie (Gold, Christie, & Friedman, 1976, mean: 1.95). Mantell 1972/1974), using a balanced F scale, found that army volunteers showed a higher level (3.84) than conscripts (3.44), whereas conscientious objectors scored the lowest (2.34). It is of importance that all of Mantell's subjects were nonstudents, and that the research was finished before the Vietnam War had ended.

Research into preferences for political candidates and parties has shown a rather stable picture, for the party members as well as for the supporters both in North America and Western Europe. In general, groups that are outspoken in their rejection of fascist values score consistently lower on the F scale than do groups that are less militant

(Adelson, 1953; Berting, 1968; Brant, Larsen, & Langenberg, 1978; Bushan, 1969; Coulter, 1953; Hagendoorn & Janssen, 1983; Kohn, 1972, 1974; Lee & Warr, 1969; Luck & Gruner, 1970; Meloen, 1983; Meloen & Middendorp, 1991; Meloen et al., 1988; Raina, 1974; Rokeach, 1960).

The Fourth Criterion

It was hypothesized that the validity of the F scale would also be supported if the variations in regional means correspond to the traditional regional differences in the United States regarding racial prejudice, readiness to support antidemocratic nationalistic leaders, and the acceptance of extremely conservative political positions. It was predicted

TABLE 3.4. Regional differences in authoritarianism: United States and Canada.

Samples	Number of samples	Years	Number of subjects	SF mean
1. Student non-South	103	1945–79	13,386	3.35
2. Student South	31	1951–78	4,424	3.65
3. Student unknown region	2	1957–66	351	—
4. Student total	136	1945–79	18,161	3.43
5. Nonstudent non-South	47	1945–79	3,542	3.74
6. Nonstudent South	16	1954–63	3,710	4.11
7. Nonstudent unknown region	10	1953–74	783	3.66
8. Nonstudent total	73	1945–80	8,035	3.90
9. Nonstudents non-South minus ex-students	42	1945–80	3,259	3.79
10. Nonstudents South minus ex-students	16	1954–63	3,710	4.11
11. Non-students non-South minus military	46	1945–80	3,494	3.73
12. Non-students South minus military	7	1959–63	918	4.53
13. Non-students non-South minus military minus ex-students	41	1945–80	3,211	3.78
14. Non-students South minus military minus ex-students	7	1959–63	918	4.53
15. Random city non-South	4	1956–80	923	3.76
16. Random city South	1	1961	266	4.72
17. Random noncity non-South	1	1959	180	4.71
18. Random noncity South	1	1959	186	4.70
19. Random non-South	3	1953	886	3.65
20. Random South	1	1953	288	4.50
21. Random non-South total	8	1953–80	1,989	3.76
22. Random South total	3	1953–61	740	4.63
23. Student non-South Coast	67	1945–76	7,949	3.34
24. Student non-South non-Coast	23	1953–78	3,314	3.49
25. Student non-South unknown	13	1969–79	2,123	3.20
26. Student non-South total	103	1945–79	13,386	3.35

that samples from the southern United States, where due to historical developments official segregation of blacks and whites had lasted at least until the 1960s, would show higher means than samples from the North. Similarly, theoretical and historical considerations regarding differences between urban and rural parts of the country were expected to show in the authoritarianism levels. Urbanites were expected to score lower than rural residents. Midwesterners were expected to score higher than people who lived on the East or West coast. The results of this examination are reported in Table 3.4.

South and Non-South

The states where the samples came from were assigned as North (or non-South) or South (including border states) using the criteria of Middleton (1976). Research samples originating from the South were compared with those originating from the remaining parts (non-South) of the United States and Canada (Table 3.4). Students from the South showed higher levels (3.65) than students from the non-South (3.35). The same was true for the nonstudent samples (South, 4.11; non-South, 3.74). This last difference hardly changed when in both groups the ex-students (highly educated) were omitted (South, 4.11; non-South, 3.79). When the military groups were omitted, the difference became even larger (South, 4.53; non-South, 3.73). The number of subjects left in this last comparison, however, was rather small. The random samples yielded similar differences (South, 4.63; non-South, 3.76) and thus confirmed these findings.

Coast and Non-Coast

The non-South groups were again divided into samples from the coast (West Coast and Northeast Coast states) and non-Coast (mainly Midwest) regions. Somewhat surprisingly, differences appeared between these regions here as well (Coast, 3.34; non-Coast, 3.49). Only student samples were available, and the difference is small; but due to the large numbers of subjects, the difference is still statistically significant. The coastal regions are typically more industrialized and more densely populated than those of the more agricultural regions, like the Midwest. Such factors may also be highly interrelated, and add up to an explanation of these regional differences in authoritarianism.

Industrial and Rural

The rural–urban differences shown in Table 3.4 may partly reflect differences between those who live in cities and those who live in rural regions. A small number of random samples are available to illustrate this point. The extent to which the comparison South versus non-South

Table 3.5. Summary of findings on regional differences in authoritarianism.

	Confirmed	Disconfirmed
South/non-South	58+	8−
Coast/non-Coast	1+	0−
City/noncity	18+	4−
Total	77+	12−

reflects this difference has already been mentioned (Table 3.4: South, 4.63; non-South, 3.76). The difference between cities and rural regions was not found in the South, however. Both appeared to have relatively high levels of authoritarianism (city, 4.72; noncity, 4.70). Nevertheless, in the remaining parts of the United States, the difference was confirmed (city, 3.76; noncity, 4.71). The South may therefore be more socio-culturally homogeneous. This would of course support the conformism hypothesis in those regions. The small number of samples here, however, limits our conclusions from these data.

Table 3.5 summarizes the findings on regional differences.

To evaluate the prevalence of the trends discussed above, the samples (in Table 3.4) were compared as to the direction of the differences between group means. A plus sign (+) is used to indicate differences in the expected direction (non-South lower than South, non-Coast higher than coast, city lower than noncity), a minus sign (−) to indicate equal means or a difference contrary to expectations. In 87% of the cases (77 out of 89 comparisons), the differences were as expected. The unexpected differences occurred systematically and only in three samples. As mentioned above, there were apparently no significant differences between southern cities and southern rural regions. This evidence leads us to conclude that regional differences occurred in a fairly consistent and predictable pattern.[5]

Summary of the Meta-Analytic Findings

According to the first criterion, high-scoring groups are associated with antidemocratic and fascist tendencies. Although the groups tested are

---

[5] Pettigrew's (1959) two *matched* northern rural and southern rural samples showed SF means of 4.70 and 4.71, respectively. Both samples are not random, however, and a random mean might be different. The level of the northern sample is somewhat higher than other samples in that region, while the southern one is almost equal to other southern samples. Pettigrew's two "means," however, result in one of the few instances of an unexpected lack of difference concerning a North–South comparison, while almost all the other available samples do support such an expected difference (see Table 3.5).

not representative of profascist movements, it is remarkable that groups showing association with ultranationalism, fascism, anti-Semitism, racism, apartheid, and national socialism also scored high on authoritarianism or F scales. In other words, they do in fact seem to have quite a number of psychological tendencies in common, although their political ideologies are phrased in different wordings. The groups mentioned all have relatively high SF scores, the most significant ones of around 5.00 and up. This indicates confirmation of the first criterion for differentiation.

The second criterion indicates that antidemocratic and profascist groups will have higher group means than the population average and that these means will be higher than those of the highest "normal" democratic groups. The results reviewed in this chapter suggest that the authoritarianism level for the general population (of Canada and the United States) for the period 1945–1980 lies between 3.80 and 4.05 (with a mean of about 4.00) and that it is thus significantly lower than the level of the high-scoring groups.

The European data look similar. Though the population means are somewhat higher, they seem to be decreasing and are in any case significantly below the means of the high-scoring groups. In the Netherlands, random samples of 1980 and 1985 showed authoritarianism means of 4.10 and 4.01 respectively (Meloen & Middendorp, 1991), which are much lower than those of the right-wing extremist Centrumpartij supporters in the same period. In Germany, Lederer (1983) showed that authoritarianism not only decreased from 1945 on, but also that high school students had comparable or even lower scores than their American counterparts. German students in the 1960s also scored much lower than the group of former SS men tested during the same time period. Finally, the higher score for Afrikaans-speaking compared to English-speaking white South Africans has been confirmed by several authors (Duckitt, 1983; Lambley, 1980; Mynhardt, 1980). These results suggest that the F-scale results can also pass the second and most important criterion for differentiation.

The third criterion holds that if low F-scale scoring groups support democratic and antifascist values, this will contribute to the validity of the F scale. Some of the many examples were reviewed here: low-scoring conscientious objectors, antiestablishment culture in the 1960s, and antifascist groups. They suggest support for the third criterion for differentiation.

The fourth criterion will be met if it can be shown that geographic areas traditionally more prone to racism and more receptive to antidemocratic political causes also score higher on the F scale. There is a broad body of research to support the claim that such regional differences do in fact exist in North America (Christie & Garcia, 1951; Middleton, 1976; Schooler, 1972; Williams, 1966) as well as in Western Europe (Meloen, 1983; Meloen & Middendorp, 1991; Schooler, 1976).

The expected differences in F-scale means were found between the regions of the South and non-South and the Coast and non-Coast. The pattern of differences between the cities and the rural regions was somewhat less clear, especially in the South, but the number of reports in this region was too limited for more definite conclusions. Differences between the more industrial and more densely populated Northeast and the West Coast, on the one hand, and the more rural Midwest and the South, on the other, were in the expected direction. Overall, the most consistently low scores were attained by the many student groups tested. Whereas the relatively great mobility of students would suggest the absence of significant differences between geographic locations, regional differences did in fact occur in the expected direction.

The results presented for the many groups examined meet the fourth criterion for differentiation in the test for validation of the F scale. On the strength of the massive evidence presented, we conclude that the F scale is an instrument for the measure of antidemocratic and fascist tendencies that has retained its validity over time.

Standardization

Nevertheless, confusing and contradicting results have been reported. Much of the existing research would present a more coherent picture of authoritarianism if the right standardization were applied. To date, no author has even attempted such a standardization, yet most authors do not hesitate to draw far-reaching conclusions from their data. From the results of this global meta-analysis, it was possible to extract a preliminary standardization. The relevant high-scoring groups mentioned all scored higher than 4.50 and can be called authoritarian. They have at least some of the characteristics attributed to authoritarians. The general population usually shows much lower levels, around the midpoint of the scale; means between 3.50 and 4.50 can be called neutral or moderate, being neither outspoken highs or lows. Scores of 3.50 or lower should be called anti-authoritarian. Such groups systematically reject authoritarianism.

These boundaries are still somewhat arbitrary but relatively parsimonious because differentiation between truly different groups proved to be possible this way. Also, a modest downward trend over decades has been reported (Lederer, 1983, in West Germany 1945–1980; Meloen & Middendorp, 1991, in the Netherlands 1970–1985; Meloen, 1983, in North America 1954–1974). A slight upward trend has been observed (e.g., Altemeyer, 1988a, in North America 1973–1987), but the relative differences may not change as the levels of both highs and lows seem to decrease or increase simultaneously. The changes in general tend to be modest and less impressive than the relative stability of the authoritarianism means over time. Results from the European countries in this overall meta-analysis indicate that there may have been somewhat higher levels in the past but that levels may now be similar to those in North America. In non-Western countries where data are available, the existence of a variation in level according to the culture is suggested. Predominantly agricultural countries tend to show somewhat higher general levels than industrialized countries.

It may be concluded that the standardization is not completely stable and that outside influences (political, social, economic) may be of importance here as has been argued (Meloen, 1983). Nevertheless, standardization provides a preliminary scheme for the interpretation of authoritarianism results, with some far-reaching consequences, as we will see.

Discussion

The global meta-analysis has produced results that on the one hand may allow more systematic interpretations and on the other hand suggest that a number of past interpretations are in need of revision. This applies to the original assumptions as well as to those of the critics. We will discuss some of the most important ones below.

Student Sample Bias

It is most surprising that *authoritarianism* research has derived its results mainly from *antiauthoritarian* samples. The student samples show systematically lower levels (3.43) than either the random (3.92) or the nonstudent samples (3.90), and this appears to have been the case from the first studies in 1945 onward. The effects of this rather systematic phenomenon can be called *student sample bias*.

These observations provide a strong argument against generalization from the frequently used student samples in social science investigations. F-scale research may have been biased, because these (mainly social science) student samples cannot be considered adequate for authoritarianism investigations. Students are not the nucleus of fascism (in Western samples and in the time period studied: 1945–present) and as a matter of fact represent almost the opposite of what authoritarian samples should be. Much of the knowledge gathered over decades is virtually without direct confirmation from studies of truly high scoring and right-wing extremist groups. In other words, we may have gathered little true knowledge of authoritarianism thus far. For example, Altemeyer (1981, 1988a) has argued that according to his results anti-intraception (opposition to tendermindedness, imagination, and subjectivity, according to Adorno et al., 1950; also called tenderness-taboo by Dicks, 1950) is not part of the authoritarianism syndrome. But this result may be limited to the predominantly student samples he investigated. The Steiner and Fahrenberg (1970a, 1970b) results show that the former SS men scored significantly higher on all four Adorno et al. (1950) F-scale items on anti-intraception, as compared to the former Wehrmacht sample, and there is certainly enough historical evidence of this aspect of SS behavior (e.g., Dicks, 1950).

Even more serious is the likelihood that many investigators have turned away from this type of research because student samples have given null results in tests of hypotheses based on *TAP*. Indeed, as we have shown earlier, fascist groups have hardly ever been investigated by authoritarianism researchers.

This student sample bias has had a much greater effect on the post–Adorno et al. (1950) follow-up investigations than it had on the original studies of the Berkeley group. In the presented meta-analysis, the majority of samples of the follow-up investigators were student samples (69%), whereas such samples made up only a minority of the Berkeley studies (8 student and 15 nonstudent groups, Adorno et al., 1950, p. 266). Adorno et al. (1950) were well aware of the disadvantages of student samples. But the follow-up research has over decades used mainly student samples in methodological, hypothesis-testing, correlational, and validation research. The critics of this research have also relied mostly on student samples.

These skewed results may be countered by applying the new standardized analyses suggested here. In a number of cases this may even lead to a complete reversal of conclusions. For instance, one may wonder how one can study authoritarian behavior by investigating low authoritarians. The highs within these groups may still not be representative of truly high-scoring groups, and their scores are often in the neutral zone of the scale. In addition, these relatively high-scoring students may not act in a truly authoritarian manner due to cross-pressures from the enlightened academic social environment. More accurately reinterpreting such groups as "lows versus moderates" makes it clear that no truly authoritarian behavior can be expected with these samples. Therefore, there is a need for a complete reinterpretation of results, as suggested by our standardization, and some conclusions may require complete revision.

The Restriction-of-Range Effect

One revised interpretation concerns the interrelations of phenomena that appeared rather weak in a large part of the research, due to low or moderate values of correlation coefficients (.30 to .40). It is now clear that most of the samples investigated have consisted of rather low-scoring (mainly social science) students, of limited age categories and with limited scopes of interest. This may suggest that groups like these are too homogeneous in important aspects.

If samples are too homogeneous, correlations derived from these groups can be expected to suffer distortions due to a restriction-of-range effect. The resulting correlations will be weaker than if more heterogeneous samples had been used. Jensen (1957), for instance, reported a weak relation (+.27) among a sample of senior students between the F scale and the Gough Prejudice (Pr) scale. Jensen noted,

This [correlation] is undoubtedly due to the very restricted range of scores on both scales in the college sample, a factor tending to lower the correlation coefficient. When the present sample was combined with a group of 96 junior college vocational students who had taken the same tests, the correlation between Pr and F rose to .65. (p. 306)

This restriction-of-range effect may therefore also lead to new interpretations.

Attitudes and Behavior

One of the effects of comparing low with moderate authoritarians instead of with true highs is the fading relationship with authoritarian behavior. In the 1970s, the highest scoring groups used in research had group means in the neutral range, around the scale midpoint. The conclusion has often been that these groups did not show "authoritarian behavior." Instead, it should have been concluded that the levels were probably not high enough to expect authoritarian behavior.

Although authoritarianism will not always coincide with authoritarian behavior, due to situational pressures, it is unlikely that there will be no relationship at all. The former SS men of Steiner and Fahrenberg's (1970a, 1970b) study, who were still highly authoritarian 20 years after World War II, were feared for this behavior. Of course, such behavior after the war was politically untenable and socially sanctioned. The non-correspondence of attitudes and behavior therefore is probably also a function of social and political power that has to this day been overlooked in the discussion of authoritarianism and behavior. For example, Ray's (1976) suggestion—that personality (by which he means his behavioral inventory of "directiveness") and attitudes (the F scale, in his interpretation) are two different things because they hardly correlated—has remained completely unchallenged. Ray's concept of directiveness, however, has been seriously criticized by Duckitt (1984), who argues that it is in no way related to the Adorno et al. concepts. Altemeyer (1988a, pp. 16–18) also criticized the directiveness concept and scale for shortcomings. In addition, it is highly unlikely, for instance, that these consistently highly authoritarian former SS men of Steiner and Fahrenberg's (1970a, 1970b) study, still clinging to dictatorship, would not have shown authoritarian behavior if they had had the chance. Also, the fascists of the Coulter (1953) study were activists, and highly authoritarian.

The discussion on the attitude–behavior issue therefore seems to be extremely flawed, and some systematic methodological biases such as using the wrong (student) samples, may have contributed to the now almost universally accepted notion of the nonexistent relationship between personality (or attitudes) and behavior, as far as authoritarianism is concerned.

It seems much more reasonable to find out when, and in what circumstances, authoritarians will show consistent authoritarian behavior. Some encouraging investigations have been carried out by Rigby, who showed that submissive behavior toward specific authorities is indeed substantially related to authoritarian attitudes toward these authorities and to peer-group evaluations (Rigby, 1984, 1987; Rigby & Rump, 1982; correlations ranging from .50 to .70). Rigby (1984) suggested a new framework, including both the directiveness *and* submissiveness concepts of authoritarianism. However, simply combining these two separate aspects may not be equal to the classic authoritarianism concept that includes support for both domination and submission within the *same* persons. In a recent test there was no positive correlation but a weak negative one $(-.22)$ between Ray's Directiveness scale and Rigby's (1984, 1987) Authority Behavior Inventory (an authoritarian behavior self report scale), thus suggesting both concepts have little in common. At the same time versions of the F Scale (Adorno et al., 1950), Altemeyer's (1988) RWA Scale, and Lederer's (1983) New General Authoritarianism Scale showed correlations between .50 and .60 with Rigby's behavior scale (Meloen, Van der Linden, De Witte, in preparation). This suggests that there is more consistency between authoritarianism and authoritarian behavior than many researchers have concluded thus far.[6]

Acquiescence Tendencies

Although many have been seriously involved in research on this tendency, one interpretation of its nature has become quite apparent, as Ray (1983b) has put it bluntly: "A person with a high F score might be simply a careless responder rather than a genuine fascist" (p. 82). The acquiescence tendency is therefore associated with the alternative explanation for high-scoring persons. This argument persisted for a long time, because no striking examples of relevant high-scoring groups were thought to exist, adding to the general doubt about the validity of the F

---

[6] This test was conducted in 1990 in Belgium in a survey of some 900 high school students. The supporters of the racist Vlaams Blok party also showed the highest mean scores on versions of the three authoritarianism scales, but not on Ray's Directiveness scale, confirming the main general propositions put forward here.

scale. Our review of authoritarianism research can help to clarify this issue. Two of the studies cited involving high scores (Sherwood's super-patriots [1966a], Kohn's students [1972]) and two studies reporting extreme low scores (Christie's counterculture [Gold et al., 1976], Mantell's conscientious objectors [1974]) used balanced F scales. Therefore, these extreme samples cannot have obtained their high or low scores as a result of response set. In addition, as mentioned above, samples did not show much difference in authoritarianism level whether this level was measured by unidirectional or balanced F scales. The estimated difference was only between .04 and .12 on the 1.00 to 7.00 SF scale, whereas the difference between the high- and low-scoring groups was as high as 2.00 points! Considering the results of the present study, the original hypothesis of Adorno et al. (1950), that authoritarianism can best be measured by unidirectional scales, seems to be much more likely (see also Rorer, 1965).

Education

The use of (social science) student samples has resulted in eliminating the differential effect of education on authoritarianism, a factor that may in some cases have an antiauthoritarian and in some an authoritarian effect. The social science samples used seem fairly predictable in acquiring less authoritarian attitudes during their stay at colleges and universities with rather liberal climates. Such a student sample bias has distracted attention from factors that may increase authoritarianism levels. Lower scores for the better educated are not universal, although they are fairly consistently reported for the U.S. and Western European student samples. Simpson (1972) reported no effect of education on authoritarianism in Mexico, whereas Liebhart (1970) in West Germany reported even *higher* group means after an educational training program than at the start of it.

It appears that an antiauthoritarian effect exists only for some types of education. The often-reported negative correlation between author-itarianism and education is sometimes interpreted without justification as if uneducated groups will start as highly authoritarian extremists, while through any type of education their levels will be lowered, and by pro-ceeding in this direction they will eventually become human!

An alternative interpretation is suggested here: Groups with relatively little education will start from a rather neutral position and move to a more or less authoritarian level, depending on the type of education. Child-rearing methods, as well as cultural levels, may also influence the base level. Although types of education that stress creativity and social relations may have an effect in an antiauthoritarian direction, this may not be the case for education in, for instance, technology, agriculture, or economy. The emphasis on education, and consequently on cognitive functioning, is not completely unwarranted, but seems to have dominated the research too much. Furthermore, the question of whether it is the highly authoritarian groups that drop out of the school system first, or whether the lowering of levels is due to educational training, has not yet been adequately answered. Much more research is needed in this field.

Conclusions

The general conclusion of this study is that the F scale is more strongly related to right-wing extremism than has hitherto been assumed. From the 1940s on into the 1980s, a number of groups consisting of activists as well as of supporters of ideologies associated with Nazism, fascism, apartheid, racism, and extreme nationalism have been shown to score high on the F scale or close F-scale derivatives. Their group scores are much higher than those of the general population, whereas clearly antifascist and antiauthoritarian groups tend to score lower than the general population. This adds considerably to the validity of the F scale as a potential fascism scale.

Whether the F scale is an authoritarianism scale as well may be a separate issue. This mainly depends on how *authoritarianism* is defined. The content of the F scale clearly addresses a right-wing authoritarian, hierarchical mentality in Western Europe and North America. At the time of the work of the Berkeley group, fascist regimes openly advocated and endorsed authoritarian state systems, and the association between fascism and authoritarianism was almost self-evident. If it can be shown that authoritarianism scales also predict support for former or existing authoritarian communist systems (as dealt with in another chapter), this would add a strong argument for the F scale's being an authoritarianism scale, one that is also independent of socioeconomic (capitalist or communist) ideology. In that case, Adorno et al. (1950) may indeed have produced the blueprint of a general authoritarianism scale. However, more evidence may be necessary.

Conservatives seem to define authoritarianism as the dominating behavior of left wingers. Yet the operationalization of this definition in the directiveness scale is not empirically associated with extremely high scores on this scale of right-wing (or left-wing) extremist groups to my knowledge, whereas the F scale has been shown repeatedly to be associated with such groups. In this respect, the F scale has full advantage over alternatives for which no extreme scores have yet been reported for extremist groups. The only exception may be the Dogmatism scale, which has been shown to be associated with right-wing extremism (DiRenzo, 1967b; Knutson, 1974; Altemeyer, 1988a, p. 261), but not with left-wing extremism, as Rokeach (1960) hypothesized. The Dogmatism scale has been shown to be highly correlated with the F scale. This also seems to be the case with Altemeyer's RWA scale so that similar results in general can be expected from the RWA and F scale.[7]

Most of the research findings discussed here were known or could have been known to major mainstream reviewers, such as Wrightsman (1977), Byrne (1974), Cherry and Byrne (1977), Dillehay (1978), and Goldstein and Blackman (1978). But the discussion about authoritarianism has ignored key information that has been available for decades and has subsequently deteriorated in quantity and quality, especially in the 1980s. The Steiner and Fahrenberg (1970a, 1970b) investigation had not been quoted until it was rediscovered by this author, nor has any major reviewer ever attempted a systematic search such as has been performed here. One is tempted to conclude either that no fascism is present in North America or that American investigators could have done a much better job to prove its existence with the F scale. The student sample syndrome of much research would tend to suggest the latter, although it is clear that both classical fascism and neofascism may be more European social and political phenomena than North American.

One may wonder about the amount of support provided by the present analysis for the authoritarian personality theory. Strictly speaking, this report shows that only the F scale has greater validity for measuring potential and actual fascism than is often assumed. Whether the original theory is satisfactory is another question. If Altemeyer (1981, 1988a) is even partly correct, it may be possible that other theories will prove more effective in explaining the empirical phenomena and that the RWA scale may be more efficient. However, his reduction of the authoritarianism concept seems historically questionable and ignores much that was already predicted by the F scale he so thoroughly "discredited," almost throwing away the baby with the bath water.

In the light of the reappearance of ethnocentric and authoritarian attitudes in the 1980s (Meloen et al., 1988), this research is too important for petty quarrels about the kind of insignificant side issues that have dominated the debate on authoritarianism for too long. Psychologists have contributed most of the studies in this field, mainly because many sociologists and political scientists do not give much credit to personal motivation and reasoning that can enhance the understanding of political phenomena. The study of authoritarianism, however, cannot be limited to psychology. Further analyses on social, political, economic, and historical levels are beyond the scope of this report, but suggestions for a more comprehensive, dynamic and multidisciplinary approach have

---

[7] In a sample of 131 Dutch psychology students the correlation between a 10-item original F scale and the 30-item RWA scale (no item overlap) was .62; the correlation of the F scale with the authoritarian half of the RWA scale (no item overlap) was even .71 (Meloen, 1991b).

been made elsewhere (Meloen, 1983, 1984, 1991a, 1991c; Meloen & Middendorp, 1991).

The relevance of authoritarianism research has been assessed in this analysis. It indicates that the results of authoritarianism research have been strongly underestimated.

4
Some Experimental Approaches to Authoritarianism: I. A Retrospective Perspective on the *Einstellung* (Rigidity?) Paradigm

RICHARD CHRISTIE

One can search the 990 pages of *The Authoritarian Personality* (*TAP*, Adorno, Frenkel-Brunswik, Levinson, & Sanford, 1950) in vain for any *experimental* evidence supporting its conclusions, although there are fleeting references to experiments by Rokeach. This is not too surprising because the authors were psychoanalytically oriented; three of them were personality psychologists, and the fourth, Adorno, a philosopher specializing in the aesthetics of music. All of the data were collected on adults, and the crucial materials dealing with childhood influences on adult attitudes and personality were retrospective. This led Else Frenkel-Brunswik (1948b, p. 295, footnote 1) to propose to the American Jewish Committee, which had sponsored the original research, that children should be studied directly. She suggested the possibility of doing *experiments* to test the implications of the theory underlying *TAP*. In the first paragraph of the concluding chapter of *TAP* it was noted,

Conventionality, *rigidity* [italics added], repressive denial, and the ensuing break-through of one's weaknesses, fears and dependencies are but other aspects of the same fundamental personality pattern, and they can be observed in personal life as well as in attitudes toward religion and social issues. (Adorno et al., 1950, p. 971)

If authoritarianism is so pervasive in personal life, why should it not show up in relevant laboratory situations?

Although the experimental research on authoritarianism–ethnocentrism (A–E) was initially impelled by studies of children, the majority of studies have been conducted on college students or other available captive audiences. The pioneering experiments by Rokeach (1948), for example, used both junior high school students and college students. The purpose of laboratory experiments is to test hypotheses based on assumptions about the theory presumed to underlie *TAP*; therefore, the kinds of samples employed should not matter if one takes as a starting point the sweeping assertion cited above.

There are more than 200 studies on A–E that can be considered experimental or close approximations thereof.[1] *Experimental*, for our present purposes, is defined as follows:

1. The use of the F scale or one(s) highly correlated wih it (e.g., the E scale) as one independent variable.
2. Experimental intervention(s).
3. The use of a dependent variable(s) to ascertain the differential performance among experimental conditions of those initially scoring at different points along the authoritarianism dimension.

This definition excludes (a) reports of correlations between the F scale and other scales, (b) case studies, (c) descriptive studies, and (d) survey studies unless there is reason to suspect that some outside (e.g., experimental) manipulation may have influenced the results.

It is an impossible task (within the space limitations of chapter) to summarize and analyze all of these studies. The focus is restricted to an evaluation of the research involving Einstellung problems, which was prominent in the early 1950s. This was not only the first experimental area in which A–E scores were used as an independent variable but also the first to achieve wide recognition. Attempted replications of this research were so ambiguous that Einstellung problems essentially disappeared as a topic of research after a decade. Many concluded that the rise and demise of the authoritarian-Einstellung syndrome proved that any experimentation on authoritarianism was doomed to failure.

My present aims are partly historic and partly heuristic. The methodological naïveté of most researchers (including myself) in the immediate post–World War II period led many to conduct research that seems incredibly simpleminded in retrospect. It should be pointed out that experimental social psychology was then literally a new discipline.

The rapid advances in experimental design and knowledge of new and more powerful statistical techniques changed the face of the field, and by the 1970s most graduate students were better trained in research methodology than many of their mentors who had been graduate students 20 or more years earlier.

Some of the comments in the following pages are critical both of the methodology used and the reporting of data in these early studies. It should be noted for the record that my remarks are based on hindsight after over 40 years of serving on hundreds of doctoral dissertation com-

---

[1] This estimate is based upon an unpublished analysis of the experimental literature on authoritarianism through 1978 by Dr. Diane Fenner Zwillenberg. She made an exhaustive critical appraisal of the relevant literature by using computor searches, tracking down references in bibliographies, and following informal leads in discovering relevant studies. She uncovered over 200 relevant studies and more have, of course, appeared subsequent to her search.

mittees. I have in the past made most of the errors that flawed the research to be reviewed and became aware of them after observing them being made by others.

The Einstellung–"Rigidity" Controversy

The first studies of experimental correlates of the A–E syndrome were conducted by Rokeach (1948) as a dissertation that was part of Frenkel-Brunswik's (1948b) project. Rokeach had known about Luchins's (1942) work on the Einstellung prior to its publication, through his under-graduate classes at Brooklyn College with Solomon Asch. In fact, he had argued with the latter that there were individual differences in susceptibility to set problems, whereas Asch had maintained the traditional Gestalt position that situational influences were all-important. When Rokeach, as a graduate student at Berkeley, became familiar with Frenkel-Brunswik's concept of rigidity in personality he immediately saw the conceptual relevance of the Einstellung problems.

Younger readers may not be familiar with the Einstellung paradigm, which was so popular in the post–World War II period that over 40% of a review chapter by Taylor and McNemar (1955) on problem solving and thinking was devoted to a section headed "Set, 'Rigidity,' and Functional Fixedness." Very briefly, the Einstellung, or set, problems involve presenting subjects with a series of problems that can be solved *only* by the use of a long set solution; that is, using a fixed series of steps is the only way to solve the problem. The experimenter then inserts one or more problems of similar appearance that can be solved by a short ("direct") solution as well as by the long set method—"critical" prob-lems. He or she may also substitute one or more "extinction" problems, which cannot be solved by the long set method but only by using a short, direct solution. Luchins and subsequent investigators have found that a surprisingly high proportion of respondents persist in using the long set solution when there is an option of solving the problem by using a short solution or, in extinction problems, to persist in using the set solution when it is inapplicable.

The first known use of the Einstellung problems was by two Gestalt psychologists, Duncker and Zener, at the University of Berlin in the early 1920s. Their work was first reported in print in an article by Maier (1930). A.S. Luchins (1942) explored the use of the problems in a lengthy monograph in which he reported the results of giving variations of the problems to groups of subjects under different conditions. His respondents varied from third graders to college professors, all of whom proved susceptible to the set, although the latter appeared to overcome it more easily. His basic procedure was to present the test taker with three hypothetical "jars" of different capacities to use as measures. The task was to obtain a given amount of "water" by filling containers and "pouring" from one to another.

Rokeach's Studies

Rokeach (1948) posited "(1) that individuals who are rigid in solving specific social problems (as measured by an attitude scale) also show up as rigid in solving non-social problems. (2) There is a general rigidity factor". (p. 260) He used critical rather than extinction problems as a measure of rigidity, a procedure that led to subsequent criticism. (See Taylor and McNemar, 1955, for a summary.) Because Rokeach (1948) defined rigidity as "the inability to change one's set when the objective conditions demand it" (p. 160), the critics argued that his use of critical problems did not "demand" a change of set and that only extinction problems that could *not* be solved by the set solution measured rigidity as he defined it. In addition, Rokeach (1948) never directly tested his second proposition.

Because most of the succeeding studies followed, although sometimes with modifications, Rokeach's (1948) use of critical problems as the criterion variable, his problems are reproduced in Table 4.1. It will be noted that the procedure used to obtain a desired quantity of water in the set solution is to (a) fill the large container in the central position, (b) pour off once into the middle-size container on the left, and (c) pour off twice into the small container on the right. The critical problems can be solved either by the long set solution or the direct solution, which involves filling the middle-size container on the left and pouring off once in the small container on the right.

In addition to defining the long solution to the critical problems as a measure of rigidity, Rokeach (1948), perhaps inadvertently, set up an experimental Einstellung of test administration. Most of the studies which followed also (a) used a group administration; (b) did not report clearly

TABLE 4.1. Rokeach's Einstellung problems.

	Capacity of jars			Desired amount
Two-jar example	39	4		Get 31
Control problem	13	29	3	Get 10
Set problems	30	40	3	Get 4
	31	61	4	Get 22
	14	59	10	Get 25
Critical problems	23	49	3	Get 20
	11	25	3	Get 8
	17	40	6	Get 11
	10	23	3	Get 7
	11	27	5	Get 6

the social aspects of test administration; (c) did not report the means, standard deviations, and almost never the reliabilities of the scales used to measure the A−E syndrome (although lack of specificity about scales was typical of many of the articles at the time). This makes it almost impossible to do an adequate assessment of many of these studies and does not permit precise replication.

In Rokeach's (1948) experiment on the Einstellung with college students, the problems were written on a blackboard and the subjects were given 2½ minutes to solve the problem and write their answers in a blue book. Of 92 subjects, 22 were eliminated subsequently because they solved the second, or control, problem by the long method or made arithmetical errors. The remaining 70 subjects were classified as high or low scorers at an unspecified cutting point on a 10-item Ethnocentrism scale (probably the one used on Form 40/45, *TAP*, Table 16, IV, p. 128).

On the first critical (sixth) problem, 23 (66%) of the 35 high scorers used the long set solution, in contrast to 21 (60%) of the low scorers, an obviously nonsignificant difference. However, on the following critical problems (7 through 10) both groups showed greater use of the short solution so that on the final problem 11 high scorers (31%) used the long solution in contrast to only 5 (14%) of the low scorers. Rokeach (1948) totaled the number of critical solutions over the five problems and found high scorers used the long solution on 2.23 problems as against 1.37 by the low scorers, this difference being significant ($p < .05$).

In a second experiment, with adolescents aged 13 to 15, a similar procedure was evidently followed. In this instance the California Attitude Scale I was used. This was a 50-item scale designed for this age group and has not, as far as is known, been published. The problems were modified so that an additional set-inducing problem was given, and 10 instead of 5 critical problems were used as the dependent variable.

There was greater attrition because of arithmetic errors (104 of 193 potential subjects were discarded) than had been true in the college sample. An additional 14 subjects were eliminated because they solved the control problem using the short solution. The remaining subjects were split at an unspecified median, leaving 37 high scorers and 36 low scorers. There was greater use of the set solution on the part of both groups than was true with the college sample; 32 (87%) of the high scorers used it on the first critical problem, as compared to 26 (68%) of the low scorers. On the 10th and last critical problem, the number of set solutions were 21 (56%) and 12 (32%), respectively, this difference being significant ($p < .05$). On all of the 10 critical problems, the high scorers used more set solutions than the low scorers, and four of these differences are reported as significant. No comparison was made of the total number of set solutions of the two samples.

Rokeach's (1948) results were widely accepted as supporting his main hypothesis that prejudiced individuals are more rigid in problem solving.

He did not directly test his second proposition—that rigidity is a general factor—although he did give a "maps" test that was based on the same principle as the numerical problems, but he did not correlate scores on the two tests.

Brown's Study

It was 5 years before Brown's (1953) research raised questions about the conditions under which Rokeach's (1948) results could be replicated. As teaching fellows at the University of Michigan, Brown and his colleagues had used Rokeach's (1948) paradigm as a classroom exercise and had been unable to find significant differences between high and low scorers in the use of the set solution. This led to reexamination of Rokeach's (1948) procedure; it was noted that Rokeach had administered the test in a large classroom setting, that the problems were described as a "test," and that the subjects had to write their names in a blue book. In other words, although the arithmetic problem had nonsocial content, the interpersonal setting in which it was given was definitely social. The instructions might be viewed as ego-threatening. This setting was contrasted with the attempted replications, which were conducted in a casual, offhand manner.

The presumed differences in the two situations were therefore tested. In an ego-involving condition

the experimenter (E) maintained an extremely grave, aloof manner, dressed formally and conservatively, and repeatedly cautioned Ss against looking at their test materials ahead of time, or conversing with one another about the tests. . . . [E] suggested that the tests to be taken (a measure of n Achievement was also given) were measures of intelligence and motivation and that the results were of great importance" (Brown, 1953, p. 471).

Subjects were also asked to sign their names on all test forms.

In the non-ego-involved group, "E wore extremely informal sports clothes and maintained a very casual, offhand manner. . . . E described himself as a 'psych major' carrying out a class project in which he personally took very little interest" (Brown, 1953, p. 471). The respondents did not sign their protocols until after completing the experiment.

The only other reported difference between Brown's (1953) and Rokeach's (1948) procedures was the omission of the latter's second control problem. Otherwise the problems were identical. It was not stated whether a 2½-minute period was allotted to each problem, although the instructions given to the ego-involved subjects suggest that some time interval was used. No mention was made of losses due to arithmetical errors or how these were handled if they occurred. Because the subjects were drawn at random from required freshman English classes, arithmetical perfection on the part of respondents seems unlikely. There is also no mention of the number of subjects tested at one time, although the word *they* in reference to experimenters suggests that the 80 subjects in the non-ego-involved group and the 82 in the ego-involved group must have been broken into smaller groups.

Brown (1953) found that members of the non-ego- involved group(s) had a mean score on the Einstellung of 8.41 and that members of the ego-involved group(s) had a mean score of 8.79. The scoring system was not specified (there were five critical problems per subject). It is impossible to tell whether these differences are significant or not because Brown (1953, footnote to Table 2) noted that the standard deviations were not presented because they were distinctly bimodal. This would indicate that those who solved the first critical problem by the set method tended to persist in its use on the subsequent problems, and those who used the direct solution on the first critical problem also persisted in its use.

The crucial comparison was the correlation between the F and Einstellung scales in the two groups. No correlation was found among the non-ego-involved and one of $+.40$ in the ego-involved group, this difference being significant ($p < .05$). Strictly speaking, Pearsonian correlations are based upon the assumption of normality in both distributions, which, as Brown (1953) noted earlier, does not apply to the Einstellung scores.

Brown (1953) used the scores on the measure of the need for achievement as an explanation for the difference in results in the two situations. Individuals scoring in the middle third on this measure were hypothesized to be "anxious about achievement," and this group showed significantly less success at using the short solution among the ego-involved group (Brown, 1953, Table 3, p. 472).

Levitt and Zelen's Studies

An article with a different thrust appeared in the very same issue of the *Journal of Abnormal and Social Psychology* as the one by Brown (1953). Levitt and Zelen (1953) investigated the use of the critical problems by Rokeach (1948) as to whether they met his definition of "... rigidity as being present where objective conditions demand a change of set." (Rokeach, 1948, p. 260) Among their experiments were two in which a 14-item E scale (Adorno et al., 1950, p. 117) was also administered. There was no control problem, but four set problems and seven critical problems were used. The only difference between the two conditions was that in one group there was a warning, "Don't be blind" (which Luchins, 1942, had found to decrease the Einstellung effect) for one group prior to the administration of the test. In this "incentive" manipulation, subjects worked at their own speed and were allowed to leave the classroom when they had finished, and one of the two experimenters checked the solutions for correctness. Bimodal distributions on the use of the set solution were found; those using the set solution performed slightly faster than those using the direct solution. Levitt and Zelen (1953) concluded from this that the use of the critical problems as a criterion did not *demand* a change of set because it was just as fast to solve them using the set as to search for and find a more direct solution. More relevant to the present chapter is that they did not find any relationship between use of the set solution and E scale scores.

Levitt and Zelen (1953) then did a further experiment; the following is a complete description of their methodology:

> Rokeach's results were duplicated with a group of 20 Ss, using Form 78 of the California E scale. The C group [direct solution] ($N = 9$) with a mean of 5.67 critical solutions (10 critical problems) has a mean E score of 30.34. the S group [set solution] ($N = 11$) had a mean E scale score of 52.82. The difference between the mean E scores is significant below the .01 level. (p. 575)

This finding is later referred to as occurring under "free conditions," the term presumably refers to a condition used in an earlier experiment in which students had an entire class hour to work on the problems at their own speed.

Lacking details, it is difficult to integrate these findings with those of Brown (1953). Taylor and McNemar (1955) raised the question as to why neither set of investigators used extinction problems in view of Luchins's (1949) earlier critique of Rokeach for not doing so. In reply, Levitt and Zelen (1955) ran two more experiments. In one, they gave the 20-item version of the E scale (Adorno et al., 1950) and used the following sequence of Einstellung problems: Five set, two critical (Cr), two extinction (Ex), two Cr, two Ex, two Cr, two Ex, and then one Cr, one Ex, and a final CR. Scoring was based on the number of extinction problems prior to the first use of the short direct solution on the Cr problems. A short solution on either of the first two Cr problems was given a score of 0, a first short solution on the third or fourth Cr problem was given a score of 2, a first short solution on the fifth or sixth CR problem a score of 4, a first short solution on the seventh Cr problem a score of 6, a first short solution on the eighth Cr problem a score of 7, and a score of 8 was arbitrarily assigned if none of the Cr problems was solved using the short solution.

Thirty-five male freshmen subjects were tested in a class hour. Six were discarded for making arithmetic errors on the set problems. The complete distribution of scores was not given, but piecing together the *ns* in various subanalyses (Levitt and Zelen, 1955, p. 335) indicates the following distribution: "Eleven subjects had scores of 0 or 2, 10 had scores of 4, 3 had scores of 6 or 7, and 5 never solved a single, critical problem using the set solution and were given a score of 8. No information is given as to how many subjects solved the extinction problems or whether the extinction problems were timed or not (did the five who never solved a single critical problem get stuck on the first block of extinction problems and never proceed further?). The use and treatment of extinction problems is ambiguous; it is not clear why they were not used as a criteria of rigidity.

The 14-item E scale (Form 78) was administered to the 29 subjects who made no errors on the set problems. A nonsignificant rank order correlation of minus .175 was found between the E scale and the scores based on the number of extinction problems given before a direct solution was used on the critical problem.

This experiment is difficult to evaluate because the description is very brief. Because specific information is lacking, it is impossible to tell what the experimenter–subject relationship was. This (as was true of the other Levitt and Zellin studies) was conducted in a single, regular class period. The subjects may well have been students in a class taught by one or the other of the experimenters.

Eriksen and Eisenstein

Eriksen and Eisenstein's (1953) approach was primarily clinical and focused on the use of a mocified Rorschach technique. Included in a battery of tests that were administered individually were 14 items from the 20-item E scale plus another 6 items drawn from an earlier version of the E scale. None of the items referred to Jews. A unique version of the Einstellung problem was used in which there were two practice problems, three set problems, and four critical problems, then five problems that could be solved either by a set solution $(A - 2B - C)$ "or by a direct method such as $A - B$ or $A + C$" (Eriksen & Eisenstein, p. 388). These direct solutions are obviously impossible because A has to be the largest container for the set formula to work and $A - B$ cannot give the same results as $A - 2B - C$, nor can adding the largest one (A) to a smaller one (an impossibility given the nature of the problem) give the same answer as the formula.

The E scale was filled out anonymously and turned in to the departmental secretary, who wrote the subject's name on the form after the subject left. The Einstellung problems were given individually to each of the 33 subjects, as were the other test materials. It is not clear from the article whether all of the test materials were given in one session; the conditions of administration are unknown. The only relevant data reported are correlations among the measures; the E scale correlated $-.06$ with Einstellung scores.

This study differs from the previous ones in that respondents were tested individually rather than in groups. It is impossible to determine from the available data what effect, if any, this had upon the results.

Applezweig's Study

Applezweig (1954) gave "the Luchins arithmetic Einstellung test" (p. 225) to three successive groups of candidates for submarine school. She gave no information as to which of Luchins's tests was employed or about the conditions of administration. Five other tests presumed to measure rigidity in previous studies were also administered. Her interest was in using natural stress as an independent variable, so one group was tested the day before they were required to escape from the bottom of a 100-foot-deep tank of water, the second was tested the day after the escape, and the third 1 week afterward. One of her measures was the 20-item version of the California E scale; she found the low scorers on the E scale solved more problems by the short solution ($p < .02$) on the day before the stressful test (when stress was presumed to be highest). The low scores used fewer short solutions on the day after ($p < .02$, not predicted), and no significant differences were found between the week-after groups.

Further, the patterns of correlations among the six tests in the three administrations were essentially random, with 21 being positive, 21 negative, and 2 being zero. This, however, is typical of studies of this nature in which tests purportedly measuring different kinds of rigidity have been used. These data are again difficult to interpret in terms of Brown's (1953) paradigm because the origin of the ego-involvement in the situations is different, being a physical challenge to one's masculinity in Applezweig's (1954) research and the forbidding nature of the experimenter in Brown's (1953) study.

French's Study

French's (1955) study is similar to Applezweig's (1954) in that in French's study a young civilian female was testing a group of servicemen, in this instance basic airmen, on a battery of tests purporting to measure rigidity. Among these were an unspecified version of the California F Scale and an unspecified version of the Luchins Einstellung problems in which "the first few items of the series" are set problems and "these are followed by several critical problems" (French, p. 114).

French's (1955) study differs from that of Applezweig (1954) in that ego-involving instructions were given to 50 airmen and relaxed ones to another 50. The ego-involving instructions stated that the tests were "selected because they give a very good picture of a person's intelligence and all-around ability. . . . The results will be of importance in your future Air Force assignment" (French, p. 114). Names and serial numbers were entered on all test booklets. The relaxed instructions were that the respondents were taking "all new tests we are trying out. We really don't know very much about them. . . . We are interested in test results only—

not in how one man does on them. You don't need to put your names on the paper at all" (French, p. 115).

The F scale and Einstellung problems were among those given to groups of five each. This, incidentally, is the only known instance in which the F scale has been given under ego-involving conditions, and the means and standard deviations for the two groups, interestingly enough, were practically identical. This is also the only study among those being reviewed in which the reliabilities of the F or E scale have been reported. The difference in reliability under the two conditions was negligible, being .78 under ego-involved conditions and .79 under relaxed conditions. One unique finding, however, is a +.22 correlation in the relaxed group between the F scale and the AFQT1, a test of intellectual ability routinely given upon entrance into service. The correlation of −.26 found among the ego-involved group is actually not as strongly negative as is usually found in a group as heterogeneous as basic airmen.

The only scale showing a difference between the two groups was a "test of insight" developed by French (1955) as a projective measure of need for achievement, which yielded higher scores (significant at the .05 level) among the ego-involved group as predicted. There were, however, no higher correlations among the rigidity measures in the ego-involved and relaxed groups and the F scale–Einstellung correlations were a nonsignificant −.06 and +.10, respectively. A further point of interest was French's attempt to repeat Brown's (1953) results by examining the relationship between high and low achievement anxiety groups and F-scale results. No significant differences were found. It should be noted, however, that different measures of need for achievement were used in the two studies and that both mean levels of achievement and F-scale scores would be expected to differ dramatically between enlisted airmen and Michigan undergraduates.

Jackson, Messick, and Solley

Jackson, Messick, and Solley's (1957) study was a straightforward replication of Brown's (1953) ego-involving experimental condition with one twist: the examination of the role of response set in Einstellung problem solving. Jackson et al. reasoned that if agreement set response was adequately controlled, many of the relationships previously found with the F scale might be different. The ego-involved group in Brown's (1953) study was chosen as a model, and Jackson et al. used the Form 40/45 California F Scale as an all positively worded scale and a specially constructed F scale with items worded in the nonauthoritarian direction to test their hypothesis. The identical Einstellung problems used by Brown (1953) were given in a group administration. Of the 77 original subjects, 10 were eliminated because of arithmetical errors. Thirty-two respondents who used the short solution remained after 13 who failed to use one or the other procedure consistently were discarded. The following ego-involving procedure was used for all subjects:

The experimenter, dressed in a dark suit, was introduced to the class as an experimenter who was going to administer some very important tests. Instructions were then read which suggested that the tests were measures of intelligence and leadership potential and that the Ss were being compared with students from a nearby state university. They were instructed to write their names on the test papers. (Jackson et al., p. 138)

Those using the long solution had significantly higher ($p < .05$) scores on the F scale than those using the short solution. The "reversed" items were not statistically reversals because they correlated positively ($+.39$) with the original F scale instead of negatively, as a more psychometrically adequate set of reversals would. Interestingly enough, the relation between Einstellung and the reversed scale was also significant, although not as strong as with the original F scale, lending credence to the authors' contention that response set might have a role in experimental results.

Of all the studies under review, Jackson et al.'s (1957) comes closest to a precise replication of Brown's (1953) ego-involving situation, in that the experimenter deliberately played an authoritarian role.

Coulter's Study

Data from a doctoral dissertation by Coulter (1956) is partially reported in two sources, a book by Eysenck (1954) and an article written by Eysenck after Coulter's premature death (Eysenck & Coulter, 1972). Coulter administered the California Form 40/45 F scale, the 20-item Ethnocentrism scale, and an unspecified modification of the Luchins (1942) Einstellung problems, along with a battery of other tests, in an individual 2½-hour administration to three groups of male, working-class respondents in Great Britain. One was a captive audience of 86 soldiers at the Maudsley Clinic; another was composed of 43 active members of the Communist party who had been recruited at a summer school, at party meetings, or from personal contacts. The third group was composed of persons attending one or more of "nearly" 100 Fascist party meetings over a 5-month period. (Because it was estimated that there were 400 or fewer Fascists in the London area—Eysenck and Coulter, 1972, p. 61—it would appear they spent a great amount of time attending meetings.)

Because members of the last two groups were volunteers, were recruited individually, and were highly skeptical about research, great care had to be taken to prevent them from breaking off during testing. It is noted,

The greatest care was taken to make the expression of the subject's attitudes as free and uninhibited as possible. They were assured of complete anonymity and reassured that their names were not needed and not wanted. The subjects were told that even the investigator would not know what scores they made as the results were to be tabulated quite independently. (Eysenck & Coulter, p. 63)

In short, by necessity if not by design, the testing situation had to be extremely low-key and non-ego-involving. Under these conditions, the correlations between the F scale and Einstellung were $+.12$ for the soldiers, $-.09$ for the Communists, and $+.15$ for the Fascists, none of these being significant (Eysenck, 1954, Table 29, p. 226). Correlations with the E scale were not reported.

Bringmann's Study

If some of the earlier studies are puzzling, a short report by Bringmann (1967) is downright perplexing. Bringmann used 10 Einstellung problems, "five *set-inducing* problems to be solved only by one method (B − A − 2C), one *extinction* problem which could not be solved either by the original or a simple procedure" (p. 1069). If subjects solved eight or more problems by the original method, they were labeled *rigid*. Because the extinction problem could not be solved by the original method, the maximum score was 9 (a point to which we will return), and this included the original set-inducing problems. Each problem was in a separate booklet, and subjects were evidently allowed to proceed at their own speed, as Bringmann noted, "Ss proceeded to the next problem only after completion of all previous ones" (p. 1069).

The subjects were 122 male undergraduates enrolled in a second required English course at a "southern state university," probably the University of Mississippi, as the author listed his affiliation as "University, Mississippi." The 122 were those who remained after an unspecified number of students who had taken courses in psychology and sociology were screened from the sample. The item mean score on "the final version of the F scale" is reported as being 3.18, with a standard deviation of .72, which Bringmann (1967) reported to be "similar to previous ones" (p. 1070). Reference is made to *TAP*, in which scores on the Form 40/45 are reported on two student samples, George Washington University women with a mean of 3.51 and testing class women (University of California at Berkeley) with a mean of 3.62, these groups being roughly half a standard deviation higher than Bringmann's. A second reference is to Roger Brown's (1965) textbook, in which there is a brief sentence noting that American college students usually score in the range from 3.0 to 4.0 (p. 527) without specifying what characteristics of schools led to different scores within that range. The third and final reference is to Rokeach (1948), who, it may be remembered, did not use the F scale in the rigidity research and did not give means! More relevant comparisons might be made to mean F-scale scores on other southern college samples: Bass (1955), Louisiana psychology students, 3.83; Christie and

Garcia (1951), Oklahoma psychology students, 4.10; Hites and Kellogg (1964), Alabama art students, 3.62; and Jackson and Messick (1957), Texas psychology students, 3.77.

The question is, Why did Bringmann's (1967) sample score so unexpectedly low compared with other southern college samples? This is an even more relevant question because Bringmann threw out those taking psychology and sociology courses, who are usually in the lowest part of the F-scale distribution.

The next source of puzzlement comes from a perusal of Bringmann's (1967) results. He divided his sample into three groups on the basis of F-scale scores: the upper 15%, the lower 15%, and the middle 70%. The mean number of set solutions is reported to be markedly bimodal, with the number using set solutions reported to be 8.5, 9.0, and 6.0, respectively (out of a maximum of 9.0), which is significantly curvilinear. Shades of Shils! (See Shils, 1954, and chapters 2 and 8 in this book.)

It strains even my bounds of credulity to imagine that *all* 17 of the lowest scorers on the F scale solved *every* problem using the "rigid" set solution, as their mean score of 9.0 indicates. This becomes even more incredible if it is remembered that they had an extinction problem prior to the critical problems, which should have broken the set for at least some of them. And making the assumption that most of the moderate group solved the set problems correctly (there is no mention of arithmetical errors), it is hard to believe that all 85 of them used the short solution a mean of 2.5 times, as contrasted to .5 for the high scorers, as against none for the low scorers. Clearly there were errors in data processing, or the laws of probability were miraculously suspended in Bringmann's (1976) study.

Summary to Date

A tally indicates the use of short solutions on critical problems in the Einstellung experimental paradigm, when related to measures of authoritarianism or ethnocentrism, has produced 6 significantly positive results, 1 significantly negative result, and 13 nonsignificant ones. An average of .316 is not an impressive average in research, however good it might be for a batting average in baseball. One might be tempted to say that the investigators have thrown, albeit inadvertently, an assortment of curves, junkballs, spitters, wild pitches, and beanballs in an attempt to baffle us.

There are a number of procedures other than tallying the good up with the bad, the clear with the murky, that may be used in an attempt to make sense out of a welter of conflicting, incompletely reported data. One such procedure is to look at studies in which one is fairly certain of what was going on. In hindsight one can say that almost all of the research reports lacked complete information about procedures that are relevant to an interpretation of the results. Within these limitations, what do the successes have in common?

The role of *authoritative experimenters* appears to be relevant. Brown (1953) surmised that in Rokeach's (1948) two positive findings the experimenter's role was crucial, in that E behaved in what might be called a formal authority role and thus aroused ego-involvement on the part of the subjects. Brown (1953) succeeded in replicating Rokeach's results only when behaving in a formal, authoritative manner. Jackson et al. (1957) replicated Brown's (1953) procedure as closely as possible and also obtained positive results. Applezweig (1954) obtained positive results when she presumably used the same (upspecified) instructions and behavior as in the situations in which she obtained a significant negative result as well as in one that was not significant. The only obvious difference among her three groups was stage of training. And we have no way of knowing how Levitt and Zelen (1953) behaved in the one condition in which they obtained positive results, or for that matter, in the ones in which they didn't. The only known case in which the experimenter deliberately tried to create ego involvement and failed to obtain a differentiation was in French's (1955) study, and this involved a civilian female experimenter with an enlisted male military sample.

Five groups were tested under what were stated to be relaxed or non-ego-involving conditions: Brown's (1953) and French's (1955) control groups and Coulter's (1953) three English samples. In none of these cases was there a significant difference in susceptibility of high and low authoritarian subjects to Einstellung behavior on the critical problems.

There is no way of determining from the published accounts the experimenter's demeanor in the studies in which no differences were found. It should be noted that some of these studies were conducted before Brown's (1953) article suggesting the importance of the experimenter role was published and all but one preceded Rosenthal's (1966) emphasis on the experimenter effect.

In retrospect, it is also clear that there were a number of other factors that mitigated against finding positive effects. In many of the studies, it is pointed out that there was attrition because of arithmetical errors. These presumably occurred most frequently among the least intelligent potential subjects. Levitt (1956), in his critique of the Einstellung problem as a psychometric device, estimated the correlation between intelligence and use of the long solution on the critical problem as about $-.20$. This suggests that some of those most prone to rigidity were screened out prior to being tested because they made errors in arithmetic on the set inducing problems, thus lowering their chances of establishing the set.

A further watering down of possible relationships occurs because of the bimodality of distributions on the critical problems used as a dependent variable. Where information is given, it appears that if subjects solved the first critical problem using the set solution, then most of them continued using it on subsequent critical problems. There are partial exceptions. Rokeach's (1948) college subjects solved 63% of the first criterion problems using set solutions and 27% of the sixth and final one. Rokeach (1948) had eliminated part of his sample, however, by using a control problem before inducing the set.

Some Personal Confessions and Reflections on the Einstellung Paradigm

When I arrived at Berkeley in the fall of 1947 as a graduate student, the research on authoritarianism that would appear 3 years later in *TAP* had been completed and the authors were writing up their results. Rokeach's (1948) as yet unpublished dissertation had been completed and was a topic of excited discussion among my peers. It was so intriguing that I was seduced into examining the Einstellung effect. Working within an interpretation of Tolman's (1932) learning theory, I hypothesized that subjects learning the set problems under high motivation would persist longer than those under relaxed conditions. Of greater interest, however, was the hypothesis that the introduction of frustration prior to the beginning of the critical problems would increase tension and lead to greater persistence in Einstellung solutions.

A pilot study was conducted in which one class of introductory psychology students was given ego-involving instructions and another task-involving instructions. Rokeach's (1948) variations of the problems were given on separate pages of blue books, and his procedure of allowing 2½ minutes per problem was followed. The two-by-two design was completed by inserting an unrelated task between the last set-inducing problem and the first critical problem. This had a 2-minute time limit and was one in which the subjects were presented with parallel rows of squares ("houses") and circles ("wells") and told to connect each house to each well with a line ("pipe") with the restriction that no pipe could cross another. Half the subjects in each group received one of two interpolated problems. Those in the nonstress condition had to connect four houses and two wells, which is easy to do. The stressed group was faced with connecting three houses and three wells, which is impossible in two-dimensional space.

My initial ego-involving induction was too strong for the time allotted for solving the set problems. The students started eagerly, but by the second set problem the faster students started looking around after quickly finishing the problem and exchanged questioning glances at me and the slower students. Shortly after the beginning of the third set problem, which the quicker students solved immediately, giggles commenced at the unexpected simplicity of the problems; soon laughter broke out, the slower students looked around in an attempt to determine what was happening, and "ego-involvement' evaporated. I made a difficult and ultimately unsuccessful attempt to maintain a proper experimental mien.

This debacle led me to reexamine Luchins's (1942) monograph more carefully. Luchins (1942) had not reported using individual administrations of the problems in his myriad variations of the Einstellung. My previous experimental manipulations of rats and men had always been on a one-to-one basis, and I felt comfortable with that situation. Individual administration had the additional advantage of permitting observation of the process by which subjects proceeded. It was decided to try again but on an individual basis. As this aspect of procedure was being changed, some additional modifications were made as well. Luchins's (1949) and Taylor and McNemar's (1955) later criticisms of the use of critical problems as a measure of rigidity were easily anticipated, so I decided to use an extinction problem that was solvable only by adding the capacity of the middle- and small-size jars. The subject was timed until the problem was solved, indicating that the set was *broken* as indicated by the attainment of the simple nonset solution. Thus, the variation was to use a criterion problem that could *not* be solved by the set solution and to allow the subject to work on it until he solved it. This would permit comparisons of the length of time to solution on the criterion problem divided by the average time spent on the set-inducing problems. This "rigidity ratio" was designed to control for wide variations in individual problem-solving speed.

As long as I was tinkering with the procedure, it seemed interesting to vary two additional aspects of the set problems. In Rokeach's (1948) and most of Luchins's (1942) problems, the jars were always in the same relative positions, so the Einstellung problems could be solved by either of two sets, for example, "fill the large container, pour once into the middle-size container, and twice into the small one" or equally logically, "fill the middle jar, pour once into the left one, and twice into the right one." Which set (or combination of them) were testees using?

The procedure employed was to eliminate the second, or position, effect by shifting the spatial arrangement of the jars from problem to problem. The second modification was to vary which of the smaller containers was poured into twice—either twice into the middle-size and once into the smaller container or once into the middle-size one and twice into the smaller one. The set could be verbalized as, "Fill the largest container (L), pour off once into both the middle-size container (M) and the smaller-size container (S), and once into one or the other smaller containers (M or S)." A pilot study indicated that 54% of subjects followed the set on a critical problem following Rokeach's (1948) procedure, and 58% did so following the modified one. The sequence of problems given is indicated in Table 4.2.

TABLE 4.2. Modified Einstellung procedure.

Problem type	Solution(s)	Container sizes			Desired amount
1. Demonstration	M − S or L − 2M	4	23	9	Get 5
2. Sample problem	L − 2M − S	5	65	8	Get 44
3. Set problem	L − M − 2S	47	10	22	Get 15
4. Set problem	L − 2M − S	11	5	57	Get 31
5. Set problem	L − M − 2S	3	57	20	Get 31
6. Set problem	L − 2M − S	25	12	69	Get 7
7. Critical problem	L − 2M − S or M − S	6	51	17	Get 11
8. Interpolated solvable/ unsolvable geometric problem					
9. Extinction problem	M + S	15	92	22	Get 37

The subjects (66 in all) were drawn from a pool of introductory psychology students who were required to participate in experiments as part of their course obligation. They were tested individually and were told they could use any number of containers and could add or subtract by pouring water from one container to another in any combination necessary to obtain the requirement amount. They were not given explicit ego-involving instructions but were told that they would be timed on each problem. Because I was sitting across a table timing them and taking notes, the situation might well be viewed as ego-involving for many individuals. The problems were mimeographed in test booklets, with ample space for arithmetical computations. Odd-numbered booklets had the interpolated control problem, even-numbered ones the unsolvable one. No time limits were imposed except for the unsolvable problem, when it was said, "This problem can be solved by college students fairly easily. The average time for solution is 29 seconds. There will be a 2-minute time limit on the problem."

Nineteen subjects made arithmetical errors on one or more of the four set problems, and their protocols were discarded. Only 32% of these used the set solution on Problem 7, the critical problem, as contrasted with 66% of those who made no errors on the previous problems. This suggests that they had not established the set and raises grounds for skepticism about the results in those studies previously cited in which there was no check on arithmetical accuracy.

The 47 remaining subjects were then classified as to those who used or did not use the set solution on the critical problem (Problem 7 in Table 4.2) and the 31 (66%) who employed the set were retained for analysis. The 15 subjects receiving the control interpolated problem had a median completion time of 33 seconds per problem on the four set problems and a median of 37 seconds on the extinction problem (range: from 6 seconds to 4 minutes and 54 seconds). Those given the unsolvable interpolated problem had a median of 28 seconds on the set problems, but on the extinction problem their median time jumped to 1 minute and 56 seconds, with solving speed varying from 16 seconds to 8 minutes and 39 seconds (with the exception of one subject who never obtained the correct solution and gave up in disgust after 15 minutes). A subsequent Mann-Whitney U test analysis of the time spent on the extinction problem by the two groups yielded a U of 42, which is well within the .002 level of confidence (two-tailed test). A similar analysis using rigidity ratios (mean time on the extinction problem divided by time on the set problems) yielded a slightly less powerful U, which was still significant at the .002 level (it had been erroneously anticipated that the rigidity ratio would be a more discriminating test). Interpolated stress created by the insoluable problem increased significantly the persistence of a set mode of procedure in a situation in which it was maladaptive.

At this point, it might be asked: What relevance does this have for authoritarianism? Because the F scale had been given in some of the classes from which the subjects had been recruited, scores described as "high" or "low" were available after the experiment for many of them. Although I had never seen a copy of the F scale at that time, it was rumored that high scorers were more likely to be prejudiced, rigid, suspicious, and everything a psychologically correct Berkeley graduate student in psychology was not supposed to be. It seemed interesting to see whether high and low authoritarians could be identified, so along with my notes on their problem-solving performance during the experiment an "H" or "L" was entered immediately after the completion of the introductory remarks and the practice problem but before the subjects started on the set problems. When the list of high and lower scorers was made available, it was checked against my guesses, which were correct in slightly over 80% of the cases. The protocols were scrutinized and the behavior of each subject was revisualized. It was clear in retrospect that my guesses were based on my gut reaction to each subject: I hadn't liked the high F scorers. Why not? As nearly as the situation could be recreated, they appeared to resent being dragooned as subjects and behaved sullenly or perfunctorily at this intrusion in their lives. This contrasted with the low scorers, who were interested in and curious about the experiment and even at the very beginning of the session displayed a distinguishably different interpersonal style.

Word of this serendipitous finding spread through the graduate student underground to Else Frenkel-Brunswik, whom I had never officially met, and she invited me to her office in the Institute of Child Welfare. Some of the graduate students working with her were launching a joint study on adolescents, and she invited me to join them. She was eager to see if the modified set of Einstellung problems would confirm Rokeach's (1948) results and was also curious about whether or not high and low scorers in a demographically different sample could be identified by a naïve observer.

The students were obtained in two separate suburban junior high schools in the Bay Area; they had previously taken a Children's Ethnocentrism scale (presumably the same one Rokeach had used on junior high school students 2 years before). They were tested individually in classrooms during the Christmas vacation week of 1948. I conducted the experiment in the first school, and a fellow graduate student, John Garcia, tested those in the second school.

There were only 45 children available as subjects, so the decision was made to run them all on the sequence using the insolvable interpolated problem and rate them on a 1- to 4-point scale as to degree of frustration because it was feared that after attrition there would not be enough subjects for a control group. (Rokeach [1948] lost 54% of a similar sample because of arithmetical errors and failure to understand instructions, and I had lost 29% of college students on this sequence of problems for arithmetic malfunctions.) In addition, to minimize the attrition of possible subjects, it was decided to monitor them and not accept a solution to problems unless the subtraction (or addition) was correct. During the set problems, then, if a subject made an error in arriving at a "solution," he was asked to check his arithmetic. Given the great difficulty in finding a solution to the final extinction problem on the part of some of the college students, the procedure on it was modified. If the solution had not been found in 5 minutes, a hint was given about remembering the original instructions. If this did not lead to a solution, more specific hints such as "You don't have to use all the containers" were given at predetermined intervals. Precisely two thirds of the subjects used the set solution on the critical problem, which is almost identical with the 66% of the college students who had solved the set problems [using] in the previous study.

Of the 30 using the set solution, 10 were rated 1 or 2 in frustration on the interpolated problem, and 20 were rated 3 or 4, that is, "high." The same directional difference was found as with college students, but the respective medians on the set problems were much higher, being 1 minute and 31 seconds for those rated low in frustration and 1 minute and 96 seconds for those rated high. On the extinction problem, the lows had a median of 4 minutes and 6 seconds, and those rated high in frustration one of 7 minutes and 53 seconds. This difference in time of solution on the extinction problem was significant at slightly better than the .002 level by the Mann-Whitney test, which gave the same level of significance to the rigidity ratio. There was no reliability check on the ratings of frustration, and the giving of hints on the last problem attenuated the time for solution. Of the 10 rated low in frustration, 6 solved the final problem before the first hint at the 5-minute mark, as against only 2 of the 20 rated high.

Observations of subjects' behavior in the earlier experiment suggested the recording of the sequence of individual subjects' problem-solving behavior. The behavior most relevant to rigidity was *the actual number of times the subject used the set sequences*: L − 2M − S or L − M − 2S on the extinction problem. Persistence in using the set when it could not possibly lead to a solution clearly is a better operational definition of rigidity than using a criterion problem that can also be solved using the set solution. Because such a distribution more nearly approximates normality, it is better psychometrically than the highly skewed time tests. Those rated low in frustration on the interpolated problem used the set on the extinction problem a mean of 2.2 times each, and those rated high a mean of 4.05. This difference yielded a *t* of 3.87, which is significant beyond the .0005 level.

The findings relating to authoritarianism were both ego-deflating and provocative. My newly discovered clinical acumen had vanished; the guesses as to whether the 22 students I tested were high or low on ethnocentrism were exactly at a chance level. I quickly went over my notes on the students, and then the light dawned. The high-scoring subjects had not displayed the initial hostility that had characterized those in the first study and had served as a differentiating cue. It was only after making the original guess and during the subjects' performance on the set-inducing problems that differences in behavior emerged. High scorers appeared oriented to me as an authority figure and were looking at me for signs of approval when they solved a problem correctly or for help when they made errors. The low scorers' attention, in contrast, was more typically focused on the problems and can better be described as task-oriented. Consider the differences in attitudes toward authority in the two situations: The conservative college highs were skeptical of me as a representative of a liberal establishment probing into "things that can never possibly be understood by the human mind," to quote part of an F-scale item, whereas the naïve junior high school high scorers saw me as an authority figure from a major university whose presence was approved by the local school system and important enough to take up part of their Christmas holiday.

Garcia and I discussed my procedures, and he agreed to make the same guesses as to high or low ethnocentrism as well as following my procedures as exactly as possible. He did one thing in addition: Before the subject started the extinction problem, Garcia, who had not been told about my hunch about experimenter orientation and ethnocentrism scores, rated the testee on a five-point scale from completely task-oriented to completely experimenter-oriented. (Parenthetically, no sex differences were noted on any of the variables we used.) Garcia was no more successful than I had been on guessing ethnocentrism scores, but his ratings on task versus experimenter orientation correctly identified the classification of 17 of the 23 subjects he ran: The probability of this is .046 (two-tailed) by the binomial expansion. A tentative post hoc explanation for differences between highs and lows in the two situations is that the latter are less affected by their attitudes toward experimenters as authority figures and are task-oriented. They are thus more likely to attend to the problems and perceive the set solution on the induction problems. When the set solution did not solve the extinction problem, they more quickly perceived its inapplicability, dropped it, and searched for an appropriate solution. Although high scorers in the two situations have different attitudes toward the experimenter as an authority figure, in both experiments their concern took their attention away from the task. The low scorers in both experiments, on the other hand, apparently had fewer concerns about the experimenter as an authority figure and worked away on the problems.

Let us return to the relationship between scale scores and the Einstellung. Of the junior high school sample, 30 subjects used the set rather than short solution on the criterion problem (Problem 7). Half of these were low scorers and half high scorers. Only 3 of the 15 who gave the short solution were high scorers, and the other 12 were low on ethnocentrism. (One of the 12 was an Einstellung-resistant female who proved she was less rigid than the experimenter by discovering a previously undetected and correct nonset solution to Problem 4). Although the greater susceptibility to the Einstellung is in the expected direction, given Rokeach's (1948) results, it fell short of significance, the chi-square being 2.59, with one of 2.71 being required for the .20 level. Ratings of frustration on the unsolvable interpolated problem did not distinguish between high and low scorers. The mean time scores on the extinction problem were 5 minutes and 57 seconds for the lows and 9 minutes and 24 seconds for the highs, the t being 1.98, which is significant almost exactly at the .05 level. (A t test is not the most appropriate one, given the nature of the data, but the key to identification of subjects as to ethnocentrism scores has long since disappeared, so it is impossible to do a more appropriate nonparametric test.)

It is not suggested that these findings are generalizable. Specific information on the distribution of scale scores and the cutting point was not available, and whether the classification of subjects as high or low was based on a median split or on the upper and lower quarters of the distribution as was typical of some of the comparisons made in *TAP*. The ratings of frustration were made by only one judge, so there was no reliability check. The project was, of course, unfunded so the only outlay were the expenses involved in dittoing the test materials. It was thus typical of many studies done in the late 1940s, which were more characterized by enthusiasm than methodological sophistication.

The Einstellung as a Measure of Rigidity

My experiences in the individual administration of the Einstellung problems, which made it possible to observe what subjects were actually doing in acquiring and breaking the set solution, led to the following conclusions.

Subjects who appeared task- (rather than experimenter-) oriented in the initial set-inducing problems were quicker in discovering the long, correct solution. When presented with the extinction problem a few found the short direct solution amost immediately. More typically, they tried the set solution (L minus M minus 2S or L minus 2M minus S) and, when it did not work, they re-examined the problem and found the non-set solution.

In contrast, individuals who were slower in picking up the set did not appear as task-oriented (e.g., they might have been more oriented toward the experimenter) and made more errors on the initial set-inducing problems. They took, on the average, twice as long in seconds to find the set solution on the first two problems; by the time they arrived at the last two set-inducing problems they were as fast in using the set as their peers. When faced with the extinction problem, they tried using the set solution roughly twice as many times as those who obtained the solution quickly. Coding of the steps taken before the solution was discovered suggests that they had a "fuzzy" set (i.e., they would start by filling the large container and try the set solutions over and over); after finding these did not work they tended to try filling the large container and engaged in nonsystematic subtraction or sometimes initially filled the middle-sized container and subtracted. Their behavior suggested that they had a nest of sets: first the actual set solution, then one starting with the large container, then a generalized subtraction set.

One conclusion from these observations was that subjects who could clearly cognize the set solution easily saw that it did not apply to the extinction problem. Once this became obvious, they looked at the problem anew and more quickly saw the simple non-set solution. Those with fuzzy sets took much longer to see that the technique did not work; they persisted longer in the use of the set solution and sometimes in bizarre variations of subtraction, before finally breaking the set and seeing the "obvious" answer.

Assuming that the foregoing is valid, it is possible to reexamine the unsystematic variations in individual problem-solving procedures as they affect the contradictory results on the authoritarianism–Einstellung relationships found in the studies reviewed. What differences might enhance or detract from problem solving efficiency as they relate to task involvement?

Discarding Subjects Because of Arithmetic Errors

Because none of the arithmetic involved in the Einstellung problems is particularly esoteric, one can argue that most errors arose because the subject was not sufficiently task-involved to have been paying close attention to what he/she was doing. Such individuals developed fuzzy sets and were most prone to have difficulty in breaking them. Discarding this subgroup of subjects for errors in arithmetic excluded some of the potentially most rigid subjects from the final sample, increasing the probability of discovering differences as sharp as one might expect. Levitt (1956) estimated that there was a +.20 correlation between arithmetical ability and high scores on ethnocentrism; this might weaken the relationship between authoritarianism/ethnocentrism and Einstellung proneness when subjects who made errors were excluded from the sample.

Discarding Subjects for Using the Direct Solution on a Criterion Problem

This procedure (which I used in my studies) to insure that the subjects had a strong set before facing an extinction problem was, in retrospect, a mistake. It eliminated 44% (12/27) of low ethnocentric subjects who had solved the set-inducing problems correctly and 17% (3/18) of the high ethnocentric subjects. The excluded subjects were ones who might be expected to quickly solve the extinction problem and their exclusion weakened the significance of the findings.

My present inclination would be never to discard arbitrarily these subjects, but to examine separately the groups of subjects failing to meet arbitrary criteria.

Critical vs. Extinction Problems as a Criterion of Rigidity

If one takes Rokeach's (1948, p. 260) definition of Einstellung rigidity seriously ("the inability to change one's set when the objective situation *demands* it" [italics added]), the use of critical problems in which the subject has the choice of using either the longer set solution or the shorter, direct one is *not* demanded. In practice it is just as fast (although not as elegant) to use the set as the short solution (Levitt and Zelen, 1953). On the other hand, an extinction problem *demands* that the set does not work.

Aside from the logical argument against using critical problems as the criteria, there are practical arguments. In practice, those who used the set solution (L minus M minus 2S) on the first critical problem rather than the direct solution (M minus S) tended to continue doing so on succeeding trials, although there was some erosion (e.g., some subjects discovered the short solution on subsequent critical problems and, once having done so, continued to use it). Those investigators who have reported on this aspect of their studies have noted that they obtained bimodal distributions. Subjects were lumped into two categories: rigid and nonrigid; those who broke the set on succeeding critical problems were scattered in a valley between them. This violates common sense observations about rigidity of behavior as a continuous rather than dichotomous variable, and creates a relatively insensitive dependent variable (as Levitt [1956] has pointed out). The tendency to repeat the solution actually used on the first critical problem yields results similar to those yielded by an attitude or personality scale with only one item (or, more accurately, a scale in which the same item is repeated over and over again).

If, on the other hand, an extinction problem with a time limit is employed, subjects will again fall into two categories: those who get the problem and those who do not. It might be possible to use a series of extinction problems with time limits. The only known report to use a modification of this technique was that of Levitt and Zelen (1955), who interspersed extinction and critical items (although it is not clear whether they used a time limit). Their technique focused on using the short solution on critical problems and not on solving the extinction problems on which no information was given. It did serve to divide the sample into four groupings: over one third found the short solution quickly, another third took a moderate amount of time, a few persisted longer before finding it, and almost one sixth never found the short answer. This distribution is better than a dichotomy but still does not provide a fine-grained discrimination. By exercising great patience and ingenuity and by varying them sufficiently using different combinations of addition and subtraction, one could probably devise a sequence of extinction problems that would make finer distinctions among individuals.

An advantage of using a single extinction problem and letting subjects continue until they solve it is that this gives a range of scores; therefore a continuous measure of the dependent variable can be obtained. There are a number of measures that can be used: (1) time spent on the last (extinction) problem, (2) a "rigidity ratio" in which the time to solve the last problem is the criterion is divided by the amount of time taken to solve the set problems, or (3) a process analysis in which the subject's responses are coded to see how many times he/she actually uses the set solution before finding the correct one. In my limited experience, the first two have given similar results. The last is harder to do but is theoretically more relevant because it provides a measure of how many times the subject *actually uses the set* before finding the solution.

Time scores on the extinction problem are highly skewed, but the distribution can be normalized for parametric analysis or analyzed by nonparametric ranking tests such as the Mann-Whitney. (The use of such tests did not come into general use in social psychology until after the publication of Siegel's (1956) book on nonparametric statistics, when most of the studies on the Einstellung had been completed).[2]

---

[2] An example of the power of more sophisticated techniques of data analysis is provided by an analysis of the time in seconds needed to solve the extinction problem (#9) in my college sample. A chi-square based on a median split that

Time scores do not, however, indicate what the subject was *actually doing* while working on the problem. In contrast, a process analysis with junior high school students of the coded steps taken to solve the problem in the experiment was done; subjects who rated low in frustration on the preceding interpolated problem used the set solution on the extinction problem an average of 2.2 times, compared with one of 4.5 for those rated as highly frustrated. The number of non-set but fuzzy set solutions (starting with the large container and attempting non-set subtraction solutions or the middle container and subtracting) was 2.3 and 4.55, respectively. Both sets of differences are significant at beyond the .001 level based on *t* scores (the distribution was close enough to normality to permit the use of a parametric test).

Use of a Battery of Different Types of Einstellung Problems

One possibility, which has not yet been explored systematically, is the use of different kinds of Einstellung problems as a dependent variable. This would provide greater generalizability about the relationship between persistence of set and authoritarianism than the use of a single type of problem. Rokeach (1948) reported a pilot study on the use of maps: a long set solution was learned, then subjects were given a map of similar appearance in which there was a shortcut from the starting point to the destination. This procedure had a number of technical problems, but Rokeach did find that, in a small sample of college students, those scoring high on an unspecified measure of ethnocentrism took longer to find the shortcut.

An interesting variation was described by Cowen, Wiener, and Hess (1953). They devised an alphabet maze in which subjects started in the upper right-hand corner and had to find a path by finding words to the lower left-hand corner of the maze. The set solution involved a nine-letter, three-word solution by taking an indirect route. The critical problems provided the same long set route with an optional short solution in which one five-letter word ran along the diagonal from the starting to finishing points. They also used the Luchins water-jar technique and found a significant phi-coefficient of .46 between the two disparate measures of Einstellung rigidity. Unfortunately for our present purposes, they did not administer the F or E scales.

These two examples suggest that the dependent variable of persistence of set might be more reliably and validly measured by the development of

---

dichotomized the data had a significance level at only the .10% level, indicating only suggestive support for the basic hypothesis. After Siegel's book appeared, the data were reanalyzed using the Mann-Whitney U test, which took into account the skewness of the data. The results were significant at the .002 level, which lent stronger support to the original hypothesis.

parallel sets of Einstellung problems using arithmetical, spatial, and verbal materials.

Group vs. Individual Administration

There is no clear indication that group versus individual administration of the Einstellung problems produces faster or greater acceptance of the set in the studies surveyed. Group administration is much more efficient in producing a large amount of data in a short period of time. The main disadvantage (given the level of technology available at the time the cited studies were conducted) is that it was not easily possible to examine the *process* by which subjects establish and maintain a set solution.

Individual administration of the Einstellung problems provides an opportunity for a fine-grained analysis of what subjects actually do in acquiring and persisting in set solutions. It is, of course, very time-consuming to examine one subject at a time. A further problem is that of the lack of reliability of ratings or codings of behavior when there is only one observer making them. It is, however, difficult to induce low stress or low ego involvement when a battery of people are focusing on what one is doing.

Gender

These studies were conducted 40 or so years ago when mostly male experimenters studied mostly male subjects. In the two studies with which I have been associated, no sex differences were found. There were three studies in which the principle investigator was female. Coulter's (1957) study of samples, probably consisting of mostly male subjects (one sample consisted of members of the military and was presumably all male), tested under nonthreatening conditions found the usual lack of relationship between authoritarianism and rigidity. In contrast, Applezweig (1954) reported both confirmatory and negative findings in her study of male submarine trainees and French (1955), in her study involving young men in the military service, is the only person to have reported not finding a relationship between specific ego-involving instructions in which the Einstellung problems were compared with authoritarianism. It is presently inferred (although it was not explicit stated in the reports) that these two female investigators actually administered the experimental materials to the two groups of young males in military service.

This point is raised because both male and female high-authoritarian subjects believe (or say they do on questionnaires) in traditional sex roles in which the men are dominant and women are submissive. It might be that the presence of a female experimenter in the role of an authority figure is disruptive enough to lessen task involvement on the part of high-authoritarian but not low-authoritarian subjects.

On the Use of Adequate Measures of Authoritarianism/Ethnocentrism

It is a given in research that there is no relationship between two variables if either or both have low reliability (e.g., do not differentiate adequately among the subjects). It has been argued that the Einstellung problems that have been used have grave but remedial defects as a dependent variable.

What about the measures of authoritarianism? Authoritarianism was tapped by the following scales: An unpublished children's authoritarianism scale (Rokeach, 1948), a ten item E scale (Rokeach, 1948), an unspecified version of the F Scale (Brown, 1953), a 14-item E scale from Form 78 of one of the Berkeley batteries of tests (Levitt and Zelken, 1953), a 20-item version of the final version of the E scale (Levitt and Zelen, 1955), a 20-item E scale that was a composite of items selected from two versions of the E scale (Ericksen and Eisenstein, 1953), the 20-item version of the E scale (Applezweig, 1954), an unspecified varsion of the F Scale (French, 1955), the Form 40/45 version of the California F scale, (Jackson, Messick, & Solley, 1957; Coulter, 1956) and the "final" version of the F Scale (Bringman, 1957). In my pilot work, both the F scale (the Form 60A given to college students at Berkeley at the time) and the unpublished children's authoritarianism scale were employed.

Clearly these measures are not completely comparable and insufficient descriptive information is given to evaluate their effectiveness in any of the studies. These studies were all completed long before Altemeyer's (1981) Right-Wing Authoritarianism (RWA) scale was available. This scale has the virtues of focusing on the core of authoritarianism, being counterblanced so that agreement-prone respondents are not combined with ideologically consistent authoritarians, and having very high reliability. These characteristics make it especially useful in experimental work (Christie, 1991); this was demonstrated by the superiority of the RWA scale when "pitted" against other measures of authoritarianism in predicting experimental results (Altemeyer, 1981, pp. 196–202).

One can only speculate what the results in the studies reviewed here would have been had had the RWA scale been available for use.

A Final Note

In four of the five studies in which ego-involving instructions were given (Rokeach [1948] twice, Brown's experimental group [1953], and Jackson, Messick, & Solley [1957]), subjects scoring high on measures of authoritarianism or ethnocentrism displayed greater Einstellung persistence than their low-scoring counterparts. French's (1955) experimental group is the only one violating this pattern.

In all five instances in which it is clear from the published research that the situation was not ego-involving (Brown's [1953] control group,

French's [1955] control group, and Coulter's [1957] three groups), no significant differences on rigidity as measured by the Einstelliung problems were found between high and low scorers on measures of authoritarianism.

It is unclear what the nature of the experimenter–subject relationship was in the other studies reviewed.

All of these studies used critical problems as the criterion measure, which, it has been argued, is a very imprecise measure of the persistence of the Einstellung. There are weaknesses in the reporting of data, in the methodology used to obtain them, and in the statistical treatment of data in these studies. Given all these problems, it is viewed as more than suggestive but near miraculous that any pattern of findings evolved.

It is suggested that the use of explicitly ego-involving instructions or other conditions that keep subjects from being task-involved deleteriously affects the ability of high authoritarians to break the Einstellung to a greater extent than that true of low authoritarians (but that under conditions in which there is no stress both groups of subjects display comparable performance). As Levitt and Zelen (1955, p. 333) noted, "The controversy over the nature of the water-jar extinction problem has to be settled in the laboratory." The present contention is that an adequately designed and executed experiment would confirm the suggested interpretation and help to resolve the controversy about authoritarianism and rigidity, at least as far as the Einstellung problems are concerned.

5
Some Experimental Approaches to Authoritarianism: II. Authoritarianism and Punitiveness

RICHARD CHRISTIE

The initial interest in experimental tests of variables hypothesized as related to authoritarianism waned with the accumulation of conflicting and often noninterpretable results. For a time, there was no popular paradigm for experimental research on authoritarianism. This changed when the social dissent of the 1960s centering on the civil rights movement and opposition to the Vietnam War led to a renewed questioning of social norms, and the relevance of the F scale to understanding the behavior of those upholding or challenging the status quo became salient. Those rebelling against the social establishment became increasingly confrontational and in conflict with the legal establishment. The authors of *The Authoritarian Personality* (*TAP*, Adorno, Frenkel-Brunswik, Levinson, & Sanford, 1950) had not concerned themselves directly with law and punishment but rather with "obedience and respect for [unspecified] authority"; and on the punishment side, "Sex crimes . . . deserve more than mere imprisonment; such criminals ought to be publicly whipped, or worse." Although the authoritarian syndrome was implicitly relevant to punitiveness toward violators of the law, it was not the subject for investigation until the late 1960s.

Studies on the Relationship Between Authoritarianism and Punitiveness

The first known experimental study[1] directed toward the relationship between authoritarianism and legal punitiveness was conducted by Boehm (1968). She was impressed by the antiauthoritarianism of pro-

---

[1] This chapter is based in large part on the literature search by Diane Fenner Zwillenberg referred to in footnote 1 of chapter 4 and upon her unpublished doctoral dissertation (Zwillenberg, 1983). The material has been rearranged and condensed to fit into this chapter. I am solely responsible for the over-simplification of her fascinating findings.

testors and developed a scale, Legal Attitudes Questionnaire (LAQ), which had three subscales measuring attitudes toward the legal system:

1. Authoritarianism, (e.g., "Too many obviously guilty persons escape punishment because of legal technicalities").
2. Equalitarianism (essentially, acceptance of legal status quo, e.g., "The Supreme Court is, by and large, an effective guardian of the Constitution").
3. Antiauthoritarianism (e.g., "Unfair treatment of underprivileged groups and classes is the chief cause of crime").

Items were presented in 10 sets of triads, each of which contained one statement from each subscale. Respondents indicated which of the items they agreed with most strongly and which they disagreed with most strongly. Comparisons were made with the F scale, and the hypothesized positive relationship was found with the Authoritarianism subscale and negative ones with the Equalitarianism and Antiauthoritarianism subscales, "with degrees of statistical significance that were acceptable, although not extremely high" (Boehm, 1968, p. 739).

An actual case was selected in which a defendant was found guilty but had his verdict overturned on appeal by a higher court on the grounds of insufficient evidence. Two versions of the case were prepared with crucial evidence in the protocols being modified so that the evidence was slanted toward guilt in one (Guilty case) and toward innocence in the other (Not Guilty case). The protocols were given in odd–even format along with the LAQ to an undergraduate sample. Three verdicts were possible given the "judge's" instructions: acquittal, manslaughter, or second-degree murder. The sample of 153 undergraduates gave significantly different sentences depending on the version of the crime they received. It was found that the 53 classified as authoritarians made "tough" errors (convictions of manslaughter or second-degree murder) in the Not Guilty case and the 48 antiauthoritarians made more lenient errors (acquittal or manslaughter) in the Guilty case (overall χ^2 $p < .001$).

There were 20 or so additional experimental studies in the 1968–81 period that dealt with the relationship between authoritarianism and legal punitiveness. Unlike the rigidity studies, they did not follow a fixed paradigm and varied from quite simple to extremely complex in design. They used measures of authoritarianism that varied widely: The original F scale, revisions of it, items selected from the F scale, other scales correlated with the F scale, and scales based on items designed to tap legal aspects of authoritarianism. There is a problem common to the studies reviewed earlier in that few measures of reliability were reported on the samples tested. When the F scale was used, it was apparently assumed that a scale based on the original California samples 15 to 25 years earlier would hold up equally well on a new generation of respondents. It is not possible within present space limitations to critique each of these studies, so we will restrict ourselves to some overall comments.

General Relationships

The following studies presented comparisons of general relationships between authoritarianism and punitiveness. Newman, Articolo, and Trilling (1974) gave summaries of "deviant" activities involving one-sentence descriptions of (a) abortion, (b) protest against government policy, (c) misappropriation of government funds, (d) homosexual relations in private, (e) failure to warn of danger, (f) incest, and (g) permitting poisonous gas to be released into the atmosphere. No differences were found on a 15-point rating scale of seriousness for these offenses among those scoring high or low on a combination of 16 F-scale items and ones from the conservative tough-minded quadrant of Eysenck's (1954) Tough-Minded Conservative scale. Sherwood (1966a) compared high- and low-scoring students on the 29-item F scale as to how a management human relations problem should be handled and found 72% of the high scorers gave coercive or arbitrary punishment, as compared with only 16% of the low scorers. Sherman and Dowdle (1974) used a complex multi-dimensional scaling technique to analyze the dimensionality of crimes; they then compared high and low scorers on the 29-item F scale and found that high scorers gave longer prison terms for such crimes "as mostly of the capital offense category (1st and 2nd degree murder, assault with intent to kill, manslaughter and child molesting)" (p. 123). The authors also note that previous studies relating judged seriousness of crime to severity of legislated punishments to be only moderate at best. Vidmar (1974) interviewed a sample ("roughly representative") of 144 adult residents of London, Ontario, Canada, about attitudes toward the death penalty, among other crime-related topics. A brief questionnaire was given that included three unspecified items from the F scale. The latter significantly differentiated ($p < .05$ by Chi-square) between high and low scorers in the expected direction.

Linear Relationships

The following studies, which involved vignettes of cases, found linear relationships between some measure of authoritarianism and severity of punishment.

Centers, Shomer, and Rodrigues (1970) presented the instance of a 17-year-old juvenile who participated in a gas station robbery with some adult confederates to a sample of 1,275 survey respondents in the Los Angeles area. The question was how severely the adolescent should be punished; high authoritarians (as measured by Sanford's, 1950, brief F scale) were significantly more punitive and recommended at least some prison sentence.

Jurow (1971) presented randomly one of two cases to a sample of 211 white, middle-class industrial workers; the murder of a liquor store proprietor by an ex-convict or the murder and rape of a college woman by a drug addict. Boehm's (1968) LAQ correlated significantly with a conviction verdict at the .01 level in the first case and the .05 in the second. Results using the F scale failed to reach significance.

Snortum and Ashear (1972) conducted interviews with 80 white residents randomly selected from two communities in the Los Angeles area. Respondents were scored on a six-item Anomic Authoritarianism (AA) scale and a four-item Police Violence (PV) scale devised by Louis Harris in conjunction with the Task Force on Assassination and Political Violence. They were then given two case descriptions: The first involved the first-degree murder charge against a liquor-store owner for shooting a man in the course of an armed robbery, the other a second-degree murder charge in which a spouse was killed during a domestic argument. Photographs of the defendant in the first case were of a white male in half the cases and a black male in the other half; the killer was male in half the cases and female in the other. The dependent variable was years of imprisonment varying from zero to 100, with the death penalty being given an arbitrary value of 110 years. There was a correlation of .20 between AA and punishment for the first-degree murder case ($p < .10$) and one of .33 ($p < .005$) in the second-degree murder case. It is also reported that when simply recommendation of the death penalty versus nonrecommendation was used as a dependent variable that "correlations of about the same magnitude . . . were found" (Snortum & Ashear, p. 293). It is of interest to note that the AA and PV scales correlated .47, because the items on the latter are described as suggesting "that the S is willing to take the more active step of endorsing fascistic police power to impose structure and induce social conformity" (Snortum & Ashear, p. 295). Further, the item "What young people need most of all is strong discipline by their parents" has the highest correlation (.49) of any single one of the 10 attitudinal items with the punitiveness index and is a slight rewording of one of the most discriminating of the 30 original F-scale items in a variety of samples (Christie, 1991).

Friend and Vinson (1974) used subscales of the F scale in a negligent homicide case in which one of three conditions of attractiveness of the female defendant were given: attractive, neutral, or unattractive. She had struck and killed a pedestrian while driving when intoxicated. Male students at the State University of New York at Stony Brook were divided into three 34-person groups, and each received a different version of the case. The high authoritarians gave the defendant an overall mean sentence of 9.86 years in contrast to the low authoritarians' 4.56 years.

Bray and Noble (1978) formed 44 six-person mock juries composed of students who were either all high or all low on Byrne and Lamberth's (1971) version of the F scale. They listened to a transcript of a murder trial in which two inebriated male defendants were accused of murdering a woman who had rebuffed their advances in a nightclub. Subjects made individual judgments as to guilt or innocence and then, if the defendant was found guilty, recommended a prison sentence. They were then asked to participate in the mock jury for 45 minutes and come to a decision. Finally, subjects repeated the individual judgments made before. High authoritarians gave significantly more verdicts of guilty ($p < .001$) before and after deliberations, and the same was true for length of sentence. In addition, the interpersonal interaction during the deliberations produced a significant statistical interaction effect ($p < .001$) in that low authoritarians were more lenient after deliberations and the high authoritarians even more punitive. Both groups seemed equally affected by interaction with their similar peers.

Griffitt and Garcia (1979) recruited subjects who had taken the Cherry and Byrne (1977) version of the California F Scale in a classroom setting. The 80 experimental subjects (half high and half low scorers on the F scale) were met individually and told that scores on one of the scales they had taken earlier had been "lost" and that to help the "other investigator" interested in their responses it was necessary to retake the test. The missing questions (from the F scale) were read by the experimenter, who recorded their responses on the usual seven-point scale. Half of each group was given verbal conditioning counter to their original responses, with the other 40 serving as controls. It worked: Low scorers were conditioned to give more authoritarian responses to F-scale items than they had originally, and the high scorers gave less authoritarian responses under these conditions. However, the successful experimental manipulation was not strong enough to eliminate the differences between the two groups on a recommended sentence for a hypothetical drunk driving case.

Other Relationships

There is another group of studies that find relationships with authoritarianism and certain classes of targets (e.g., "defendants") or for different types of crimes, but not a clear-cut linear relationship.

Gladstone (1969), in a report that defies easy summary, used a 3 × 2 × 2 factorial design in an experiment. There were three types of transgression—against persons, against propriety, and against property—with four examples of each. The actual stimuli used are unclear. Two transgressions in each condition were carried out by a high-status person and two by a low-status person. Subjects were 25 matched pairs of high scorers and 25 matched pairs of low scorers on the F scale (version unspecified) selected from "several different types of college classes and . . . several dormitories" at Oklahoma State University. "Reasonable" punishments for each transgression were evidently summed for the dependent variable.

There was a main effect for authoritarianism, which was significant at the $p < .005$ level for the subject variable, score on the F scale (Gladstone, 1969, Table 1, p. 287). No means are given, but the present inference is that the high scorers on the F scale were more punitive, because it is noted that "the significance of F × T [the F scale of the respondent by transgression interaction] was significantly more punitive on the propriety transgression only" (Gladstone, p. 287). Interestingly enough, there was no main effect for the status variable and, as might be expected, a significant one ($<.005$) for the transgression variable. As the author notes, "HF and LF [high and low authoritarians as measured by the F scale] may differ little or much in punitiveness depending upon the type of transgression involved" (p. 288).

Attractiveness of the perpetrator was manipulated by Mitchell and Byrne (1973) by rigging information presented about him that completely agreed or disagreed with responses on five attitudinal areas on a questionnaire previously taken by each subject. The offense was stealing a copy of an examination to be given in a course in which the culprit was enrolled. The 139 subjects (Purdue University introductory psychology students) were dichotomized into high and low scorers on the Byrne and Lamberth (1971) counterbalanced F scale. Among other judgments made were those of severity of punishment on an eight-point scale, varying from giving a warning to permanent expulsion from school. The high authoritarians were marginally more punitive ($p = .054$), but the interaction between F-scale scores and attractiveness was significant ($p < .02$). This reflected the fact that low scorers gave almost identical punishment to similar and dissimilar others, whereas the high scorers recommended more severe punishment to the dissimilar defendant than the subjects in the other three conditions ($p < .01$).

It is also of interest to note that Mitchell and Byrne (1973) did a follow-up study that replicated this one except for the manipulation of presumed similarity and found no significant differences in the punitiveness of high and low authoritarians.

Berg and Vidmar (1975) reported a highly similar study in which they used the Mitchell and Byrne (1973) cheating paradigm but manipulated the status of the offender rather than his attitudinal similarity to the subject. The high-status offender, the son of a business executive, was an honors chemistry student planning to go into medicine. He had very good grades and was captain of the football team. The low-status offender was a son of a factory worker with no plans for the future who barely managed to pass his courses. Once again, the main effect for authoritarianism was at a marginal level of significance ($p < .06$), but the interaction of authoritarianism and status of offender was significant ($p <$ .05). Low authoritarians did not discriminate between offenders of differing status, but the high authoritarians were much more punitive toward low-status offenders.

Vecchio (1977) used recommendations to a parole board as to how much of a convict's remaining sentence should be served as one dependent variable in a $2 \times 2 \times 2 \times 2$ factorial design. The six subjects per cell were drawn from an introductory psychology class at Notre Dame University. The independent variables were (a) high or low authoritarianism as measured by the Byrne and Lamberth (1971) version of the F scale; (b) severity of crime, with the contrast being between bank robbery with concomitant assault on a bank guard versus breaking and entering a private residence; (c) an extremely favorable or unfavorable recommendation for parole by a rehabilitation officer; and (d) an attractiveness measure based on similarity of opinion of the convict and the subject. High authoritarianism, severity of crime, and unfavorable recommendations were all significantly associated ($p < .01$), but the attraction variable was not. A three-way interaction of authoritarianism × severity × recommendation was significant at $p < .05$. The high authoritarian judges discriminated on severity of crime when the rehabilitation officer's recommendation was favorable but not when it was negative. The low authoritarians discriminated on severity only when the recommendation was negative.

Garcia and Griffitt (1978a) reasoned that overconcern with sexual deviance ("Exaggerated Concern With Sexual 'Goings-On' " was the title of one of the nine hypothetical clusters characteristic of authoritarians in *TAP*, p. 235) should elicit greater punitiveness on the part of high authoritarians than physical violence. On a pretest, 80 male and 80 female introductory psychology students were dichtomized at the median on the Cherry and Byrne (1977) F scale. In the experiment they were presented with the hypothetical case of a 35-year-old male schoolteacher with no criminal record who either (a) showed his 13-year-old son (or, in half the cases, daughter) sexually explicit films, fondled him or her around the genital area, and forced the adolescent to reciprocate (ending in the latter masturbating the offender); or (b) repeatedly hit the son (daughter) with his fists and a belt, leaving multiple bruises. In all cases these indignities occurred several times, after which the victim reported to a relative who in turn notified authorities. Respondents were asked to (a) judge the defendant guilty or not guilty on a seven-point scale, (b) assume the defendant guilty and sentence him to prison for 10 to 30 months, and (c) determine the number of visits per year the child should be allowed to see his or her jailed father. Date were analyzed in a 2 (authoritarianism) × 2 (sex of child) × 2 (sex of subject) design for each of the crimes separately. As predicted, the high authoritarians gave significantly longer sentences ($p < .01$) and allowed fewer visits

($p < .05$) than their low counterparts in the incest case, and there were no other main or interaction effects that approached significance. The high authoritarians were slightly more punitive in the physical abuse case.

Altemeyer (1981), as part of his research on right-wing authoritarianism, gave vignettes of five crimes to a sample of 954 University of Manitoba introductory psychology students. Positive correlations between the PWA scale and sentencing (presumably scored on a 0–9 point scale— see Altemeyer, 1981, Table 6, p. 199, and a reference to such a scale, p. 233) was found (.34 and .38) in the cases of both black and white unskilled laborers convicted of raping a white woman; one of .27 was found in the case of an unemployed white male convicted of armed robbery; and one of .12 in the case of a 52-year-old Caucasian businessman who first denied, then pleaded guilty to, tax evasion (with 956 respondents, even this correlation is significant: $< .001$). The fifth case, however, involved a white policeman accused of beating a handcuffed Ojibwa Indian as he was being driven away after being arrested in a demonstration. Here the correlation was $-.17$. These findings illustrate the old saw about authoritarians kicking the asses of those viewed as inferior and kissing the ones of authority figures.

These findings were replicated in three other smaller samples of students at the Universities of North Dakota, Alberta, and Western Ontario as well as 56 adult males from the Winnipeg population. The correlations with RWA were .45, .39, .47, and .43, respectively, when the police brutality case was omitted.

Altemeyer (1981) then turned his attention to exploring the relationship between RWA and the severity of sentences given to different categories of individuals convicted of crimes. Four were "unsavory" criminals and the other three were "respectable" persons. Cases in the first category involved, "a juvenile delinquent with a long police record, a political agitator convicted of creating a public disturbance, a drug addict convicted of bank robbery, and an 'ex-con' convicted of rape" (p. 232). Counterposed were the police brutality case alluded to above, an accountant who assaulted a "hippie" panhandler, and an American Air Force officer who led unauthorized bombing raids against Vietnamese villages. The samples were composed of 779 students at five American Universities: Alabama, Indiana, Penn State, Virginia, and Wyoming. Correlations averaged .48 between RWA and severity of sentencing for the "unsavory" cases and from $-.11$ to $-.01$ for the other grouping. Reference is also made to a correlation of .54 between the sum of sentences imposed in 10 unspecified trials (presumably all of the "unsavory" criminals) and RWA in both a sample of 233 Manitoba students and one of 237 parents of the students (Altemeyer, 1981, p. 233).

The indefatigable Altemeyer (1981) reported yet a further study of 687 students drawn from the apparently inexhaustible Manitoba subject pool.

In this instance five crimes were used: (1) child abuse, (2) common assault, (3) bank robbery, (4) defrauding the government, and (5) beating a child molester in jail. "Low-status criminals" were the culprits in 347 instances and "high-status criminals" were involved in 340 cases. The former were, respectively, (1) unwed mother, (2) hippie panhandler (hits accountant), (3) tramp drug addict, (4) welfare recipient (defrauded the government of $3,000), and (5) another prisoner. Their high-status counterparts were (1) wife of an investment counselor, (2) accountant (hits hippie panhandler), (3) insurance salesman, (4) millionaire industrialist (defrauds government of $50,000), and (5) the chief of detectives. In all instances the low-status perpetrators were given the more severe sentences by the high scorers on RWA. (In Cases 2, 4, and 5, the differences were significant at the .01 level or better.)

An analysis of variance on these five cases indicated that there were significant interaction effects in the assault (2) and the defrauding of the government (4) cases due to the high RWA scorers giving disproportionately stiffer sentences to the low-status rather than the high-status defendant. An interaction was also found in the fifth, or beaten prisoner, case, which was attributable to the high scorers being less punitive to the chief of detectives than the low-status fellow prisoner.

No Significant Relationships

In contrast to the previous studies, in which positive relationships were found between authoritarianism and punitiveness, there were five in which no significant relationships were found.

Hatton and Snortum (1971) showed a film in which a car backed out of a parking space and struck a woman. The driver and a male companion of the woman had a brief scuffle. The 90 volunteer undergraduates at Claremont College who viewed the film were then given one of four different bits of possibly biasing information: (a) The driver had a record of driving violations; (b) the woman, the mother of two, had stopped off to shop on her way home from a volunteer hospital job; (c) the woman had a history of unsubstantiated major claims, or (d) no biasing information (a control set). The subjects then took Rokeach's (1956) Dogmatism scale, and the dependent variable was whether or not the driver was guilty of reckless driving. No differences were found relating guilt to dogmatism.

Steffensmeier (1975) conducted a field experiment in which a shoplifting episode was staged in a department store or one of two grocery stores in a small midwestern city. The "shoplifter" was either neatly dressed or in the garb of a disheveled hippie. After an object was shoplifted (the value of most of the objects was less than $3.00), a randomly selected shopper who witnessed the incident was observed to see if he or she reported the incident to an accomplice dressed as a clerk who was standing nearby. If the incident was not reported, a second accomplice in similar clerk attire approached and told the shopper that the shoplifter was being watched because of suspicions on the part of the management and asked if he (or she) seen anything. If the shopper said "no," a more direct probe was made. Another accomplice then debriefed the shopper and obtained the name and address; subsequently, the shopper was interviewed at home and given the Trodahl and Powell (1965) short form of the Dogmatism scale. (Scores on the latter were not found to be related to subjects' reporting or not reporting the theft.)

Sue, Smith, and Pedroza (1975) were concerned with the problem of how pretrial publicity and awareness of bias affected decisions about guilt in an experiment on jury simulation. They administered the Byrne and Lamberth (1971) version of the F scale to a class of 119 introductory psychology students at the University of Washington. Two months later they all served as experimental subjects, and each was given a four-page booklet containing instructions, an alleged newspaper account of a robbery and murder case, and a summary of the case. They were then asked to make ratings of the strength of the arguments by the prosecution and defense as well as judgements of guilty or not guilty. The biased subjects read a newspaper account that said the defendant's gun had been found through ballistic analysis to be the murder weapon; in the neutral condition the subjects received a version saying the gun had not been found to be the murder weapon. When admittedly biased jurors, who were significantly more likely to find the defendant guilty, were excluded from the analysis it was found that high authoritarian subjects did not find the defendant significantly more guilty or give more severe sentences even though they rated the prosecution's case as stronger ($p < .02$).

Garcia and Griffitt (1978b) utilized an actual highly publicized trial—that of Patricia Hearst, the California heiress who had been kidnapped and subsequently joined her abductors in bank robberies—to test hypotheses about the differential recall of prosecution and defense evidence. Their 50 Kansas State University introductory psychology students were divided into high and low scorers on the Byrne and Lamberth (1971) F scale, and it was found that there was no significant difference in the amount of prosecution evidence recalled but that the high authoritarians recalled significantly less ($p < .05$) evidence favorable to the defense. No differences were found in whether or not Ms. Hearst was believed guilty.

An extremely complex experiment was conducted by Penrod (1980) in a study that is especially interesting because the sample was composed of 367 actual jurors in two courts in the Boston metropolitan area during the period in which they were impanelled and waiting to be called for voir dire. Audiotapes had been prepared which were based on four actual cases. For each there was an opening statement by the prosecuting/plaintiff's attorney summarizing facts and charges, statements summarizing evidence by prosecution witnesses, the defense attorney's opening statement, the defense witnesses testimony, and the attorneys' closing statements. The procedure was closed by the judge's instructions. The entire procedure required 3 hours, not including breaks. The four cases were "garden variety" (Penrod, p. 16) involving, respectively, a barroom stabbing murder, a gasoline station robbery, a rape, and a motor vehicle negligence case. The dependent variables were the actual verdict options, which varied for each crime. There were minimal correlations across crimes, indicating within these data no tendency toward conviction proneness. The predictor variables were responses to a questionnaire that had 12 attitudinal questions relating to crime, some of which might be expected to be related to authoritarianism. Penrod did an exhaustive analysis of his data and found no patterns of significant relationships among the attitudinal variables and none between them and the dependent variables (severity of sentence). Neither did he find correlations between the severity of punishment assigned for the various crimes.

Summary of Experimental Studies on Legal Punitiveness to This Point

The correlations between authoritarianism and punitiveness in sentencing for putative crimes range from a high of $+.54$ found by Altemeyer (1981) in comparing RWA scores to an index of severity for a group of 10 crimes involving "unsavory" criminals to the nonsignificant findings reported above. Among the variables involved are severity of the crime, status of the defendant vis-à-vis the victim, attractiveness of the defendant, the strength of the evidence, the often unknown psychometric adequacy of the measure of authoritarianism employed, and the differing nature of the dependent variable used to measure severity of sentencing. Interpretations of the differences among the studies is complicated by their lack of comparability.

It is interesting to note that in two of the five cases where no differences were found (Hatton & Snortum, 1971; Steffensmeier, 1975) the Dogmatism scale was used as a predictive variable. Altemeyer found (1981, Table 6, p. 199) the Dogmatism scale to be a much weaker predictor of punitiveness than either the F or RWA scales. Christie (1991) reviewed evidence indicating that the Dogmatism scale was not designed to be a measure of authoritarianism and subsequent research indicated that it measured something else. The status of the defendant(s) in the Penrod (1980) study and in the study by Sue, Smith, and Pedroza (1975) was ambiguous, and in the Penrod study it was found that the authoritarian-type items did not intercorrelate highly enough to scale. In the Garcia and Griffith (1978b) study in which Patricia Hearst was the highly publicized defendant, the students might reasonably be expected to have differential knowledge about the facts of the case, which may have affected the lack of differences.

Zwillenberg's Study

Diane Zwillenberg (1983) analyzed the previous studies in detail and decided to put some of the variables she deemed important into one overall experimental design so the effects of the interactions could be observed. A $3 \times 2 \times 2 \times 2$ factorial design was used, which tapped three levels of authoritarianism: high versus low severity of crime, presence or absence of mitigating circumstances, and high or low status of offender.

Altemeyer's (1981) 24-item RWA scale was chosen as the best available measure of authoritarianism because it had the highest reported reliability and best construct validity. The respondents were divided into three groups: 121 low scorers with item means that varied from 1.13 to 3.13 ($M = 2.47$), 253 middle scorers with scores varying from 3.17 to 4.75 ($M = 4.00$), and 129 high scorers with scores ranging from 4.79 to 6.42 ($M = 5.38$). It will be noted that the high and low groupings fit Meloen's criteria for high and low authoritarians (see chap. 3, this volume) even when one makes allowance for the fact that the RWA scale has a .33 higher item mean than the Form 40/45 California F Scale (see Altemeyer, 1981, Table 1, p. 181). Readers familiar with distributions on measures of authoritarianism will note that this is an unusually wide range of scores. This was no accident. The respondents were students at nine different schools known or suspected to vary widely in levels of authoritarianism, and cooperation was elicited through professional colleagues who were responsible for the test administration in each school. The item mean scores for the individual schools varied from 2.83 in a sample of predominantly humanities majors at Columbia College to 4.63 in students in a criminal justice class at an urban private eastern university, which shall not be named for reasons of public relations. The alpha reliability for the combined groups was .91, which is extremely high for a counterbalanced scale.

The crimes allegedly committed included eight of high severity, varying from aggravated assault with a knife to felony murder plus rape, with magnitude estimation ratings from .99 to 1.4 on the Sellin and Wolfgang (1964) scale. There were also eight crimes of low severity, ranging from disorderly conduct to being proprietor of a gambling house, with ratings of −1.39 to .00. The defendants had all been found guilty, and the task for the respondent was to assign sanctions varying from no punishment to the death penalty with intermediate degrees of punishment, on a 16-point scale.

Mitigating circumstances were manipulated in the vignettes, which described each crime and the participant(s) by the circumstances surrounding the deed. Weak mitigating circumstances were defined as a situation in which the information given suggested true personal causality on the part of the actor. Strong mitigating circumstances included such matters as personal safety of the actor, strong provocation on the part of another person or persons, behavior which the person at the time of the incident did not believe was criminal, and so on. Vignettes were written and rewritten until a group of judges rated them as significantly different along the dimension.

The social status manipulation was based on Temme's (1975) ratings of occupational prestige. Occupations selected for the high-status defendants had values of 65 to 90 on Temme's occupational prestige scale, and low-status defendents had values of 1 to 35. In each vignette, other information was given about the defendant that was congruent with the occupation such as educational level, place of residence, and income. Because some crimes are associated with race and ethnicity in popular lore, if not in real life, clues were provided so that these could be deduced without specific identification, for example, a rapist "with matted blond hair" who was a garbage collector or a corporate lawyer named Cabot Brewster Lodge who followed in his father's footsteps by attending Harvard College and Harvard Law School. Vignettes of defendants committing high and low severity crimes were counter-balanced on the status variable so that every low-status criminal with an Anglo-Saxon (or Greek, Hispanic, etc.) surname had a high-status counterpart. The same was true for the mitigating circumstances variable.

Each respondent received one of a set of four packets of 16 cases out of 64 protocols for making ratings. Complete counterbalancing of the variables within the cases was contained in each packet. In half the cases the RWA scale was taken before and in the other half after making the judgments about punishment, and because order made no difference all cases were combined in an overall analysis of variance.

For the benefit of readers who are not familiar with analysis of variance— and for those who are but occasionally can become understandably confused when interpreting interaction effects—a graph is presented in Figure 5.1 that illustrates the mean sentencing scores on a 16-point scale along the ordinate. The punishment option available to respondents is on the left of the vertical line, and the conversion to a numerical score is on the right. The height of each bar indicates severity of punishment for the particular combination of conditions in the experimental design. These are indicated along the abscissa. The experimental conditions are listed across the bottom, with 16 cells indicating different combinations of experimental conditions. Extending upward from each cell are two bars. The left, unfilled bar is the punishment assigned by the lowest quarter of the entire sample on the RWA scale. The right, filled bar in each of the 16 pairs represents the punishment assigned by the high (upper quarter) scorers on RWA. Liberal readers familiar with Western movies are free to define the unfilled bars as occupied by "white hats" or good guys

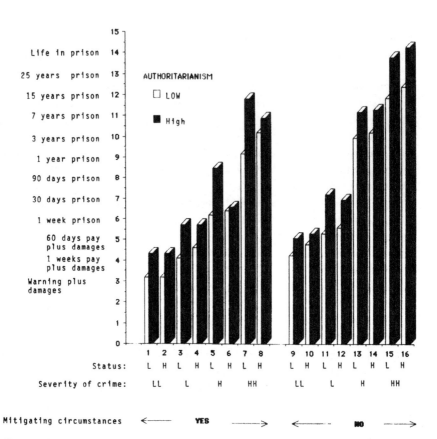

FIGURE 5.1. Authoritarianism and severity of assigned punishment as related to the presence of mitigating circumstances, severity of crime, and status of perpetrator.

(and gals) and the filled bars as symbolizing black-hatted "baddies." Conservative readers may prefer to label the unfilled bars as reflecting the emptiness of liberal ideology and the filled bars as representing the sentences preferred by solid citizens. It will be noted that responses of the middle half of the distribution of RWA scorers have been eliminated from the figure. This was done to simplify the presentation and, because these middle scoring subjects almost always scored between the high and low scorers, does not distort the overall results. They are included in the analysis of variance reported.

The next major manipulated variable, status of the defendant, did not have significant main effect. It had, however, a significant interaction effect ($p < .00001$) in combination with authoritarianism because low scorers assigned harsher punishment to high-status criminals while high authoritarians were more severe in sentencing low-status defendants. By inspection, one can see that in seven comparisons the lows follow the pattern with the sole exception occurring in Cells 1 and 2. The high scorers are less consistent since they give only slightly stiffer sentences to low status defendants in three comparisons (Cells 1–2, 3–4, and 11–12), dramatically stronger ones in two comparisons (Cells 5–6 and 7–8), and are slightly more harsh to higher status defendants in the remaining three comparisons, all of which occur under cases in which there are no mitigating circumstances.

The triple-order interactions in the analysis of variance are psychologically even more interesting because they indicate under what combinations effects are found; note that the authoritarianism × status × mitigating circumstances interaction is significant at the $p < .00001$ level. The high authoritarians are significantly more punitive under both strong and mitigating circumstances ($p < .0001$). The status × authoritarianism interaction ($p < .0001$) occurs only under strong mitigating circumstances but not under weak mitigating circumstances (p of only .42).

Although Zwillenberg's (1983) analysis was more complex than the above might indicate, her findings give a framework for interpreting earlier studies involving hypothetical criminal cases.

It will be remembered that in one group of studies (those involving linear relationships) high authoritarians were more punitive than low authoritarians whatever the particular crime. The highest correlations between authoritarianism and punishment were reported by Altemeyer (1981), who found correlations as high as the .50s when dealing with "unsavory" criminals who committed serious crimes. Zwillenberg (1983), using the same RWA scale as a measure of authoritarianism, found an overall correlation of .38, based on defendants who were counterbalanced in terms of social status, and covered 16 separate crimes, which varied from relatively minor to extremely serious; in addition, in half the cases there were strong mitigating circumstances and in the other half, few or none. Clearly, it is possible to manipulate the magnitude of the relationship by varying the circumstances of the crime as Altemeyer (1981) has demonstrated.

There is another group of studies (those described under the heading Other Relationships) in which high authoritarians were more punitive in punishing criminals in high-but not low-severity crimes or in which similarity of the defendant to the subject was manipulated. This apparently contradicts Zwillenberg's (1983) finding that even in low severity crimes high authoritarians were more punitive than their low-scoring counterparts. Possible explanations might include the fact that she had a more reliable measure of authoritarianism, and a more sensitive measure of punishment since it was based on judgments about 16 different cases for each respondent. Her study also employed a large and more heterogeneous sample on authoritarianism than any of the other samples of college students, and a broader sample (eight) of low severity crimes than was true in the previous studies. Her finding that the magnitude of the punishment assigned by high and low authoritarians was significantly less for low- than for high-severity crimes is also a possible contributing factor. The present assessment is that for one or more of these reasons the experimental net used in the earlier studies was not meshed finely enough to pick up differences at the low severity of crime end of the continuum, and they slipped through.

One very interesting and unpredicted finding was the tendency of low-authoritarian respondents to give slightly but significantly harsher sentences to high- rather than low-status defendants when all other variables were counterbalanced. The only other study in which they displayed such a bias was in Boehm's (1968) pioneering study, in which the evidence was slanted prodefendant in one vignette and antidefendant in the other. In the latter case the lows made more "lenient" errors in assigning guilt. It may be noted that Boehm standardized her LAQ measure of authoritarianism on Northern civil rights college students in the South in the summer of 1965. Although this sample was given the Christie et al. (1958) counterbalanced F scale, no mean score is reported although other studies on similar groups found low F-scale scorers to be typical. The sample used in the study proper was not given the F scale but only the LAQ. It was composed of undergraduates at the University of California at Berkeley where low scores on the F scale as compared with most other schools are typically found. These were not randomly selected students but were in an abnormal psychology course, which means that they had taken at least one other psychology course and psychology students, along with those in the social sciences and humanities, are noted for being low scorers. It is not known what effect the Free Speech Movement at Berkeley at that time or what effect the course professor's active involvement in the early protests against the Vietnam War might have had upon the antiauthoritarianism of the respondents. The inferential evidence strongly suggests that this group of Berkeley students would have contained a large number of low scorers on the F scale. Because Zwillenberg's (1983) sample had been successfully selected to yield a sizable contingent of low scorers on the RWA scale, these two samples probably contained a higher proportion of antiauthoritarians than any of the other studies reviewed.

The most striking interaction effect uncovered by Zwillenberg (1983) was created by the disproportionately harsher sentences imposed upon low- rather than high-status defendants in the high-severity crime condition when there were mitigating circumstances (see the graph for experimental cells 5 and 7 in Fig. 5.1). Mitigating circumstances were not manipulated as such in the earlier studies although Boehm shifted the weight of evidence in her two vignettes. A status effect might be inferred in Centers et al.'s (1970) use of a juvenile as an accessory in a crime in conjunction with adults, and in Vecchio's (1977) rehabilitation officers' letters of recommendation for or against parole. In Boehm's (1968) experiment, high scorers made punitive errors, in Centers et al.'s survey high authoritarians assigned harsher punishment, and in Vecchio's study there was a significant triple interaction with authoritarianism, severity of crime, and favorable or unfavorableness of recommendation. Results from these three studies are consistent with Zwillenberg's finding.

Summary of Authoritarianism and Punitiveness

The present assessment of experimental findings is that authoritarians are not only significantly more punitive in assigning sentences to target persons who are "guilty" of committing crimes varying from trivial to extremely serious but are consistent in doing so across the range of severity of crimes. Low authoritarians give harsher sentences to high than low status individuals whereas high authoritarians show the opposite pattern especially strongly when the criminal is a low-status person committing a high-severity crime when there are mitigating circumstances.

The eight cells on the left (1–8) indicate cases in which there were mitigating circumstances in the crime protocols; the eight cells on the right (9–18) are ones in which there were few or no mitigating circumstances. Inspection of the graph indicates greater punitiveness in cases in which there were fewer mitigating circumstances. In analysis of variance terms, the main effect was significant ($p < .0001$). Aside from concurring with common sense, this indicates that the experimental manipulation was successful.

The severity of crime variable was broken into four rather than the two categories used in Zwillenberg's (1983) analysis in order to better illustrate interaction effects (to be discussed later). Inspection of Figure 5.1 reveals that within each half of the graph that there is a progressive rise in assigned punishment as we move from cells 1–2 to 7–8, and from cells 9–10 to 15–16. Again, the experimental manipulation was successful ($p < .0001$) and concurs with expectations: The worse the crime, the greater the punishment.

The third manipulated variable (status of the defendant, defined in terms of social position and controlling for race and ethnicity) is reflected in the odd-numbered cells, which are ones in which the defendant had low status, and the even-numbered ones, in which he had high status. Eyeballing the figure, one can see discrepancies but not an overall pattern for the simple reason that there is none. The main effect when tested by analysis of variance was resoundingly nonsignificant (p of only .29). Incidentally, this lack of an overall relationship had been predicted by Zwillenberg (1983) from her analysis of earlier studies.

The fourth, nonmanipulated, variable was scores on Altemeyer's (1981) 24-item scale of right-wing authoritarianism. Again, back to the graph in Figure 5.1. It can be seen that in every one of the 16 cells, which systematically varied combinations of the three independently manipulated variables, low scorers on the RWA scale had lower scores on punitiveness than did their high-scoring counterparts. The main effect by analysis of variance is significant ($p < .0001$). Expressing the same relationship in correlational terms, we find an r of $+.38$.

As we turn to the interaction effects of authoritarianism and manipulated experimental variables, which tell us under which conditions high and low authoritarians are differentially punitive, it will first be noted that the interaction of authoritarianism and mitigating circumstances alone is not significant ($p = .26$). In short, overall we cannot predict greater or less punishment by high and low scorers if the presence or absence of mitigating circumstances is the only information we have.

There is, however, an interaction between authoritarianism and severity of crime ($p < .00001$), which reflects the fact that high scorers give relatively harsher sentences the more severe the crime as compared with low scorers. For all eight high-severity crimes combined, the scale mean is 10.57 (which translates along the ordinate to about 5 years in prison) compared to the low's 9.60 (slightly over 2 years in prison). The means for the eight low-severity crimes are 5.03 for highs (fined a week's pay) as against 4.60 for lows (slightly over halfway between a day's and a week's pay). Inspection of the height of the bars for particular severity of crimes indicates that in general the actual penalty assigned by highs is greater by about a two-to-one ratio throughout the range. When these are converted into scale scores the magnitude of the difference increases from .46 for all low severity crimes to .97 for all high severity crimes as we go up the scale and this accounts for the statistical interaction.

A Closing Note on Authoritarianism and Experimentation

Our sample of experiments typical of work done in the fifties (chapter 4) and the seventies shows a shift from an emphasis on the expectation that high authoritarians would behave differently from lows in almost any situation to one in which increasingly the emphasis has been upon the kinds of situations in which they would behave differently. Another difference that may be noted is that in almost all the rigidity studies the interaction I believe important was that between the experimenter as an authority figure and the subject literally as one subjected to authority. The later studies on authoritarian punitiveness became increasingly ones in which the personal relationship between the two was minimized and the interactions were among the differing descriptions, vignettes, or other aspects of the cases presented and the respondent's authoritarianism. The greater complexity of experimental designs over time represented the development and growing use of more sophisticated research methodology.

One wry note may be in order about the reporting of research, which has not improved dramatically. One cardinal rule of experimentation is that studies should be reported in precise enough detail so they can be replicated, and in all too many reports of research one has to have the acumen of a Sherlock Holmes to determine who did what to whom with which under what conditions. In some cases this is impossible for an amateur sleuth to determine from the published account; for example, in one instance an article was published in a prestigious, highly refereed journal on response set in which the California F Scale was used. The results were baffling. I wrote a letter of inquiry to the author, and he informed me that he had not used the standard seven-point scoring system but a five-point one. His findings were then interpretable.

The review of the literature on rigidity strongly indicated there were two conditions that were relevant to eliciting greater Einstellung tendencies (rigid behavior) on the part of high rather than low scorers on the F scale: (a) The experimenter behaves in an authoritarian rather than a causal manner, or (b) there is an experimentally induced increase of stress between the set establishing problems and the critical problems. As far as is known there is no study combining the two variables to see if they are additive in effect. Although there is no evidence that any measurable difference in rigid performance on the Einstellung problem differentiates between high and low scorers when neither of these conditions are present, the problem is, in my judgment, an open one. Most of the studies produced dichotomous groupings of more or less rigid behavior. A more refined and relevant scoring system might produce a system especially if Einstellung problems of differing types (arithmetic, maze, spacial, etc.) were used to permit a composite score. In effect, the argument is that a more refined dependent variable might show differences that haven't appeared hitherto similar to Zwillenberg's (1983) finding of differentiation between highs and lows in the low severity crime condition which had not been picked up earlier because of the crudeness of the measures.

The evidence reviewed on the relationship between authoritarianism and punitiveness in sentencing for hypothetical crimes indicates a consistent and significant relationship. This is enhanced with severity of the crime and is especially discrepant when there are mitigating circumstances and the defendant has low social status. There are a number of possible other interactions with such variables as attractiveness of the defendant, the types of arguments used by attorneys such as rational versus emotional, and so on, which have been tested in isolation from those Zwillenberg (1983) found important and not in one overall design.

One factor that enhances the possibility of finding relationships is the use of a highly reliable counterbalanced scale. (Altemeyer's, 1981, RWA is the best available one to date.) It is a statistical truism that the strength of a relationship cannot be adequately determined with an unreliable measurement device. There is also evidence that some individuals high and low on a unidirectional F scale are misclassified as high and low authoritarians and that those high in agreement or disagreement tendencies perform differently in experimental situations from ideologically "pure" high and low scorers (Christie, 1991).

Another statistical truism is that chances of finding differences in authoritarianism are enhanced the greater the variability of the sample on a measure of authoritarianism. Because most investigators don't have the resources to select a random sample of the population, one possibility is to do as Zwillenberg (1983) did and select samples from colleges that draw students from quite different populations. Using mean SAT scores of freshmen entering different colleges is a fast way of assessing probable variability on the F or RWA scales. Yet another possibility within a large school is to select students enrolled in both liberal arts and applied fields, because the scores of students in these areas usually differ markedly on measures of authoritarianism. A little ingenuity in sample selection can go a long way in increasing its heterogeneity.

It has been possible to cover briefly only two of the topics relating to authoritarianism that have yielded unclear messages in terms of research findings. My perusal of other experimental literature on authoritarianism, which is probably at least five times as extensive and sends as many mixed messages as that reviewed here, leaves me with the impression that a similarly sympathetic but skeptical approach to this literature would lead to similar conclusions. The demand characteristics of the situation are of crucial importance in eliciting authoritarian behavior on the part of individuals who display differences along the dimension. The degree of frustration or stress and variations in the authority relationships between experimenter and subject are crucial determinants of the differences in performance of high and low authoritarians.

6
Authoritarians and Their Families: Qualitative Studies on the Origins of Authoritarian Dispositions

CHRISTEL HOPF

With the publication of *Studien über Autorität und Familie* (Horkheimer, 1936) and *The Authoritarian Personality* (*TAP*, Adorno, Frenkel-Brunswik, Levinson, & Sanford, 1950), the family situation of authoritarians became a central component of theoretical attempts to understand authoritarian dispositions. The structure of the family, its historical context, the nature of relations within the family, the affection shown by parents, and the sanctions they employed—all were to provide information on how the readiness to act, think, and feel in an authoritarian way develops. *Authoritarian* is defined broadly here as the receptiveness to prejudices and aggression toward those weaker than oneself (especially ethnic minorities) and the readiness to subordinate oneself to those more powerful.[1]

Despite the importance assigned to family background and early childhood experiences by the early writers on authoritarianism, there have been few empirical studies dealing with this topic. Reviews of literature have therefore focused on standardized procedures and scales (cf. Christie & Cook, 1958, p. 179; Kirscht & Dillehay, 1967, p. 2; or Altemeyer, 1981, p. 33). These reviewers conclude that the results of these studies are not adequate to substantiate or disconfirm the importance of early childhood experiences. Bob Altemeyer (1981) found no support for the theses advanced by the authors of *TAP* (the "Berkeley group") on the relevance of early childhood experiences (p. 49). He administered the Right-Wing Authoritarianism (RWA) scale to students and their parents, and also questioned them about their experiences in the family (cf. Altemeyer, 1981, p. 259). The subjects were asked to describe the punishment used by parents (Parental Punishment scale), the childhood offenses criticized by parents (Parental Anger scale), and their interest in the activities of the growing child (Parental Interest scale). In a later publication, Altemeyer (1988a) summarizes the results of his research:

---

[1] This broad use of the concept contrasts to other usages, for example, in connection with the F scale (cf. Kirscht and Dillehay, 1967, pp. 5, 6).

Both students and parents told admirably consistent tales on these measures; alphas ranged from .87 to .92. Unfortunately, the children and their parents often seemed to be from different families, for stories within a family bore little resemblance to each other (Would you be surprised to learn that parents described themselves as less angry, less punitive, and more interested in their children than the children recall?) But even more unfortunate, for the Berkeley theory, nobody's version of the past explained much of the student's present authoritarianism. The largest of 28 "validity coefficients" was .24, between students' RWA Scale scores and their accounts of mother's anger. (p. 53)

Altemeyer (1988a) concedes that these results alone cannot disprove the Berkeley theory (p. 53). Clearly, the parents who are the holders of power remember (or say they remember) using their power benignly, whereas their children who were the subjects of power remember their parents as behaving more authoritatively. Because the two groups are viewing the same events from completely different power perspectives it is not surprising that there is disagreement, and the truth of the long-past events cannot be determined from a literal interpretation of their scale scores. Nevertheless, Altemeyer (1988a) maintains that the approach used by the Berkeley group and its basic psychoanalytic orientation is obsolete. In his opinion, their theory is not verifiable and should be replaced by learning theory models. This verdict seems to be problematic for several reasons. First of all, as I would like to show in the second part of this chapter ("Family and Authoritarianism: Qualitative Analyses in *The Authoritarian Personality*"), it is based on a selective and biased adoption of certain parts of the studies on *TAP*. Altemeyer focuses mostly on the parts written by Else Frenkel-Brunswik, which contain the results of semistructured "clinical" interviews with authoritarians and nonauthoritarians, and in which the most important assumptions about the origins of authoritarian dispositions had been formulated and discussed.

My second objection to Altemeyer's conclusion is that, even if there may be good reasons to revise the Berkeley theory, this does not invalidate psychoanalytically oriented social psychology. A psychoanalytic orientation can lead to conclusions different from the Berkeley group's—Nathan W. Ackerman and Marie Jahoda's (1950) psychoanalytically oriented analysis of the origins of anti-Semitism (see the section headed "Functions and Origins of Prejudice in the Family" of this chapter), is tangible proof of this fact. One must also bear in mind that psychoanalytic theory has continued to evolve in the last 40 years.

In modern psychoanalysis, approaches have gained in importance that give more attention to the primary social relationships within the family—the "object relations approaches" (cf. Kernberg, 1980; Kutter, 1989). At the same time, the "attachment" research approach, in which ethological and psychoanalytic research traditions are integrated (cf. Ainsworth et al., 1978; Bowlby, 1988) provides a broad range of conceptual and theoretical instruments for the analysis of social relationships in the family. In my opinion, the closer attention being paid to the "pre-oedipal" patterns and the more exact analysis of the consequences of disturbances in the mother–child relationship as a result of these developments are of great importance to research on authoritarianism.

Finally, methodological objections may be raised. It seems to me problematic to test hypotheses generated on the basis of qualitative interviews and differentiated insights into developmental processes and family dynamics with standardized procedures, which are often deficient in complexity and differentiation. Therefore, in my opinion, more valid answers to the question of links between family experiences and personality development can be found through studies using qualitative approaches similar to those favored by Else Frenkel-Brunswik in her chapters of *TAP*. Such studies include the following:

1. Nathan Ackerman and Marie Jahoda's (1950) study of the social and psychological prerequisites of anti-Semitism, in which case studies collected with the help of psychoanalysts are reported on in great detail.
2. David Mantell's (1972/1974) qualitative study of Green Berets and war resisters.
3. A study conducted in West Berlin on the socialization of skilled workers (cf. Hoff, Lapper, & Lempert, 1983, for information on methods used), which, among other things, also contains information on hostility toward foreigners and on the family origins of the subjects.
4. A study by Mary Main and Ruth Goldwyn (1984) in which mothers with disciplinary problems were questioned about their own childhoods.

In the following discussion, it will not be possible to present these studies in their entirety. My emphasis will be placed upon selected topics relevant to authoritarianism research: Characteristics and problems in the mother–child relationship of authoritarians and "idealization" of the parents. Idealization of parents is a topic that Else Frenkel-Brunswik may have dealt with inappropriately in *TAP* (see also Hyman & Sheatsley, 1954, p. 82); however, it appears as a relevant trait of authoritarians in the other studies.

The broad definition of the term *authoritarianism* used in this discussion is bound neither to the F scale nor to other efforts to define the concept of authoritarianism in terms of revised scale content (e.g., Ray, 1976; Altemeyer, 1981). Rather, accenting the inclinations toward prejudice, authoritarianism is defined here in the broad sense underlying the title *The Authoritarian Personality*. As is generally known, this title was not agreed upon until relatively late, after the completion of the research. It was supposed to refer to earlier publications (*Studien über*

Autorität und Familie, Horkheimer, 1936; Fromm, 1941; Maslow, 1943).[2] The study was not developed using the term *authoritarian* as a theoretical concept. Rather, it dealt with anti-Semitism, prejudices toward minorities, and fascist potential. Emphasis was placed on prejudice and *not*, as one might possibly expect, on a comprehensive analysis of the personality structure and the *actions* of authoritarians *in various contexts* (see Sanford, 1956, p. 256). The personality structure was analyzed in the study as far as it appeared necessary for understanding prejudice and fascist potential; the making of authoritarian personalities was not an independent, central subject matter.

In order to understand *The Authoritarian Personality*, it is also important to mention two aspects of the meaning of *authoritarian*: Authoritarian dominance and authoritarian subordination—kowtowing to those above and stepping on those below, a syndrome symbolized in Germany by the image of the bicycle rider who bends his back as he bears down. I stress the two-tracked definition of *authoritarian* because in our daily usage the term *authoritarian* generally is taken to refer to authoritarian dominance. In *TAP*, however, the emphasis is placed on authoritarian submission[3]—the deference expected of children in the relationship to their parents; more generally, the relationship between individuals and authorities. "Stepping on"—that is, authoritarian dominance—becomes most visible in the acting out of prejudice toward minorities. The origin of such prejudices and their relation to family experiences are dealt with in those chapters of *The Authoritarian Personality* in which the qualitative interviews are analyzed. The conclusions drawn in these chapters are the topic of discussion in the following section.

---

[2] See Sanford, 1956, p. 255; 1973, p. 142, for a history of the term. See also Wiggershaus, 1986, p. 458, for controversies over the title: Adorno was afraid that the other authors could choose a *lammfrommen* (placid) title like, for example, *Character and Prejudice*. "The title under which the book was published in 1950 manifested the late compromise, since this concept was only used in Horkheimer's foreword. In the book itself fascist, potential fascist or prejudiced personalities and the (Fascism) Scale were spoken of" (Wiggershaus, 1986, p. 458). See also Hopf (1987) for conflicts within the Berkeley group.

[3] This accentuation of the term *authoritarian* is even more pronounced in *Studien über Autorität und Familie*. In his foreword, Max Horkheimer (1936) explains: " 'Autoritar' ist in diesem Bande im Sinne von autoritäts-bejahend (von Seiten des Autoritäts-Objektes aus) gebraucht, während 'autoritativ' ein autoritätsforderndes Verhalten (vom Autoritäts-Subjekt aus) bezeichnet" [In this volume "authoritarian" is used in the sense of authority acceptance (on the part of the authority object), whereas "authoritative" describes an authority demanding behavior (on the part of the authority subject)] (p. ix).

Family and Authoritarianism: Qualitative Analyses in *The Authoritarian Personality*

Preliminary Remarks to Methodology

Research on authoritarianism usually concentrates on the F scale, ignoring the qualitative parts of *The Authoritarian Personality* (see also Hopf, 1987, with regard to the FRG). Therefore, it is necessary to discuss briefly the lesser known methodological procedure and analysis of the interviews with people high and low on prejudice. These clinical interviews were semistructured qualitative interviews. During the questioning, the interviewers proceeded along interview guidelines. These protocols, used flexibly, were comprised of a broad (by today's standards too broad) spectrum of questions on social status and occupation, family history, relationships to parents and siblings, sexual and marital relationships and friendships, self-image, and political and religious attitudes. (See *TAP*, p. 313, for interview guidelines; p. 300, for further information about the interviews.) The subjects were selected on the basis of their answers to the items of the Anti-Semitism scale or the Ethnocentrism scale. Those men and women were chosen who were either high (in the upper quartile) or low (in the lower quartile) on one of these scales. (See *TAP*, p. 294, for more details on sampling procedures, like the attempt to control for sex and other variables, such as age or religion. Younger respondents— 30 years old and younger—made up the larger part of the sample.)

Various methods of analysis were used in *TAP* to evaluate the interview responses. They were analyzed in part as individual case studies, as in chapters 2 and 20 on Mack and Larry, written by Nevitt Sanford. The political and ideological sections of the interviews were dealt with on the basis of particular extracts and summaries in the chapters by Theodor W. Adorno (chaps. 16–19). Frenkel-Brunswik's chapters integrated quantitative and qualitative analysis. She assessed the personal and biographical data of the interviews—the so-called clinical data (a total of 80 cases). In addition, TAT tests were carried out with many of the subjects questioned in the qualitative interviews (see chapter 14, by Betty Aron). Frenkel-Brunswick occasionally drew upon the results of these tests in her interpretation of the data on the subjects' social relationships.

The procedures used for the analysis and quantification of the qualitative interviews must be pictured as a combination of theoretically guided research and exploratory, descriptive analysis. Its categories were in part shaped by psychoanalytic social psychology, in part chosen on the basis of intensive, exploratory analysis of the interview data. (See TAP, p. 325, and Frenkel-Brunswik, 1948a, Section II, for information on the origin of the scoring manuals and the coding procedure.) In this respect, the analysis served to verify previous hypotheses and to develop new ones.

In their well-known methodological critique of *TAP*, H. Hyman and Paul B. Sheatsley (1954, pp. 65, 79) also criticized the procedures used to implement and analyze the qualitative interviews. Part of the criticism is justified—for example, the criticism of speculative interpretations based on a shaky empirical foundation. Part of it, however, misses the point—for instance, the criticism that the interviewers were informed about the other empirical data collected on the subjects. One must wonder if the exploratory nature of the study—pointed out by Sanford (1956, p. 266)—was discerned at all by Hyman and Sheatsley.

The qualitative sections of *TAP* represent one of the first attempts to deal with psychoanalytic and social psychological problems using a qualitative exploratory procedure on a broad scale—and not simply in individual clinical case studies. Dick Christie (personal communication) noted that the critics were concerned with the crucial matter of *how* the qualitative ratings were converted into *quantitative scores*.

The procedure used was as follows:

1. The principle investigators, who were familiar with the implicit theory underlying *TAP*, had two stacks of interview protocols. They examined them and set up coding categories that differentiated between the two groups.

2. The investigators then gave the protocols to coders, who were also familiar with the underlying theory for rating the individual scoring categories. After reading and studying the complete protocols, the raters examined them for the presence or absence of the individual scoring categories. *Quite simply, this means that each individual rating was not made independently of the overall context of the protocols.* In other words, judgments of whether or not a particular event was present or not was *not* statistically independent of knowing what the same individual said in another context.

3. Despite this lack of independence, the authors of *TAP* then treated them as statistically independent.

4. Christie (1954) pointed out that the overall judgments of the raters as to whether the subjects were high or low were right five out of six times, which is not surprising given access to the total protocol by both the coders and those interpreting the code. It was also pointed out that this was the same ratio as the summed accuracy on the coding categories.

This then led to the discovery that when the coders were right on guessing whether the respondent was high or low almost all of their judgments about individual characteristics conformed to theory. But *when the overall evaluation was wrong, the individual characteristics were scored in the reverse direction.*

What does all of this mean? First, that some of the scoring categories must have been right, or otherwise the raters would not have been able to distinguish between the protocols of the high and low scorers. It also means, unfortunately, that there is no way of determining with any accuracy which scoring categories were the most discriminating. Thus, the study leaves much open to question, and its methods are not without fault. These shortcomings, however, should act as incentives to further qualitative study of the origins of prejudice and authoritarian dispositions.

"Control" and "Acceptance" as Aspects of Parent–Child Relationships

Frenkel-Brunswik's interpretations of the link between family experiences and authoritarianism have been summarized by Sanford (1956) as follows:

The high-authoritarians came, for the most part, from homes in which a rather stern and distant father dominates a submissive and long-suffering, but morally restrictive mother, and in which discipline was an attempt to apply conventionally approved rules rather than an effort to further general values in accordance with the perceived needs of the child. (p. 307; see also Sanford, 1973, p. 147)

Altemeyer (1981, p. 253; 1988a, p. 52) refers essentially to this résumé in his criticism of the approach used by the Berkeley group and in his attempt to test the Berkeley group's conclusions through development of his own instruments for assessing the family background of his subjects. The scales Altemeyer used refer to the content of norms and rules that are imposed upon children, and to the manner in which they were enforced (character of the disciplinary action, cf. 1981, p. 260). Moreover, Altemeyer attempted to tap the dimension of parental acceptance (Parental Interest scale). Whether he succeeded seems questionable, for the scale might be more suitable to analyze a general program of child rearing and recreation activities than to deal with the affective quality of parent–child relationships.

Sanford's (1956) summary of familial antecedents of authoritarianism, however, mainly addressed questions of parental control behavior, focusing on parental discipline standards and techniques. Another important dimension of the parent–child relationship, acceptance or responsiveness toward children's wishes and signals, is mentioned only briefly. This dimension, which Altemeyer (1988a) covers only superficially in his analyses of the family background of authoritarians, has gained in importance in discussions on the developmental process of children over the last decades and is of central importance for the explanation of elementary security in their relationships to adults (cf. Ainsworth et al., 1978; Sroufe & Fleeson, 1986, p. 56).

"Control" and "acceptance in the parents' behavior toward their children may possibly be closely linked to one another empirically, but they can be analytically distinguished, and may be independently relevant aspects of the socialization process as can be concluded from Diana Baumrind's studies on authoritarian, authoritative, and permissive

TABLE 6.1. A two-dimensional classification of parenting patterns.

	Accepting, responsive, child-centered	Rejecting, unresponsive, parent-centered
Demanding, controlling	Authoritative-reciprocal, high in bidirectional communication	Authoritarian, power assertive
Undemanding, low in control attempts	Indulgent	Neglecting, ignoring, indifferent, uninvolved

Source: Maccoby and Martin, 1983, p. 39. From P.H. Mussen (ed.), *Handbook of Child Psychology*, 4th ed., © 1983. Reproduced with the permission of John Wiley & Sons, Inc., New York.

styles of child rearing (cf. Maccoby & Martin, 1983, p. 40). Eleanor E. Maccoby and John A. Martin illustrated the necessity to systematically differentiate between control and acceptance as aspects of parental behavior with the help of a table (see Table 6.1).

The affective acceptance and responsiveness factor, accentuated here, was emphasized in Else Frenkel-Brunswik's interpretations of the family background of authoritarians, but not in Sanford's (1956) discussion and Altemeyer's (1988a) adoption of it. In her final deliberations on the origin of authoritarian dispositions, Frenkel-Brunswik stressed that, although strict discipline is found in the authoritarians' families, there are important accompanying emotional difficulties. Authoritarian parents are not able to show their children affection without reservation; it is contingent upon the child's good behavior (Adorno et al., 1950, p. 482). In the summary of her chapter (chap. 10) on the family backgrounds of authoritarians and nonauthoritarians, Frenkel-Brunswik emphasizes that nonauthoritarians were shown more love and acceptance in comparison to authoritarians, and they felt "more basically secure" in their relationship to their parents (Adorno et al., 1950, p. 388; see also Frenkel-Brunswik, 1954, p. 236). This acceptance made conflict with the parents easier; criticism of the parent is possible without fear of a fundamental rejection.

Empirical evidence for the thesis that nonauthoritarians experience greater security in the relationship to their parents is rather sparse in *TAP*. However, there is indirect evidence. The description of the current child–parent relationship is, in my opinion, one example of such indirect evidence. The bond between nonauthoritarians and their parents more likely results from the need for affection, the emotional bond to the mother being of particular importance to the men. For authoritarians, in contrast, the relationship to the parents is determined by the orientation toward "getting things" ("dependence for things vs. dependence for love," Adorno et al., 1950, pp. 353, 341). In addition, the non-authoritarians are able to describe their parents more precisely and vividly—the parents are more present as individuals. Their descriptions differ in this perspective from those portrayals offered by authoritarians, which tend more toward stereotyping and glorification (cf. Adorno et al., 1950, p. 340). These problems of idealization will be taken up later in another context.

On the Father-Oriented Bias in The Authoritarian Personality

Sanford's summary, quoted earlier, also discusses father-dominance in the families of authoritarians; his conclusions concur with Frenkel-Brunswik's. Based on the interviews (Adorno et al., 1950, pp. 370, 363), it was concluded that most authoritarians had a dominant father (or, in some cases, a strong, or "henpecking," mother). In the families of non-authoritarians, in comparison, either the mother was more important or the relationship between the parents could be described as a partnership of equals. For Else Frenkel-Brunswik, this was an important result; were it to be confirmed in a broader study it would support the older hypotheses (such as Erich Fromm's) that authoritarian dispositions originate above all in father-dominated families (cf. Adorno et al., 1950, p. 370).

The thesis that father-dominance is an important condition for the development of authoritarian dispositions is part of the folklore that has grown up around *TAP*. The idea is often repeated—it fit so well with the theoretical concepts laid down earlier by the Frankfurt School's *Studien über Autorität und Familie* (Horkheimer, 1936). Erich Fromm's (1936) explanation of the authoritarian or sadomasochistic character, recapitulated in part in *Escape from Freedom* (1941/1965), referred exclusively to the father–son relationship. Daughters went practically unmentioned, and mothers entered the picture as objects of competition in the oedipal triangle (see Fromm, 1936, p. 82) rather than as pertinent teachers and parents in their own right.

This father–son presupposition can also be detected in *TAP*, though it has been toned down a bit. *TAP* referred not only to authoritarian and nonauthoritarian sons but also to authoritarian and nonauthoritarian daughters. In addition, the mother's role in the socialization process is more clearly open to study, though with an unusual slant. Mothers are the focal point when dealing with the interpretation of nonauthoritarians and their satisfactory relationship to their mothers. However, in the interpretation of authoritarians, aside from a few henpecking mothers, they are allotted a shadowy existence. It is hardly mentioned that mothers can inflict disappointments; reject or be inconsistent in their affection; beat their children; and thus, independent of the father, contribute to authoritarian development.

Else Frenkel-Brunswik's interpretation of the following information is in this context revealing: Of the 20 men classified as authoritarian, no less than 7 lost their mothers through death as young children or in their early teens, whereas none of the nonauthoritarians suffered such a loss (see

Adorno et al., 1950, p. 382). Frenkel-Brunswik comments briefly; to her, this observation is additional proof for the hypothesis that the mother-orientation (see Adorno et al., 1950, p. 370) is important for the development of nonauthoritarian dispositions (p. 382). Fathers, and a few rare henpecking mothers, are responsible for authoritarian developments, and mothers in general are responsible when dealing with nonauthoritarian developments. In her brief comments, Frenkel-Brunswik completely ignores the fact that illness and early death of mothers—or fathers—is always difficult for children and that such an experience leaves a lasting impression on an individual far into adulthood. John Bowlby (1980) pointed out in *Attachment and Loss* that the experience of loss shapes a person more, the fewer opportunities the child is given to consciously comprehend and mourn the loss of persons central in his or her life.

Because *TAP* contains no additional information on the manner in which the authoritarian men experienced and reflected on the illness and death of their mothers, it would be futile to speculate further. For my part, this detail of the study is simply one reason to be skeptical and to question whether it would not be important to deal with the mother–child relationship in more detail. If early separation experiences are in fact significant for the development of authoritarian personality structures, then the mother–child relationship and experience of early separation should be included as independent variables in studies of the development of authoritarianism.

Functions and Origins of Prejudice in the Family

Nathan W. Ackerman and Marie Jahoda's study (1950) on the psychological and social conditions of anti-Semitism contains an analysis that differentiates the role of the father–child relationship from that of the mother–child relationship in the development of authoritarian dispositions. Ackerman and Jahoda explicitly characterize their study as exploratory (p. 17). The study, based upon unusually multifarious data collected in part through intensive biographical reconstructions, shows great methodological resourcefulness. One of the failings of subsequent research on authoritarianism is that this study has seldom been carefully attended to. Beyond the bias against such qualitative research, two important reasons for this neglect may be (a) that the study is quite complex in its argumentation, and (b) that its results do not quite fit into the traditional picture that is presented by *TAP* and related research.

Ackerman and Jahoda's (1950) study is based on interviews and discussions with psychoanalysts on case histories of anti-Semitic patients.[4]

---

[4] Comparable case histories were also analyzed with the aid of psychologically qualified personnel from charitable institutions. They are not considered here because they were less informative.

The interviews and discussions with the analysts covered as a rule several sessions (see Ackerman & Jahoda, 1950, p. 15). An opening interview was followed by two or three sessions in which the case studies described by the psychoanalysts were discussed in greater detail using discussion guidelines. A research group including a psychoanalyst[5] evaluated and condensed the acquired data into initial case interpretations. In a further session with the therapists involved in the study, initial interpretations were introduced and modified where necessary. Of the case histories acquired in this manner, for the most part only those with complete family histories will be considered in the following discussion. In addition, the cases of Jewish anti-Semitism that Ackerman and Jahoda included in their study will not be discussed because of the differing pattern of family dynamics (anti-Semitism as hatred of the parents in a direct sense). Therefore, out of a total of 27 male and female patients analyzed, we will examine only 15 cases—9 men and 6 women.[6]

The patients were predominantly members of the middle class, living in and around New York (Ackerman & Jahoda, 1950, pp. 17, 58, 74). They began psychoanalytic therapy not because of their anti-Semitism, but because of other problems. Their anti-Semitism ranged from harmless negative attitudes to massive annihilation wishes. The anti-Semitic prejudices and aggressions were in part linked to a specific construct of symptoms (Ackerman & Jahoda, p. 59), and in part inspecific and unselective: "'Unselective' anti-Semitism is expressed either in name-calling alone—'dirty Jew' or 'kike' are typical examples—or in an almost unlimited number of accusations. In these cases, projection is used to externalize diffuse hostility" (p. 60).

A few characteristics and psychological dispositions were found in all of the anti-Semites. To begin with the clinical picture, in none of the cases analyzed were the patients suffering from deep depression (Ackerman & Jahoda, 1950, p. 50). In the opinion of the authors, this absence is not a chance phenomenon resulting from the limitations of the data, but rather a plausible correlate of externalization tendencies of anti-Semites. Feelings of guilt and self-accusation belong to the classical picture of depressive illnesses, whereas anti-Semitic reactions are linked to the tendency "to blame the outside world rather than one's own self" (Ackerman & Jahoda, p. 26). The following characteristics are described as universal for anti-Semitic patients (see Ackerman & Jahoda, 1950, p. 27):

---

[5] Nathan Ackerman. Other members of the research team also were interested in psychoanalytic theory and knew, as is emphasized, the practical side of psychoanalysis from their own therapy.

[6] See appendix to the study (p. 95) for an overview of all cases—also those recorded in the charitable institutions. Above all, the following cases are being considered: 1, 2, 4, 7, 10, 11, 13, 14, 15, 17, 18, 19, 22, 23, 26.

1. A vague feeling of fear, linked to an inner picture of the world around them that appears to be hostile, evil, and difficult to master.
2. A shaky self-image, identity problems, and fluctuations between overestimation of oneself and self-derogation.
3. Difficulties in interpersonal relationships manifested in part in a high degree of isolation and hidden in part behind functioning facades. "But at best such disguises deceive the outer world and sometimes the self; they never lead to the establishment of warm, human relations" (p. 33).
4. The tendency to conform and fear of attracting attention.
5. Problems in coping with reality; often, there are weak bonds not only to other persons but also to external "objects" (content of work, occupation in one's leisure time, etc.). For instance, only one of the subjects analyzed reported having a genuinely positive relation to the contents of his own occupation (p. 90). On the other hand, commitments to improving social status were more pronounced (cf. p. 88).
6. Problems in the development of an autonomous set of ethics; there is little evidence for the presence of an internalized, mature system of values and norms that shaped reactions of conscience and feelings of guilt. Genuine feelings of guilt are in some cases completely missing— for the authors, another opportunity to point out the link to the absence of genuine depression (p. 38).

If one compares these general traits with those extracted by Frenkel-Brunswik from the qualitative interviews with authoritarians and non-authoritarians (see particularly chaps. 11–12 of *TAP*), one discovers parallels in practically every point. In this respect, the differences in the two studies are not to be found in the general characterization of the prejudiced individual. However, important differences become clear when one examines the more specific interpretations of the function of prejudice and aggression, and the analysis of their origins in the family.

Self-Image, Family Background, and Anti-Semitism

The mechanism of displacement is of marked importance for the interpretation of the connection between family constructs and prejudices in *The Authoritarian Personality*: Aggression that cannot be expressed toward the all-powerful and idealized parents can be verbalized or acted out toward underdogs. Generally, these are members of minorities that, depending on the social and cultural context, have drawn negative attention in various ways. Such displaced aggression provides relief for a short time.

The same pattern of argumentation can be found in Ackerman and Jahoda's (1950) book (see p. 47); it is, however, of no great importance in the overall context of the argumentation. The anti-Semites' feelings about themselves—characterized by insecurity, feelings of discrimination, and self-rejection—are much more important to Ackerman and Jahoda (see, above all, p. 55, but also p. 79). Anti-Semitic aggressions fulfill an important function in helping to cope with these feelings of insecurity and to stabilize the self-image. This function is commented on by Ackerman and Jahoda as follows:

Basically they reject themselves and envy others. To find a semblance of balance in spite of their frustrations, they mobilize against their anxiety and self-hate a variety of defense mechanisms. In the interlocking pattern of these defenses, anti-Semitism seems to fulfill a functionally well-defined role. It represents an effort to displace the self-destroying trends in the personality. At the psychic level, anti-Semitic hostility can be viewed as a profound though irrational and futile defensive effort to restore a crippled self. At the social level, it can be regarded as a device for achieving secondary emotional and material gain. (p. 55)

According to this explanation, anti-Semitism and prejudice are components of a comprehensive tendency toward externalization of one's own problems, insecurities, and inner conflicts. Of special importance to the defense system of anti-Semitic patients is the mechanism of "projection." Projection shapes in a more diffuse or more selective way the character of their anti-Semitic reproaches (see Ackerman & Jahoda, p. 56).

Ackerman and Jahoda (1950) interpret the insecurities in the self-image and the tendencies toward a fundamental, although denied, self-rejection against the background of family experiences of the group studied. Such defenses are the plausible result of a specific socialization process. In the course of socialization, rejection by one or both the parents was a relevant experience (see p. 45). Deviating from the father-centered world view of *TAP*, Ackerman and Jahoda highlight the role of the mother in the development of the prejudiced personality. Her role in socialization becomes even more evident when one examines the individual case descriptions contained in the appendix (Ackerman & Jahoda, p. 95) and in other materials of the text itself (discussed below).

To begin with, it is remarkable that not father-dominance but rather mother-dominance typified many hostile relationships between parents and anti-Semitic patients. The mothers played more often the aggressive dominant and the fathers more often the weaker, masochistic part (Ackerman & Jahoda, 1950, p. 45). This alone does not defeat the thesis of father-dominance as a condition of authoritarian development, considering the small and select sample of patients (cf. contradictory results of Mantell, 1972, pp. 45 and 398, in which father-dominance is more prevalent). These results add a critical perspective to a thesis that has often been passed on without reflection in the reporting of research on authoritarianism.

If one closely examines the case histories chosen for a more exact analysis (see footnote 6), then one will notice that in all cases the subject matter of rejection plays a part in the description of the mother–child relationship.[7] Rejection by the mother is in part the dominating experience, as evidenced in the following case (Case 26), a male, between 40 and 50 years old. In this case, the anti-Semitic tendencies are a problem for the patient himself because they do not fit in with his leftist-liberal conception of himself. His family background is given as follows:

The patient was the son of a German father and an Irish mother. The father was a weak person who suffered ostracism in this country during the First World War because of his German origin. He spent little time at home and died abroad when the patient was a child. The mother was an aggressive, cunning, efficient, money-greedy person who worked her way up to considerable wealth. She frequently abandoned her son to a wealthy woman friend; however, when she discovered that the child became too attached to that woman she took him away. The patient, therefore, had no chance of identifying with his father, nor with his mother to whose domination he meekly submitted. From early childhood on, he suffered from a feeling of isolation and a lack of belongingness. (Ackerman & Jahoda, 1950, p. 118)

The mother's rejections more often than not are accompanied by the father's rejections or his pronounced inclination to punish. The following cases illustrate.

Case 2 is a man about 45 years old, the content of whose verbal anti-Semitism is shaped by a fear of superiority and contempt. His family background is given as follows:

[He] experienced rejection during early childhood through the father's sadistic beatings and the mother's more subtle, but equally cruel, ridicule. In relation to his enuresis and a physical handicap (a congenitally exposed urinary canal), she told him again and again, 'you are not like other boys.' (Ackerman & Jahoda, 1950, p. 45)

Another case (Case 4), a woman between 30 and 40 years old expressed anti-Semitism in conversation and in jokes; she inclined toward a clear social segregation from Jews. Her family background included rejection by both parents:

Patient felt rejected as a child by mother and father. Mother was a forceful aggressive person who never permitted the child any warm intimacy. The patient felt that both parents were most interested in her brother; her own interests and needs always had to be subordinated to the special care required by a sick sister.

---

[7] In a few cases the "rejection" is complicated to grasp and describe; for example, in one case (17), the mother suffered from a mental illness that had serious consequences for interaction and identification; in another case (23) feelings of desolation and rejection resulted from early death of the mother and problems with the stepmother; a seduction by the mother is reported on in a third case (22); and finally, one subject (15) reports on mother's indulgence coupled with dominance and the establishment of sustained dependence.

The parents never showed each other affection; all relationships in the family were rigid, conventional, and without warmth. This was true also in respect to religion. The patient received formal teachings, but never had deep religious feelings. This emotional climate, together with her own problem of deep-rooted envy, has led her to continue the attitude toward Jews which prevailed in her parental family. (Ackerman & Jahoda, 1950, p. 98)

Ackerman and Jahoda's (1950) case histories report harsh, even sadistic, punishment (e.g., Case 2) or a general restrictive and conventional family milieu (Case 4). These reports are included in their interpretations, but their key concept is *rejection*: This strong emphasis on rejection distinguishes their theory from that put forth in *TAP*. Their observations lead them to conclude that experience of multiple rejection and the feelings of insecurity in relationship to the parents early in life lead (a) to a failure to identify with the parents—a central prerequisite for the development of conscience—and to an inability to sufficiently master oedipal conflict patterns[8]; and (b) to a fundamental feeling of insecurity concerning one's own self-image and relationships to others.

Ackerman and Jahoda (1950) did not claim that insecurity and failure of identification are necessarily linked to anti-Semitism; rather, they argue that individuals with these dispositions are susceptible to anti-Semitism when it is accepted in their social and cultural environment that it is permissible to discriminate against others (p. 55). The object of discrimination depends on the situation: Under other circumstances, these people could just as well have feelings of hatred toward Turks, be avid supporters of a greater restriction of the right to asylum, or be employers who harass their subordinates. Thus, sociological and psychological interpretations are linked here in two ways:

1. In a socialization theory sense: Social experiences in the family and patterns of relationship within the family are related to the development of individual dispositions.
2. In a contextual, historical sense, the manner in which the experiences within the family and the respective psychological characteristics are transformed is determined to a great extent by the current situation, the prevailing political and cultural environment, educational influences, and influences of the media. In this respect, there is no straight path from early social experiences to specific patterns of prejudice in adulthood.

---

[8] Cf. Ackerman and Jahoda, 1950, p. 48. The authors comment that their evidence here is rather sparse and that they deduce the incomplete solution of the oedipal conflict from circumstances later in life (p. 48). They note, in addition, that they had difficulties in establishing clear-cut relations between oedipal conflicts and later anti-Semitism. A closer connection between the two could be found in the case of Jewish anti-Semitism (cf. p. 50).

Problems of Generalization

For Ackerman and Jahoda (1950), receptivity to prejudice and the readiness to show aggression toward minorities depend on two conditions:

1. The presence of a deep-seated insecurity in the self-image and the tendency toward self-rejection which, however, are denied and are therefore not openly expressed.
2. Insecurity in the relationship to the parents, which precedes the above-mentioned insecurity, and experiences of rejection, especially by the mother. The willingness of the parents to punish and the tendency toward harsh punishment also plays a part; these are, however, of secondary importance as compared to the influence of experiences of rejection.

These results and their possible generality depend upon our evaluation of methods used in the study. The case descriptions on which Ackerman and Jahoda's conclusions are based derive from extensive communication in the course of therapy. In one sense they contain more information than is usually gathered in social research. At the same time, the results are bound to the peculiarities of the cases analyzed: Not only are the patients emotionally distressed, but also they let it be known, by the fact that they seek out psychoanalytic treatment, that they have problems that are not solely due to a hostile environment but also to personal difficulties. They deviate in this respect from the known ideal types of authoritarian dispositions. The classical authoritarian would more likely maltreat his wife or defame "persons seeking asylum" than degrade himself to a subject of psychoanalytic therapy.

Ackerman and Jahoda (1950) were quite conscious of the special character of their sample and stressed the "essentially explorative" nature of their work (p. 17). It is my opinion that one should take this self-definition seriously, and that in the consideration of their work one should stress above all their contribution to the development of hypotheses. Their theses can contribute to an enrichment of the discussion in authoritarianism research, which has become bogged down and unproductive. I would like to illustrate this by discussing various studies and theoretical insights, developed particularly within the scope of attachment research.

Authoritarianism and Attachment Research: An Attempt at Integration

According to Ackerman and Jahoda's (1950) argumentation, the dominant problems of those who are inclined to prejudice and aggression toward minorities are problems of self-assessment and the sense of self-worth. These feelings are denied and are therefore not directly evident. They must be deduced from indirect indications, such as the tendency toward exaggerated sensitivity to criticism, the inclination to boast and show off, tendencies to put blame on others and to resist self-criticism, and the inclination to show arrogance toward others. Although these traits and behavioral tendencies of authoritarians were also described in the analysis of the clinical interviews in *The Authoritarian Personality* (cf. Adorno et al., 1950, pp. 393, 409, 423, 430), they drew little attention.

The thesis that one of the central problems of authoritarians is the denial of problems with the self appears plausible. I cannot, however, produce satisfactory proof of this thesis; its verification is a task for future research. Evidence of its soundness can be found, however, in studies that seek to analyze the problems of authoritarianism on the basis of standardized questionnaires. In these studies, among other things, the moral self-righteousness of authoritarians (Altemeyer, 1988a, p. 157) or their negativity toward the environment and other people (e.g., Schumann 1984b, p. 12; Altemeyer, 1988a, p. 168) is emphasized. Altemeyer (1988a, p. 183) goes so far as to describe the tendency to self-righteousness as a particularly important explanation for authoritarian aggression.

Assuming the plausibility of relating authoritarian dispositions to the latent narcissist problems we have described, then it is also plausible that the origins of these problems may lie in early experiences in interpersonal relationships. It is important, them, to direct attention to the first years of life and to the development of the relationship between the child and the mother (or some other person who is primarily responsible for the welfare of the child and toward whom the child's attachment behavior is directed). (See Bowlby, 1969, 1973, for a discussion of the development of attachment behavior in small children.) These early relationships can make the child secure to various degrees, or they can produce insecurity. Thereby, attachments are of long-term importance to the development of self-concepts and expectations toward others, as was demonstrated in longitudinal studies of children who were observed from their first year to the preschool and school years (see Bretherton, 1985, p. 14, for an overview).

In the analysis of degrees of security in the child–mother relationship, we follow in the tradition of attachment research, employing a classification scheme that has been developed by Mary Ainsworth. On the basis of observations in natural and experimental conditions, Ainsworth (1967; Ainsworth et al., 1978) differentiates between children who have secure attachments to their primary caregiver and those who do not.

The children who have secure attachments are children for whom there is a harmonious balance between exploration and seeking the mother. In experimental situations in which the time spent with the mother was interrupted by brief periods of separation (the "Strange Situation") these children rejoice over the reunion at the end of the separation. They are readily comforted and are able to respond to their environment with curiosity because of the secure relationship to the mother. (See Sroufe & Fleeson, 1988, p. 31, for summaries of this and the following points.)

Children insecure in their attachments can be described in two variations. *Avoidant* children react primarily to the experimental separation and reunion situations by distancing themselves from the mother—they tend to ignore her after the brief separations. Among *ambivalent*, or resistant, children, the desire for closeness and clinging prevails. They react to separations with panic; even after the separation had ended, they do not let themselves be readily comforted; they often angrily reject repeated attempts to comfort them. At the same time, they are particularly wary of novel situations and show little interest in exploring their environment.

Whether a secure or insecure, avoiding or ambivalent attachment to the mother develops in the individual case depends to a great extent upon the mother's quality of interaction with her child, and on the mother's responsiveness to the child and her ability to react to the child's behavior and signals appropriately (cf. Ainsworth et al., 1978, pp. 137, 310). In the case of insecure avoidant children, the mother is consistently rejecting. There is often a strong avoidance of body contact, an inclination to ridicule the child, and high restrictiveness (Main & Weston, 1982, p. 45). For insecure ambivalent children, inconsistency of attention toward the child is the more important determinant of insecurity.

Both variations of insecure attachments are of great significance to the development of self-concept and of social relationships, including those outside the family. This makes these adjustment patterns relevant for research on authoritarianism, as shown in a longitudinal study conducted by L. Alan Sroufe (1983) in Minnesota. The infants involved were observed in their relationship to their mothers during the first year. Judging from their behavior in preschool classes, the authors found that, in comparison to secure children, insecure children had fewer resources and flexibility at their disposal to aid them in mastering their environment and difficult situations ("ego resiliency"), a lower sense of self-worth, and a smaller capacity for feelings of empathy (which held especially true for the avoidant children). Finally, they were more likely to fall into dominance–subordination patterns in their relationships to peers ("victimizing relationships") (Sroufe, 1983; Sroufe & Fleeson, 1988).

I do not advocate replacing the thesis of father-dominance as a condition of authoritarian development, with an antithesis in which only the mothers are considered in their relationship to their children. It is a much more complex composition of factors that leads to the development of authoritarian dispositions. What I am urging instead is that models of research should be conceived that allow the role of the mother–child relationship to be assessed appropriately in longitudinal studies or in retrospective biographical studies and that its importance for the development of authoritarian dispositions be discussed.

Indications that research models including relationships with all early caregivers could be fruitful are found also in other qualitative studies. One important example is David Mantell's (1972) investigation, based on extensive semistructured interviews with American war resisters and volunteers who participated in the Vietnam War as members of a close combat troop, the Green Berets. The Green Berets characterized their mothers as being very similar to their fathers in restrictiveness and emotional distance (Mantell, 1972, p. 74). They reported that their mothers carried out the bodily punishment of children more often than their fathers (p. 72). Mothers of Green Berets distinguished themselves also by their lacking of understanding and empathy in their relationship to their children (p. 74).[9]

As Mantell's (1972/1974) report indicates, the Green Berets' receptiveness to authoritarian aggression and their cynical relation to human life represent a type of authoritarian disposition in which sadistic components are particularly salient. Mantell's results, therefore, must be compared to studies in which "average" authoritarians are dealt with— potential supporters of fascist movements in times of crisis who may not necessarily become violators. One such investigation is the longitudinal study on personality development of young skilled workers conducted by Ernst Hoff, Lothar Lappe, and Wolfgang Lempert (1983) in Berlin.[10] This study does not deal primarily with authoritarianism, but with moral development and assessment of locus of control. However, the present author's reanalysis of those parts of the semistructured interviews concerning biography and some of the moral dilemmas employed reveal their significance for the topic of authoritarian dispositions.

---

[9] See also Grossmann, 1984, p. 146, for a discussion of Mantell's study within the attachment research context.

[10] See Hoff et al., 1983, for methods of the research conducted at the Max-Planck-Institut für Bildungs forschung. Included were 21 skilled workers who were on the average 23 years old at the beginning of data collection (1980/81). Their professional career and personal development have been followed without interruption (see Lempert, 1988, for a current publication of this project). In my reanalysis I concentrated on interviews conducted in the project's initial phase (biographical interviews and selected sections of the interviews on moral dilemmas). From the 21 cases, I included only 19 in my analyses. Two subjects were left out because they did not participate in the later parts of the project. I would like to thank the research group for giving me access to their data and to the individual case analyses compiled by them. I would also like to thank Heide Hempel and Martina Sanden-Marcus for their assistance, and Teresa Jacobsen for helpful discussions.

The Socialization of Young Workers

Four respondents interviewed by Hoff et al. (1983) were especially hostile toward foreigners and more or less denied the right to asylum. During the interviews, all of them reported difficulties early in their lives with their mother or the primary attachment figure. In one case, the early disturbances in social relationships were particularly prevalent. Its detailed description further illustrates the tendencies toward idealization and denial, so important for the understanding of authoritarians:

The subject (24 years old at the time of the interview; working in the automobile industry) lived with his grandparents in East Berlin up to the age of four. Both parents worked and initially lived with the grandparents, and later moved into their own apartment in West Berlin. The subject joined his parents after the mother had a second child, a daughter, and quit work. The separation from his grandparents, which was particularly drastic because of the Berlin wall, was very difficult for him, as became clear during the interview. The grandmother in comparison to his mother continued to be the more important attachment figure; and he liked his grandfather more than his father even though the former had beaten him more than once.

The parents' marriage was full of conflict after the separation from the grandparents. The parents divorced later after a peaceful interval of some years. The mother, who was described as the more strict parent in his upbringing, dominated the subject's depiction of his childhood. This is concluded, however, from descriptions of events later in his life: The mother, for example, had the habit of tearing out pages of her son's exercise book that were not neatly written and of forcing him to rewrite the homework, even though she was not in a position to judge the adequacy of the content of the work, especially as the young boy grew older.

The subject's father was not as restrictive, but showed little interest in his son. The subject later reproached his father for this —though with a guilty conscience (he felt he really had no right to do this). The son–father relationship was especially troublesome because the father drank excessively, particularly during the time in which the son had to cope with the separation from the grandparents. The mother often tried to find the father in local bars and to coax him home, taking her son with her on these excursions.

The fact that the mother could not give him her undivided attention because of his little sister was also quite difficult for the subject. The sister was always seen as interfering; the two were arch enemies ("*spinnefeind*"), sticking together at most when confronted with a third person. For the subject, the presence of the sister sharply contrasted the more pleasant situations at his grandparents. ". . . *Vorher war ich der King, der Kronprinz, und auf einmal war noch jemand da*" (". . . I used to be the king, the crown prince, and then suddenly there was someone else there").

Others with similar childhood experiences might have openly objected to their fate, be hateful of their parents, tend to be depressive, and so forth. This was not the case with the subject.

At the most, the father is criticized moderately. Only for the sister—as a rival—does the subject openly demonstrate antipathy. In addition, the efforts to generate a positive picture of his own childhood is predominant: burdensome memories tend to be denied—mentioned, but made light of, or simply not mentioned—the positive ones emphasized. Pertinent examples of this are the following statements: *"Meine Kindheit ist ganz normal verlaufen."* ("I had a very normal childhood") or *". . . ich denk im grossen und ganzen gern (an die Kindheit) zuruck . . . gloob ick also; fast nicht—ausser auf von vaterlicher Seite hat's mir an nichts gefehlt . . . Vielleicht zuviel des Guten."* (". . . on the whole I enjoy thinking back [on my childhood] . . . I think so; almost nothing except on the father's part, I wanted for nothing . . . Perhaps too much of a good thing".) The grandparents spoiled him rotten (*"von vorn bis hinten"*), the mother as well.

At one point in the interview the subject mentioned himself his tendency to deny certain childhood events. He was asked whether he still has recollections of the move away from his grandparents to his parents: *"Nee. Det, weess nicht, ist irgendwie weg. Vielleicht weil es zu unangenehm fruher war dass ick—so im Hinterstubchen hab ich da so'n Gedanken dran."* ("No, don't know, it's somehow gone. Perhaps, because at the time it was too unpleasant, or so, that I repress it somehow, until I—no longer that I—so somewhere in the back of my mind I think about it.")[11]

The case illustrates, on the one hand, the situation of insecure attachment in the childhood and the insecurity in the relationship to primary attachment figures (grandmother, mother). It documents, on the other hand, how difficult it is in social research to trace such experiences when the subject, at the same time, plays down problems—separation experiences, disappointments, rejections—and transfigures the past. What should one rely on in the interpretation?

Altemeyer, whose criticism of the theoretical approach of *TAP* has been mentioned several times in this article, is inclined to make this problem of data collection and interpretation the basis for a radical solution. He criticizes the concept of idealization, or glorification, of the parents that is given a central role in *TAP* (cf. especially Adorno et al., 1950, p. 338) and is used to describe the tendency of denial in Hoff et al.'s (1983) Case 165. Altemeyer thinks the concept of idealization is misleading. He maintains that assuming denial and idealization makes the theory of *TAP* untestable, for the data can be interpreted arbitrarily:

Suppose one finds that High RWA subjects gush with praise of their parents; it is the expected overglorification. If, on the other hand, they describe their parents as beasts, it is taken as proof that the parents *were* cruel and harsh. And if, of the behavior in both positive and negative terms (which is what they do), it is

---

[11] Source: Interview protocol and individual case study of Case 165 of the study conducted by Hoff, Lappe, and Lempert (1983) on the socialization of young skilled worked workers.

explained as a mixture of overglorification and accurate recollection. That may be the case, but how could we ever find out the theory is wrong, if it is wrong? It has all the angles covered. (Altemeyer, 1988a, p. 54)

Altemeyer's criticism is, for several reasons, not very pertinent. First of all, as to the theoretical approach of the Berkeley group and Frenkel-Brunswik's interpretations: They did not arbitrarily speak of glorification at one time and, when it happened to fit in well, of harshness at the next. Rather, it was the specific connection of difficult experiences *and* tendencies of idealization and denial that led to the alleged effect. Altemeyer's contention that the theoretical approach is not verifiable can be doubted on methodological grounds as well. He rules out the possibility that problematic aspects of socialization may be adequately recorded and that tendencies of denial and glorification may be confirmed on the sole basis of slightly structured interviews and differentiated text analyses. In the case described above, the respondent helped the interviewer in putting him on the right track himself. But even when the respective indications are less direct, the situation is far from hopeless.

One way of dealing with the issue of idealization of parents may be illustrated by a paper written by Mary Main and Ruth Goldwyn (1984). They report on semistructured interviews with mothers whose children were observed in the Strange Situation (see above). Their theoretical interest was focused on the question of the reproduction of relationship patterns within families. In the article, special attention was paid to mothers who were particularly rejecting of their children and whose children reacted in a insecure avoidant manner to the Strange Situation. Many of the mothers reported that they had been rejected during childhood by their own mothers. In the interview they had great difficulty in recollecting childhood experiences, and in looking back they tended to idealize their own mother (Main & Goldwyn, p. 213). Main and Goldwyn's approach to the empirical verification of the idealization concept is informative. Unlike the approach used by the authors of *TAP* or that used by Milton Rokeach (1960, p. 357), Main and Goldwyn did not simply use the general statements about the subjects' own mothers and the degree of their assumed stereotypy and exaggeration. Rather, the general statements about the mothers were systematically compared with other more precise accounts in the interview:

A mother who stated that her mother was warm and accepting, and who then could supply concrete supporting evidence, was not considered to have idealized her mother. A subject was considered to idealize when praise of the mother was unqualified, but the subject was unable to offer concrete supporting evidence. Idealization also referred to seemingly unconscious discrepancies between positive general descriptions of the mother or the relationship and actual negative experiences of the parent as described in specific episodes. (Main & Goldwyn, 1984, p. 212)

Main and Goldwyn (1984) illustrated their interpretation procedure using the example of one woman who, in their opinion, idealized her mother to a great extent (See p. 214). This woman described her mother generally as a "good" mother and spoke of a very good relationship to her. When asked to whom she turned as child in a crisis, she answered that in such a situation she usually ran away. She gave a supportive example: Once, when she fell and broke her hand, she did not have the courage to go to her mother, for fear that her mother would be angry. In my opinion, this case illustrates that it is possible to analyze accounts of childhood experiences in such a way that the idealization concept is empirically justified. As a prerequisite, however, the childhood experiences must not be recorded in a standardized form, but rather in a manner that promotes unconstrained narration, reflection, and the conveyance of vivid descriptions of childhood memories. In this way, contradictions, inconsistencies in the relation between general and specific statements, and massive gaps in memory can emerge.

Main and Goldwyn's (1984) study was used here to show that interpretations dealing with the tendencies to idealize parents or to deny negative experiences do not necessarily lead to ambiguous conclusions, as Altemeyer (1988a) suggests. One of the study's main results, however, is of equal importance for research on authoritarianism. This is the finding that problematical childhood experiences are more likely to be reproduced in other contexts, the less they are recognized and reflected upon. The attempt to more adequately detect specific defense mechanisms of authoritarians and to describe their development is of great strategic importance for authoritarianism research. Is it true that authoritarians deny negative experiences in a particularly conspicuous manner? If so, what causes this? Why does a situation appear wonderful and satisfying to them that others would describe in their recollection as burdensome, disappointing, or humiliating? Have their parents raised them in such a way that happiness is considered a virtue and plaintiveness a vice? Do narcissistic wishes play a role—one is exemplary because one's parents were exemplary—or was the disownment and denial of parental rejection during childhood simply functional in order to maintain a relationship that would have been intolerable without skillfully turning one's eyes off?

Unfortunately, these questions cannot be answered convincingly at the present state of research on authoritarianism or of attachment research. I believe, however, that defense mechanisms are central to the understanding of the development of authoritarian dispositions, for I believe that it is the particular combination of difficult childhood experiences *and* their denial that will explain why comparable childhood experiences lead, in one case, to the development of depressive reactions, and in the other, to the externalization of problems and the development of aggression toward minorities.

Conclusion

I have attempted to show that the consideration of generally neglected qualitative traditions in research on authoritarianism can contribute to a deeper understanding of the origins of authoritarian dispositions. A reconsideration of these traditions can point the way for new emphases in research. The present review suggests that, in comparison to the approach used in the research tradition of *TAP*, emphasis should be placed on following topics:

1. A stronger emphasis on narcissistic problems in the behavior of authoritarians.
2. A more intensive analysis of those aspects of parental behavior described as acceptance and responsiveness, which are of particular importance for the development of security in relationships to the parents.
3. The withdrawal from the father-centered world view of *TAP* and a stronger focus on the role of mothers in the interpretation of authoritarian development. More generally, attention should be given to the attachment figure primarily responsible for the care of the growing child.
4. A more intensive analysis of the defense mechanisms of authoritarians, specifically their tendencies toward denial, justification after the fact, or playing down of burdensome experiences. The question of the idealization of parents, or one of the parents, should be seen as a partial aspect of this general problem.

The research designs for the topics discussed here must, as I have attempted to show in different ways, differ from the prevailing models of research on authoritarianism. On the one hand, sampling problems must be given more attention. In this regard, David Mantell's (1972/1974) study of Green Berets and war resisters is very interesting. Sampling of respondents should not follow the way of convenience and easy access, as has been common in authoritarianism research with the ever popular student survey, but should be directed by theoretical considerations and the need to systematically survey the social behavior of the selected groups. On the other hand, methods of securing data should be favored that allow for flexible forms of interviewing or observation.

The possibility of cooperating with psychoanalysts (as did Ackerman & Jahoda, 1950) should be left open. To me, the insight is important that a psychoanalytically oriented or, more modestly, a psychoanalytically *informed* social psychology, continues to be relevant for developing further research on authoritarianism. The perspective cannot, as Altemeyer implies, simply be dismissed by criticizing the work of the Berkeley group. *The Authoritarian Personality* was written 40 years ago; since then great progress has been made both in socialization research and in psychoanalytically oriented developmental psychology. Research on authoritarianism should, at last, take notice of this development.

7
Authoritarianism: Left and Right

WILLIAM F. STONE AND LAURENCE D. SMITH

In a prepublication discussion of *The Authoritarian Personality* (Adorno, Frenkel-Brunswik, Levinson, & Sanford, 1950) research, Edward Shils (1948) was liberal in his praise. The researchers, he then believed, had "succeeded in isolating the set of personality and attitudinal character-istics which make for receptivity to anti-Semitic ideas. The relevance of psychoanalytic categories and hypotheses, flexibly used, in the under-standing of social cleavages is better demonstrated in this study than anywhere else" (Shils, 1948, p. 29). The preliminary report that Shils cited was on the anti-Semitic personality; he did not mention the equation of this personality with prefascist leanings. About the time Shils was making this assessment, the concerns of United States policy and public opinion makers were refocusing. Fascism had been defeated; the new enemy was communism. The name of Joseph McCarthy was coming to be synonymous with irresponsible attacks on people in government, academia, and the arts who had left-wing sympathies. By 1950, anti-communism had come to the fore as the engine of U.S. foreign policy.

Many formerly liberal commentators and social scientists caught the spirit of the times and perceived the threat posed by communism. Among the intellectuals so affected were Norman Podhoretz, Daniel Bell, and notably Edward Shils. By the 1960s even many members of the U.S. Socialist party were imbued with the spirit of anticommunism. The term *neoconservative* came to be applied to these former liberals.

In 1954, Shils revised his earlier opinion of *TAP*. His rethinking was expressed in a chapter entitled "Authoritarianism, Left and Right" in the critical volume edited by Christie and Jahoda (1954). In this chapter, Shils criticized *TAP*'s focus on the conventional left–right distinction, calling it a "deforming intellectual tradition" (p. 31). Despite the his-torical focus of authoritarianism theory and research on attraction to fascism, Shils insisted that there was a neglected species of authoritarian on the left. Whether left-authoritarians (attracted to communism) and right-authoritarians (attracted to fascism) were subspecies of the authori-tarian type or whether they were highly similar people who were simply attracted to extreme political movements was left uncertain by Shils. The main point was that there *are* authoritarians of the left as well as authoritarians of the right.

If we focus on the core characteristics of the prototypical authoritarian personality—a threat-oriented, defensive individual whe copes with threats by conventionality and obedience and who shows hostility generally toward weaker members of outgroups—there is a certain plausibility to Shils's (1954) thesis. Setting aside the historical origins of the discovery of this personality syndrome, we can countenance the hypothesis that such a person could accept the authority of a strong and convincing leader *or* the authority of a dedicated party, left or right. A moderate party or leader might be less attractive to such a person than one with clear-cut, black-and-white solutions to the individual's own problems. Milton Rokeach (1960) was later to focus on such black-and-white, or dogmatic, thinking as the core characteristic of authoritarianism.

However, if we look at the *content* of left and right ideologies, the "extremism" hypothesis concerning ideology and authoritarianism becomes less believable. There may be some similarities between the extremes, but surely there are vast differences between individuals drawn to an ideology that stresses equality above all (communism) and one that stresses hierarchy and the superiority of a master race (fascism). Rokeach (1960) recognized these differences in the following passage:

Communism, considered purely as an ideology, is humanitarian and antiauthoritarian. Its ideological aim is to establish a classless society, to wither away the state, and to take care of the individual according to the doctrine: "From each according to his abilities, to each according to his needs." However, in the case of fascism, particularly naziism, the ideological content is frankly antihumanitarian. It advances as its ideological aim the establishment of the Aryan race as a master race, to rule and subjugate forever the rest of mankind. (p. 127)

Thus, although it is logically possible that persons of the same personality type could be drawn to differing ideologies, each promising certainty and security, due regard for the content of extreme left and right ideologies makes this hypothesis of mirror-image authoritarianisms seem less viable.

Nevertheless, Rokeach (1960) makes a distinction between the *structure* of ideology and the content of that ideology. Given that both communists and fascists embrace formula thinking and hierarchical authority in pursuit of their goals, the *structure* of both ideologies is authoritarian. Thus, the authoritarian individual who is exposed to the ideas of fascism encounters an ideology that is attractive both in content and in structure. "But in the case of a person who embraces communism," writes Rokeach (1960), "there is a sharp discrepancy between content and structure" (p. 127). He concludes that this misfit causes communist recruits considerable agony. There is, consequently, a high turnover among communist party neophytes—they are drawn to the party through idealism, but repelled by the totalitarian structure and methods used. This reasoning is supported by the empirical observations of stronger linkages between authoritarianism and fascist sympathy that Meloen has demonstrated in chapter 3 of this volume.

Personality and Ideology

The controversy of interest here has numerous ramifications. Although many writers have entered the fray, the basic differences can be framed in terms of *TAP*'s position and the 1954 dissent by Shils. *TAP*'s findings on ideology and personality were cautiously stated by Daniel Levinson in his conclusion to a chapter that reviewed in detail the correlational evidence:

There appears to be an affinity between conservatism and ethnocentrism, liberalism and anti-ethnocentrism. The relationship is, however, quantitatively imperfect (r = approximately .5) and qualitatively complex. It is proposed, in further studies, to break down the right–left dimension into numerous ideological patterns. One of these—perhaps the most significant in terms of potential antidemocracy— is the *pseudoconservative*. (Adorno et al., 1950, p. 207)

There was also some discussion in *TAP* about the "rigid low" subjects, who scored extremely low on the Anti-Semitism and F Scales. Thus, although they never explored the idea fully, the authors of *TAP* recognized the possibility of a dogmatic left syndrome.

Following the attempt by Rokeach (1956) to develop a measure of "general authoritarianism," and the suggestion made by Shils (1954) that authoritarianism exists on the left as well as the right, the idea of left-wing authoritarianism has come to be generally accepted. Besides sociologists like Shils, historians (Schlesinger, 1949) and social psychologists (Gergen & Gergen, 1986; Wrightsman, 1977) have accepted the belief in an authoritarianism on the left. Specific empirical studies addressing the issue have been meager, however. Stone (1980) reviewed the evidence, including the influential but suspect reports by Eysenck (1954; Eysenck & Coulter, 1972), and found the arguments for left-wing authoritarianism to be generally without substance.

The criticisms of *TAP* have persisted in the literature, despite the fact that they are typically based on casual observations regarding similarities between far-left and far-right regimes. McCloskey and Chong (1985), for example, appealed to intuitive evidence in their comment about the "similarities in political style, organization and practice" among left- and right-wing dictatorships (p. 331). This passage will be cited more fully in connection with our discussion of the dangers of making inferences about the psychology of individuals from observation of social systems; here, it suffices to note that this type of evidence has been sufficiently persuasive such that the belief in authoritarianism of the left has become entrenched among American social scientists.

Rokeach (1956) developed a notion of authoritarianism that dealt with the cognitive processes. Thus, "dogmatism" was considered to be general authoritarianism, and low and high authoritarians were conceived—as indicated by the title of Rokeach's 1960 book, *The Open and Closed Mind*—to be relatively open-minded or closed-minded. His theory held that the Dogmatism (D) Scale, as a measure of general authoritarianism, is unrelated to political ideology. However, although it is widely acknowledged that the D Scale is less ideologically loaded than the F Scale, D scores are positively correlated with conservative beliefs (Parrott & Brown, 1972).

Stone (1980) reviewed studies of the dogmatism scores of members of politically active groups. He found little support for the left-wing authoritarianism hypothesis. The showcase study, by Gordon DiRenzo (1967b), surveyed members of the Italian House of Deputies. DiRenzo found the 25 Communist deputies to have the lowest Dogmatism scores, and the 24 members of the neofascist Italian Social Movement to have the highest scores. On the basis of the evidence reviewed, Stone concluded that there *is* no good psychological evidence of left-wing authoritarianism and that the concept is a myth perpetuated for some as-yet-unknown reasons (although what he called the centrist bias is strongly implicated).

Another, very different sort of evidence has been used to support the notion of authoritarianism of the left. In *Roots of Radicalism*, Stanley Rothman and Robert Lichter (1982) challenged the social scientists who had found the radical students of the 1960s to be exceptionally healthy (e.g., Keniston, 1971; Flacks, 1967). The main research technique employed was the scoring of TAT stories written by radical and mainstream students. Although the authors conclude that left-wing radicals are authoritarian, the limitations of their research methodology do not permit such conclusions. A search of the literature turned up only one major review (Flacks, 1984) of Rothman and Lichter's book, by a social scientist they had criticized. Flacks (1984) characterized *Roots of Radicalism* as a neoconservative effort "to debunk both the New Leftists themselves and those in the social science community who saw in the student movement potentialities for social regeneration" (p. 92).

Authoritarianism or Extremism?

The study of authoritarianism since the 1950 publication of *The Authoritarian Personality* has been marked by considerable disagreement and conceptual confusion. Many investigators seem to take the position that authoritarianism is rigidity (or whatever the person defines it to be). The following discussion begins with two of the many investigators who have tried to clarify the issues, Jim Sidanius and Bob Altemeyer.

Jim Sidanius (1985) formulated the alternatives in the debate on authoritarianism and ideology by contrasting *authoritarianism* theory with *extremism* theory. (As we shall see, he also added a quite different model, *context* theory.) Authoritarianism theory is the traditional theory that authoritarian personality characteristics go with right-wing ideology. Extremism theory represents the view that the pathologies of thought and mood that characterize authoritarians are shared by people at both political extremes, typified by fascism and communism in our time.

The left-wing authoritarianism debate contrasts authoritarianism and extremism theories. It begins with *TAP*'s findings of the relation of authoritarianism to conservatism. The correlations between the Conservatism Scale (PEC) and the F Scale averaged 0.52 over a large number of groups.

Authoritarianism Theory

The important research on authoritarianism by Bob Altemeyer is mentioned by several of the present contributors and will be reviewed in more detail in chapter 8 of this volume. His 1981 book reviewed the vast literature on authoritarianism and described development of the Right-Wing Authoritarianism (RWA) Scale. Altemeyer found that the literature showed inconsistent support for the entire psychological syndrome described in *TAP*. Three traits, however, did recur with regularity in people scoring high on the F Scale. "Consistently," he wrote, "the data suggested that submissiveness, conventionalism and aggressiveness [went together] but that other traits, including superstition and dogmatism, did not" (1988b, p. 32). These observations were incorporated in his alternative to the F Scale, the RWA Scale.

Are submissiveness, conventionality, and aggressiveness peculiar to right-wing authoritarians? The question entails problems of definition. Altemeyer (1988b) noted Milgram's (1974) findings: There is broad compliance to authoritative commands to shock an innocent victim. But, he noted, even in Milgram's (1974) experimental situation some people were more ready than others to attack a victim upon the command of the legitimate authority. Thus, Altemeyer (1988b) formulated an argument that supports naming aggression in the service of established power, *right-wing aggression*:

The question of what motivates such behavior in the name of higher authorities is hardly an idle curiosity; some of the most horrifying events of our time—from the Holocaust to the My Lai massacre; from the persecution of dissidents in Chile to the deaths by torture in South African prisons—have been acts of authoritarian aggression. Such atrocities are not unique to any political or economic system; Communist and anti-Communist dictatorships seem equally capable of violent repression. *But to the degree that such violence is committed in behalf of a society's established traditions and authorities, it can be called right-wing. In this sense, the mistreatment of Soviet dissidents is no less right-wing than is Guatemalan repression* [italics added]. (p. 32)

Extremism Theory

Are liberals and conservatives alike in some important psychological respects? Extremism theorists argue that the more extreme partisans of each persuasion *are* alike. They tend to focus on members of way-out fascist and communist groups.

Edward Shils

In his chapter of a volume devoted to criticism of *TAP*, Shils (1954) equated the psychology of the masses of people in communist and fascist countries. To him, the right-wing authoritarian's extreme hostility toward Jews and other outgroups is equivalent to the Bolshevik's demand for complete and unqualified loyalty to the Party; the anti-Semite's authoritarian submissiveness is equated with the submissiveness of the Russian people to Stalin.

Shils's (1954) theme was taken up in a recent paper by McCloskey and Chong (1985), who similarly confuse leaders and followers, parties and people:

The findings derived from the available research studies, especially those using the F-Scale, do not correspond to what is obvious from even the most casual observation of political regimes of the far left and far right. No particular expertise is required to discern the striking similarities in political style, organization, and practice among, on the one side, such left-wing dictatorships as the Soviet Union . . . East Germany . . . and, on the other side, such right-wing dictatorships as . . . Spain under Franco, Nazi Germany. . . . (p. 331)

The key word in the foregoing passage is *regimes*. Without acknowledging having done so, McCloskey and Chong (1985) have shifted the perspective from *person* to *regime*, thereby clouding the issue of *personality's* relation to political beliefs. For example, where would this shift in the level of discourse leave us when trying to discuss Gorbachev and the critics of his liberalization? We question the attribution of similar psychological motives, say, to the Italian citizen whose political identification is with the Italian Communist Party (MCI) and the citizen who joins the neofascist Italian Social Movement. The former, a strong believer in equality and the solidarity of the working classes, feels that the triumph of communism will bring a better life for all. The fascist, on the other hand, believes in a strict social hierarchy; the better classes should dominate the lesser, and thus he preaches hatred of certain groups. Is there any reason to believe that people holding such dissimilar beliefs and attitudes have similar personalities?

Left- and Right-Wing Compared

McCloskey and Chong (1985) chose responses from three sample surveys to characterize the respondents as being "far left" or "far right." Far leftists endorsed a goodly number of items such as choice (a) in the following pair:

The sacrifices made by the people in the communist countries:
(a) are necessary and will benefit the people in the long run.
(b) are not really in the people's interests.

Far rightists were characterized by endorsement of the (b) alternative in questions like this one:

How would you feel if the United States were to lose its role as leader among nations?
  (a) I doubt it would bother me very much.
  (b) I would consider it tragic and humiliating.

The individuals surveyed also answered a number of personality items; the theoretical analysis predicts certain similarities between left and right extremists. There are, of course, predictable differences; in general, the left group is more in tune with the center than is the right-wing group. This can be seen, for example, in the percentage agreement on the following issues:

	Left	Middle	Right
Conventionality	0%	6%	71%
Racial equality	98%	72%	1%
Welfare	98%	67%	1%

The closeness of left and center on these and many other issues is minimized by McCloskey and Chong (1985), who note only that "the political moderates . . . hold attitudes that are *somewhat* [italics added] closer to the far left than to the far right" (p. 342).

It is the similarities, of course, that these theorists are looking for. "These similarities," they note, "are of essentially two varieties. Certain of them result from the mutual estrangement of the radical left and right from the political mainstream, while others reflect the common political and psychological style that infuses and colours right-wing and left-wing rhetoric and activity" (McCloskey & Chong, 1985, p. 343). These stylistic tendencies include intolerance of ambiguity and intolerance of opposing viewpoints; these variables were operationalized from the survey data.

Intolerance of ambiguity is measured by agreement with items such as "I believe that you're really *for* something or *against* it, and anything in between is just an excuse to avoid the issue." Percentages of agreement were left, 61%; middle, 39%; and right, 78%. The similarities here suggest *either* intolerance of ambiguity *or* a greater degree of conviction, which is generally part and parcel of taking a position. In any event, the items chosen seem to have little in common with the concept as defined in Budner's (1962) Intolerance of Ambiguity Scale.

The strongest support for McCloskey and Chong's (1985) argument is the data they presented on tolerance for others' views. They claim, for example, that leftist support for civil liberties is selective. As an example, they cite the proportion of political leaders in one study who finished the statement "If a speaker at a public meeting begins to make racial slurs, the audience should . . ." as follows:

	Left	Middle	Right
(a) Let him have his say and then answer him	40%	84%	70%
(b) Stop him speaking	40%	4%	15%

(The remaining 11 to 20% in each group declined to choose either alternative.) The "toughmindedness" of the two extremes is purportedly shown by agreement with the statement, "To bring about great changes for the benefit of mankind often requires cruelty and even ruthlessness" (left, 26%; Middle, 13%; right, 24%). A "final proof" of the personal similarities of right and left extremists was said to be that even though the F scale is loaded toward right-wing appeal, some items appeal to the extremes more than the center (e.g., "People can be divided into two distinct classes, the weak and the strong"). In the sample survey of the general population that used this item, 30% of the far-left respondents, 19% of the centrists, and 56% of the rightists agreed.

In conclusion, although McCloskey and Chong (1985) demonstrated some similarities between left and right extremists, the differences still stand out. The case for personality similarity between left- and right-wing adherents seems forced.

A recent correlational study by Hope Tarr and Maurice Lorr (1991) analyzed RWA-scale responses of 339 university students, together with their answers to items measuring rule following and liberalism-conservatism. Their analysis showed considerable overlap among RWA, conformity, and conservatism. Conformity and conservatism correlated 0.55; their correlations with RWA were 0.59 and 0.57, respectively. "Are there 'left-wing authoritarians'?" Tarr and Lorr asked; "As far as personality structure is concerned, there appears to be no supportive evidence" (p. 310). They do note the data collected in the Soviet Union (see chapter 10, this volume) that shows high RWA scores among supporters of rigid one-party (communist) rule; these people are right-wingers by Altemeyer's (1988b) definition, quoted earlier.

Ideology and Integrative Complexity

Tetlock (1984) takes quite a different approach to the problem of personality similarities between left and right extremists. Dealing exclusively with one hypothetical attribute of the authoritarian, cognitive rigidity, he has investigated integrative complexity in a number of samples of political elites. In one study, Tetlock (1983) found support for authoritarian personality theory in that U.S. senators with extremely conservative voting records were more simplex in their policy statements than their more moderate or liberal colleagues. It could be argued, however, that there are no extreme leftists in the U.S. Congress.

Tetlock (1984) interviewed British MPs, whose ranks do include a wider spectrum of ideology than do their U.S. counterparts. In this study, he found evidence that would support the idea of left-wing authoritarianism, in that extreme socialists and extreme conservatives were both lower on integrative complexity than were their more moderate counterparts on the left and right. However, he also found that moderate socialists were more cognitively flexible than moderate conservatives. His preferred explanation is not in terms of what he calls the "ideologue hypothesis" (both extremes harbor authoritarians) but in terms of the "value pluralism model," an idea that will be discussed below.

Left- and Right-Wing Authoritarianism in Perspective

In order to evaluate the issues we have been discussing in wider perspective, we need to consider more broadly the determinants of ideology, going back in time to the insights of Rokeach (1960) that preceded his value theory, and the ideas of Tomkins (1981; Stone, 1986). To open this discussion, let us briefly consider the framework used by Sidanius (1985) in his examination of these issues. Sidanius's research attempts to pit against one another three "theories" concerning the relationship between cognitive functioning and ideology. One theory is the authoritarian personality model that has accrued much support, in the many demonstrations of authoritarian traits in the supporters of right-wing groups. Tetlock (1984) calls this the "rigidity of the right hypothesis." The second theory Sidanius calls extremism theory. This is the familiar idea that authoritarianism is a phenomenon of left and right extremes alike (Tetlock's "ideologue hypothesis"). Finally, Sidanius proposes context theory, which focuses on more positive aspects of left and right ideologues, including greater interest, greater knowledge, and even in some circumstances greater cognitive complexity than the people holding centrist ideology. A fourth perspective, dogmatism theory, may be added as well. This is the view taken by Rokeach (1956, 1960), that authoritarian characteristics are independent of ideology; theoretically, they may inhere in any individual regardless of ideology. In a number of studies Sidanius has found support for authoritarian personality theory and for context theory, depending upon the psychological variables measured. In a sense, then, both he and Tetlock have broadened the debate from the focus on *TAP*.

The Determinants of Ideology

We have long held the belief that personality is one determinant of acceptance of left/right ideology. However, we must recognize that ideology is a social product, a set of ideas that generally has some coherence either because it has been formalized or because it is implicitly accepted by a group of people whose life circumstances are similar. In other words, an ideology can be *objectified*, and as Stone (1983) has argued, it is a mistake to confuse the personality characteristics that affect a person's choices among competing ideologies with the ideology itself. Thus, Tomkins (1981) has written about two contrasting modes of socialization of children (normative and humanistic) that are thought to produce personality differences. However, these personality tendencies at first lead only to *attraction to* a radical or reactionary ideology, as opposed to *commitment* to it.

Other determinants of ideology include explicit teaching or modeling by parents, and the child's identification with or rebellion against those parents. Also, peer pressure, fads and fashions, the mood of the times, and self-interest enter into the picture. These factors can be thought of as one-way determinants of ideological choice, but obviously there are "feedback loops" such that our personalities *and* our friendships are modified by our ideological choices. As we make commitments, our ideological scripts (Tomkins, 1987, 1991) are elaborated and consolidated. Modern personality theory deemphasizes fixity and early determination in favor of flexibility, growth, and change: Personality determines ideology, but ideology also determines personality.

With these clarifications in mind, let us return to the question of left-wing authoritarianism. First, let us recall Rokeach's (1960) discussion of tenets of extreme ideologies, cited in our introduction. The problem with Rokeach's argument, as Meloen points out in chapter 3 of this volume, is that most of our research has been with more moderate samples, and even in these samples, dogmatism is higher the more conservative the subject.

Value Conflict

More recent than Rokeach's work on cognitive structure is his emphasis on *values* (Rokeach, 1973). There has been considerable discussion of his attempts to characterize ideologies and their proponents in terms of the relative weight accorded to freedom and equality. In this scheme, fascists are said to hold both values in low esteem, whereas socialists place them both high in their value hierarchies; conservatives like Barry Goldwater place a great deal of emphasis on freedom, but give low priority to equality; and communists are believed to value equality much higher than freedom.

This is not the place to go further into Rokeach's (1973) theory, but we should mention Tetlock's (1986) use of Rokeach's analysis to explain ideological differences in integrative complexity. Tetlock (1986) suggests that political activists who highly value two important concerns—as the socialists with freedom and equality—will have greater conflict when the realization of the two goals is incompatible. This theory, then, explains the greater complexity of the socialists, the lower complexity of the moderate conservatives, and the low complexity both of communist left-wingers (who value equality much more than freedom) and of extreme conservatives (who weight freedom relatively more than their moderate siblings, as in Tetlock's 1984 study of British MPs).

Analysis of the Case for Left-Wing Authoritarianism

The advocates of the theory of left-wing authoritarianism typically base their case on intuitive evidence—"casual observation," as McCloskey and Chong (1985) put it—concerning apparent similarities between regimes of the far left and far right, rather than on a systematic review of the empirical data on personality and ideology (as in Stone, 1980). In so doing, they appeal implicitly to what philosophers of science refer to as *plausibility arguments*. Issues of plausibility *do* play legitimate roles in science (Salmon, 1967), sometimes decisive roles; but plausibility arguments must be used cautiously, because their legitimacy depends on their *relevance* to the theoretical and empirical issues at stake. In the present controversy, the use of intuitive evidence to support left-wing authoritarianism fails to lend credence to that view.

There are three bases for this conclusion. First, the defenders of left-wing authoritarianism typically fail to consider that the issue is at bottom a *statistical* issue. The relevant question is whether people who adopt left-wing political orientations are both statistically more likely than moderates to be authoritarian and equivalent to right-wingers in authoritarianism. When the issue is properly framed in these terms, it becomes obvious that the mere citing of examples will do nothing to establish the thesis or even to advance its plausibility. Those who cite casual evidence in arguing that one can find examples of left-wing authoritarianism just as easily as examples of the right-wing variety are evading the crucial question of whether, statistically speaking, the same rate of authoritarianism is found on the left as on the right.

A second and related point is that the empirical generalizations of science always involve ceteris paribus clauses, which state that *other things being equal*, the generalization is true. Such caveats apply equally to statistical and to deterministic generalizations. Thus, the thesis that left-wingers are just as likely to be authoritarian as right-wingers, other things being equal, cannot be adequately addressed by casually citing examples. If one wishes to cite oppressive left-wing regimes in support of the left-wing authoritarianism thesis, some effort should be made to make comparisons across large numbers of regimes. Preferably, such comparisons should control for such cultural traditions as xenophobia and governmental traditions such as hierarchical systems of authority. (See Toulmin, 1970, for a telling discussion of how well-entrenched cultural practices survive both political and scientific revolutions.)

Our third point is crucial. In citing examples of authoritarian leftist regimes, the proponents of the left-wing authoritarianism thesis have implicitly shifted the level of analysis from a psychological to a socio-logical one. It is not clear what bearing, if any, examples of regimes of various sorts have on the psychological issue of whether differing ideologies (e.g., left, right) attract people having different personality traits (e.g., authoritarian, egalitarian). Notably, none of those who cite examples of authoritarian "leftist" governments in support of the con-nection between authoritarian personality and attraction to far-left ideology have taken the step of actually *measuring* the traits of persons in those governments (or for that matter, their behavioral commitment to leftist ideological principles). And, as we have argued, any inferences about persons living as subjects under those regimes will be at a further remove from any bearing on the thesis of left-wing authoritarianism.

In sum, the intuitive "evidence" does not in fact bear on the issue, and it involves serious non sequiturs even when advanced as a plausibility argument. The meaning of an authoritarian trait such as "submissiveness" is necessarily suspect in the case of those who live under totalitarian governments. The issue of left-wing authoritarianism will eventually be decided on the basis of studies like DiRenzo's (1967b) study of Italian parliamentarians, studies of people who have some degree of free choice in matters of political affiliation, and in which comparisons are made on a within-country basis to control for cultural differences (as required by the principle of ceteris paribus).

The existence of regimes that proclaim leftist ideology while engaging in authoritarian governance may indeed by "obvious from even the most casual observation," but it is neither obvious nor correct to make the several inferential leaps required to translate this observation into evi-dence that authoritarian personality traits are as common among leftists as among rightists. The casual citing of authoritarian leftist governments as evidence for the latter claim is a non sequitur that has been committed since the time of Shils (1954). As to why so many competent social scientists have glibly acceded to this reasoning, we will not here offer an explanation, although both the "centrist bias" (Stone, 1980) and the anticommunism of social scientists seem to play a part.

Conclusion

Some years ago, Roger Brown (1965) reviewed the status of authoritarianism. His review, which still stands as the most balanced evaluation of the topic, suggests that the proof of the left-wing authoritarianism hypothesis requires examination of the citizens of a regime that offers free choice of group affiliations. We have tried to develop this idea further. In Italy, Norway, and England the choices are wide. In the United States they are less varied, and in countries like the former Soviet Union or Iran there are few or no choices. Consequently, the choice of relevant situations to study is limited. Our objections to previous formulations are based on common principles of scientific method, and we must concur with Brown's (1965) conclusion that "it has not been demonstrated that fascists and communists resemble one another in authoritarianism or in any other dimension of ideology" (p. 542) (or, we may add, any other dimension of personality).

The psychology of ideology is much more complicated than the political psychologists of the 1930s, 1940s, and 1950s had thought. What Adorno et al. (1950) called the authoritarian personality seems to be a robust phenomenon, but it occurs mainly in people holding conservative beliefs. We must consider various aspects of personality as well as the individual's sociopolitical context and degree of involvement; clearly, greater theoretical effort is needed to untangle these issues.

Part III
Recent Developments in Authoritarianism Research and Theory

8
Psychodynamics, Cognitive Functioning, or Group Orientation: Research and Theory in the 1980s

WILLIAM F. STONE

The Authoritarian Personality (*TAP*, Adorno, Frenkel-Brunswik, Levinson, & Sanford, 1950) research was known to many social scientists before the book's publication. Edward Shils (1948) commented enthusiastically on this unprecedented research prior to its publication, and M. Brewster Smith (1950) was first off the blocks with his review of the completed book. Smith's enthusiasm is reflected in his statement that the book was "a landmark in the development of social psychology and personality study" (pp. 775–776). Its investigation of anti-Semitism, he went on to say, "is certainly the most extensive and sophisticated research on the topic yet contributed by psychologists" (p. 776). These comments were typical of the early reviews of this ambitious undertaking.

Criticisms were not long in coming, however. Two books published in 1954 both contained serious criticisms of *TAP*. In the previous year, in *Uses and Abuses of Psychology*, Hans Eysenck (1953) had found the authoritarian personality study's results "to be rather striking in their cogency, and in their power to create a personality picture which agrees with a great variety of more objective research findings" (p. 278). In the same popular account of authoritarianism as a cause of anti-Semitism, Eysenck (1953) also cautioned that this was a *conservative* phenomenon, and that "evidence is available to show that communists share with fascists that 'tough-mindedness' which is such a marked feature of the personality description of the ethnocentric" (p. 279). In *The Psychology of Politics*, Eysenck (1954) found more fault with *TAP*, in that he now verified authoritarianism not as a basic psychological characteristic or tendency, but rather as a combination of "toughmindedness" and extreme right- or left-wing political attitudes.

The second critical volume, *Studies in the Scope and Method of "The Authoritarian Personality"*, edited by Richard Christie and Marie Jahoda (1954), was entirely devoted to a careful critical assessment of the work. In her introduction, Jahoda praised *TAP*'s authors for their awareness of preceding work:

There is in social psychology and the social sciences in general, too much work going on based on the foolish and arrogant assumption that no one else has ever given thought and effort to the problem under investigation. *The Authoritarian Personality* is free from that sin. (p. 19)

The criticisms made by the contributors to the Christie and Jahoda (1954) volume include an almost complete turnaround from his earlier praise by Shils (1948); his critique was discussed in chapter 7 of this volume. The Hyman and Sheatsley (1954) chapter is a careful criticism of the various methodological steps in the study, not focused completely on the F Scale itself, as were later critiques. Richard Christie (1954) contributed the first careful review of the earliest follow-up studies of the authoritarian personality. Thus, his chapter necessarily focused on the F Scale. He concluded that the F Scale seems to tap fascist orientations but not other political ideological orientations such as communism, that it does discriminate authoritarian behaviors in interpersonal relations, and that high F-Scale scores do predict ethnic prejudice and ethnocentrism, likely because of suspiciousness and general hostility. Finally, Christie (1954) noted:

Both the strength and the weakness of *The Authoritarian Personality* lie in its basic assumptions that are rooted in psychoanalytic theory. Such an orientation has led to the uncovering of a host of data which in all likelihood would not have been discovered by investigators with differing theoretical viewpoints. (p. 196)

Nevitt Sanford's contribution to *The Authoritarian Personality* cannot be measured by the order of authorship, because it was decided to list the contributors alphabetically. He is indeed "a truly great personality/social/ political psychologist" (Campbell, 1989) and a major contributor to *TAP*. Thus, his 1973 review of the status of the theory, in Knutson's *Handbook of Political Psychology*, is of interest whether or not he was "the chief architect of *The Authoritarian Personality*" (an attribution made by M.B. Freedman, 1987, and quoted approvingly by Campbell in his 1989 review).

In his 1973 chapter, "Authoritarian Personality in Contemporary Perspective," Sanford reviewed the basic personality makeup that we call authoritarian. The first three characteristics that he mentions are *conventionalism, authoritarian submission*, and *authoritarian aggression*. It is interesting to note that these characteristics of the authoritarian have stood the test of time, in that Bob Altemeyer (1981, 1988a), perhaps the most active researcher today, defines authoritarianism in terms of these three characteristics. There ends the agreement between these two theorists, however. Sanford (1973) holds to the description of the author-itarian *personality*, a syndrome held together by the unconscious dynamics established early in life by experiences in the family. Altemeyer's author-itarian, no less dangerous to society, is constructed on a more social-psychological model, with heavy reliance on social learning theory. His focus is on authoritarian attitudes: These attitudes do form a cluster or *attitudinal* syndrome, as shown by the correlation of aggressive, submissive, and conventional responses to items on the Right-Wing Authoritarianism (RWA) scale.

Thus, in comparing Altemeyer's (1988) and Sanford's (1973) views, we contrast the cognitive view of the authoritarian with the psychodynamic perspective. Whereas Altemeyer conceptualizes a sticky network of attitudes and beliefs that would predispose a high authoritarian to accept related ideas down the road to fascism, Sanford believes that there are behavioral manifestations beyond conventionality, aggression, and submission that support belief in a deeper structure of the authoritarian personality. This structure consists of a "strong, punitive and ego-alien" id; a strict, rigid superego; and a weak ego that copes with conflicts only through use of defense mechanisms, particularly the mechanism of projection. The behavioral evidence for this personality structure includes the three tendencies already mentioned, which indicate a weak ego. Such behaviors as anti-intraception, superstition, exaggerated attraction to power and toughness, and ambivalent attraction to sexual matters are attributable to the operation of the ego-alien id and rigid superego.

These two important competing explanations of the origins of authoritarian behaviors—the cognitive (attitudinal) and the psychodynamic—do not exhaust the possible approaches. They approach the problem through personality or individual differences. In the 1980s, Bob Altemeyer's is the most sustained personality approach, from a cognitive-learning perspective. Also in the 1980s, the cognitive approach has been emphasized in the work of Philip Tetlock (1983, 1984). In some ways, Tetlock's work can be seen as a continuation of Rokeach's (1948) study of the mental rigidity of prejudiced people and of Rokeach's (1960) study of the authoritarian, *The Open and Closed Mind*, in a different context. However, in the Netherlands there has been a sort of *TAP* revival that has provided support for the psychodynamic hypotheses (Meloen, 1983, chapter 3; Hagendoorn, 1982; Middendorp, 1978; Meloen & Middendorp, 1985; Meloen et al., 1988).

Other research emphases that were prominent in the 1980s are less easy to categorize. There has been a steady stream of publications by John J. Ray. Hans Eysenck (1982) has repeated his views from the earlier authoritarianism controversy. Work begun during the 1970s in Sweden by Jim Sidanius comparing three theories—"authoritarian personality," "extremist," and "context"—has been continued by that author in the 1980s. We will comment on these approaches and then mention the Potsdam Conference on Authoritarianism that was convened at the State University of New York in 1984. We will discuss the paper by Deborah Browning (1985) on ego development and authoritarianism; a paper presented by Michela von Freyhold (1985), who devised a German authoritarianism scale (the A Scale); and a paper by the most prominent of several South African scholars who published on authoritarianism in the 1980s, John Duckitt (1985).

John Duckitt (1989) has developed a theory that we will emphasize for its novelty. This much-discussed theory conceives of authoritarianism as a particular orientation to the ingroup; it is a new perspective on authoritarianism. Finally, in line with the emphasis on situational causation in social psychology, we will focus on follow-ups in the 1980s of Stephen Sales's (1972, 1973) investigations that utilize archival data to investigate the effects of societal stress on authoritarianism.

Personality Explanations of Authoritarian Behavior

The Authoritarian Personality stressed "the *potentially fascistic* individual, one whose structure is such as to render him particularly susceptible to anti-democratic propaganda" (Levinson & Sanford 1982, p. 1). The studies were conducted in California, but the results implied that the *character* of the German people in part explained the Germans' acceptance of such a strong but demented leader, Adolph Hitler. The style of child rearing employed by German parents was thought to make their children particularly susceptible to real and imaginary threats and to look toward strong authority figures in search of protection and relief. There has been empirical support for this hypothesis; Christie and Cook (1958) summarized the results of their review of the early literature as follows: "The bulk of the evidence supports the hypothesized relationship between strict practices in childrearing and intolerant beliefs" (p. 180). They observed further that the Freudian scenario that purports to account for these relationships has not been tested: "The actual specification of what parent behaviors or combinations of them led to a higher probability of authoritarianism in children is little advanced beyond the factors noted in *The Authoritarian Personality*" (Christie & Cook, p. 180).

Reviews of the literature (e.g., Byrne & Kelley, 1981) reveal little new evidence on the effects of parenting on authoritarianism. Generally, the results of studies are not discriminative between psychodynamic and social learning explanations. Authoritarian parents *do* seem to transmit authoritarian attitudes to their college-age children of the same sex (Byrne, 1965; Altemeyer, 1988a). An autocratic home atmosphere, as measured by the Traditional Family Ideology (TFI) Scale, does produce more authoritarian children as shown by the strong link between TFI and F-Scale scores (Levinson & Huffman, 1955). Likewise, Lederer (1981, and chap. 9, this volume) has found a decline in authoritarian attitudes in Germany since 1945, presumably because of changes toward more permissive parenting. The mechanisms were suggested by Hart's (1957) finding that authoritarian parents used "non-love-oriented" punishment, and by Block's (1955) finding that *restrictive* as opposed to *permissive* fathers had much higher F-Scale scores. A puzzling complement to these rather consistent findings was Baumrind's (1972) finding that the daughters in authoritarian black families are relatively more independent and assertive. Christel Hopf, in chapter 6 of this volume, takes this discussion of the familial origins of authoritarian character further.

Much of the research that followed publication of *TAP* was, as Samelson (chap. 2, this volume) recounts, concerned with measurement issues. The personality type distinguished by high scores on the F Scale does behave differently from those low on the scale in many studies, but questions are continually raised as to what this "type" denotes. Is the "authoritarian" simply a person of poor education who easily finds agreement with F-Scale items?

The most dogged modern worker in the authoritarian vineyards is Bob Altemeyer, whose research (1981, 1988a) has been widely acknowledged, discussed, and criticized. Therefore, we will devote considerable space to his criticisms of *TAP*, to his reformulation of the problem in learning theory terms, and to his empirical work.

Bob Altemeyer: Friend of Freedom

Bob Altemeyer began work on authoritarianism in the late 1960s, out of concern that the problem had been prematurely laid to rest because of the methodological criticisms of the F Scale and the contradictory findings that are documented by Christie in chapter 4 of this volume. Despite the decline of interest in the topic during the 1970s,

all the problems in our culture associated with the authoritarian personality have remained, and in many respects they have grown. Ironically, they were creating headlines, and enormous internal turmoil, at the very time behavioral scientists abandoned the quest. The dateline was "Saigon" And "Washington" And "My Lai" And "Kent State." . . . My research has been driven . . . by the perception that there exists a vast potential for the acceptance of right-wing totalitarian rule in countries like the United States and Canada. (Altemeyer, 1988a, p. xviii)

Altemeyer's Critique of *TAP*

Despite his community with the authors of *The Authoritarian Personality* concerning the potential for fascism in America, Altemeyer believes that the underlying theoretical conceptualization of *TAP* is faulty. He has pointed out that the tracing of authoritarian personalities to early childhood experiences had not been very successful. In theory, authoritarian children are repressing hostility toward parents whose punitive, strict discipline has created a well of resentment within them. This anger is displaced and finds its way into aggression toward outgroups. The process is largely unconscious.

Much of the data supporting this model of the genesis of authoritarianism was collected by Else Frenkel-Brunswik, as reported in *TAP*. The evidence, says Altemeyer (1988a), is unconvincing: "Hyman and Sheatsley (1954) identified many flaws in Frenkel-Brunswik's data-collection procedures and analyses. Subsequent research, which has often been cited as supporting her model, has mainly produced inconclusive or contradictory findings" (p. 53). To make his own test of Frenkel-Brunswik's theory, Altemeyer (1981) measured parental anger over misdeeds and parental use of punishment as recalled by college students and their parents. These scores on the parental anger and parental punishment scales were correlated with the students' Right-Wing Authoritarianism (RWA) Scale scores. The results showed little relationship between parental punitiveness, either as remembered by parent or student, and the student's RWA score. Of 28 so-called validity coefficients, the largest was .24, between students' RWA and the extent of mother's anger, as reported by the student (1981, p. 264). Altemeyer realizes that the "Berkeley theory" cannot be dismissed on such slight evidence, but he points out that psychoanalytic concepts are very difficult to test. Therefore, he has endeavored to construct and test a simpler model.

Cognitive Contents

Altemeyer (1981) presented a conception of authoritarianism that builds upon the work of *The Authoritarian Personality*. His focus is on right-wing authoritarianism, in accord with his belief that the major threat to western democracy is from those who would trample on civil liberties under the guise of conventional values. His answer to those who, like Eysenck (1982), question his neglect of authoritarianism of the left was cited in chapter 7 of this volume.

In his second book, *Enemies of Freedom*, Altemeyer (1988a) described the continuing development and validation of the Right-Wing Authoritarianism (RWA) Scale. He concluded that the authoritarian syndrome consists of attitudes of (a) submission to authority, (b) conventionality, and (c) righteous aggression. This conceptualization is both simpler and better documented than the nine-cluster syndrome put forth in *The Authoritarian Personality*. Thus, in conception, the theory of RWA eschews the psychoanalytic hypotheses that enlivened the work of *TAP* in favor of social learning theory. Altemeyer is especially indebted to Albert Bandura (1986).

In *Right-Wing Authoritarianism*, Altemeyer (1981) presented the RWA Scale and described its development through 10 years of research. The RWA Scale is a balanced Likert scale that contains 15 proauthority and 15 antiauthority items, including two original F-Scale items. He continually revised and added new items to maintain high internal consistency, striving to achieve unidimensionality (the lack of which is a flaw in the F Scale). In the main, his subjects were University of Manitoba students and their parents. Despite the changing composition of the RWA Scale, Altemeyer has maintained 12 constant items upon which he can compare scores of samples from 1973 to 1987; he finds a trend of increasing scores over the period. The mean scores have increased from 60 to 69 in the period, an increase that relates to the decrease in subjects scoring low and very low, with an increase in moderately high scores but not in very high scores (Altemeyer, 1988a, pp. 24–27).

There is considerable evidence for the RWA Scale's validity. One study found high RWA scorers tolerant of government injustice during the Watergate scandal. This study found that U.S. college students with high RWA scores maintained their belief in President Nixon's innocence in the Watergate scandal longer than their low RWA counterparts. High RWAs have a law-and-order orientation; they impose longer sentences in mock jury deliberations. Zwillenberg's (1983) research confirmed Altemeyer's sentencing findings; this research was described in chapter 5 of this volume. High RWAs also shocked peers more strongly in a learning experiment similar to Milgram's (1974) obedience study. Greater prejudice, greater acceptance of home religion, and preference for rightist political parties also characterize high RWA scorers. In a study of white South African students, Duckitt found greater prejudice among right-wing authoritarians; RWA correlated 0.53 to 0.69 with various measures of antiblack prejudice (cited by Altemeyer, 1988a, p. 15).

Social learning of RWA attitudes was supported by Altemeyer's (1988a) Experiences Scale (ES) results. This scale included a variety of statements about the subject's life experiences. One item, for example, read: "The homosexuals I have known seemed to be normal, decent people, just like everybody else, except for their sexual orientation." Experiences of this sort correlated with low RWA scale scores to a high degree over several studies (r's were generally in the 70s).

To the basic question; Is there a consistent, relatively integrated syndrome that can meaningfully be called authoritarianism?, Altemeyer answers, "Yes, there is such a syndrome, and its constituents are submissiveness to authority, extraordinary conventionality, and unusually strong verbal aggressiveness toward outgroups and norm violators." While it has long been held that some psychodynamic mechanisms hold these items together, Altemeyer advocates social learning explanations. For example, he employs these concepts in the explanation of the origins of authoritarian aggression: modeling, aversive stimuli, consequences, and cognitions.

RWAs have learned social norms that support aggression against unconventional people. Support for this hypothesis is given by low positive correlations between student and parent responses on aggression items, prejudice, and tendencies to support violation of the civil rights of government critics. Parental modeling is evident in one result that also supports authoritarian personality theory: There is greater incidence of physical violence within the families of high as opposed to low RWA scorers.

Altemeyer (1988a) concluded that *fear* of social chaos produces impulses to aggress against bad people; *self-righteousness* disinhibits the restraints against aggression. He cited Bandura's (1977) writings in support of this formulation. Also, social norms as to the acceptability of aggression are important in the explanation of authoritarian responses. Support for this norm-following interpretation is given by the findings (a) that high RWA scorers seem more aggressive than low scorers toward socially acceptable targets, and (b) that they acknowledge less hostility toward minority group members but admit relatively more prejudice toward gays. (Generally, prejudice against gays is more socially acceptable than against blacks.)

Evaluation of RWA

Early reviews of Altemeyer's (1981) presentation of his RWA Scale and the evidence for its validity were generally favorable (see Christie, 1984; Ward, 1982). The reviewers were pleased with the development of a scale that corrected the major faults of the F Scale: The RWA Scale was balanced, reliable, and valid in the context of extensive research by its author. Also, it was based on a simplified theory that did not speak of projection, superstition, or anti-introspectionism, concepts reflected in F-Scale items that grew out of its psychoanalytic roots. Not all reviewers were enthusiastic, however. Eysenck (1982) found many "distortions and errors," particularly in Altemeyer's critique of Eysenck's work. Altemeyer is faulted for his neglect of left-wing authoritarianism and for his pursuit of high interitem correlations, which shows that he "does not understand the notion of higher order factors" (Eysenck, 1982, p. 352). Other critics have raised questions about the alleged superiority of the RWA over the F scale. Jos Meloen (1990) is one such critic; his evaluation is based upon the study summarized below.

Meloen (1990) has reviewed research undertaken in the Netherlands to evaluate Altemeyer's claim that the RWA Scale is superior to the F Scale. Meloen and his colleagues (1988) had administered a translated version of the full 30-item F Scale (Form 40/45) to a random sample of magazine subscribers and a group of evening class students ($N = 216$). These data were compared with those for 131 psychology students at Nijmegen University who took the Dutch version of the RWA Scale. The two scales (in 12-item nonoverlapping versions) correlated + .62 in the Nijmegen sample. The 12-item F Scale correlated .72 in this sample with the 15 authoritarian-worded items on the RWA Scale.

The two scales were quite comparable in reliability: Alpha reliability of the F Scale was .89, of the RWA Scale .85. The slightly higher reliability of the F Scale, as well as its higher mean interitem correlation (.21 versus .16) can be attributed to the greater heterogeneity of the F-Scale sample. There is slight evidence for greater validity of the RWA Scale in that authoritarian scores on RWA predict right-wing party preference (r = .55) better than do F-Scale scores (r = .35).

Although the RWA Scale is balanced with 15 proauthoritarian and 15 antiauthoritarian items, Meloen (1990) found no distinguishable advantage to the balanced format. He computed correlations between balanced and proauthoritarian versions of the RWA Scale and found no significant differences in their relation to external criteria. In sum, Meloen's (1990) study suggests a slight advantage for the RWA Scale over the F Scale, but this difference is not so great as to render the F Scale either invalid or useless.

In sum, Altemeyer has created a useful new authoritarianism scale that dispenses with the "disguised" items used by *TAP*'s authors to tap basic personality dynamics. That these two scales correlate highly suggests that they are measuring much of the same variance. Altemeyer's contribution has been in the creative testing of hypotheses about the behavior and motivation of high and low RWA scorers. It could be argued that Altemeyer's theoretical perspective is implicit rather than explicit, and that his major contribution is in the establishment of empirical relationships between RWA and certain behaviors. Thus, he has not proven that the social learning approach more aptly describes the authoritarian than does the psychoanalytic approach underlying the F Scale. The existence of those two scales will suggest better tests of these alternative models to some enterprising investigators.

A TAP Revival: Dutch Authoritarianism

In 1983, Jos Meloen completed one of the most extensive reviews ever undertaken of studies using the F Scale. (He reviewed all of the studies published between 1950 and 1980.) His reports to conferences and contacts with English-speaking colleagues generated considerable interest in this work, but it has been generally inaccessible to the English-speaking audience. We are pleased to make available a portion of Meloen's findings in chapter 3 of this volume. His project was stimulated in part by the menacing increases in support for a neo-Nazi party in the Netherlands; this was part of a rather extensive effort by social scientists in the country to investigate the causes for this resurgence in authoritarianism. Among these workers were Hagendoorn (1982) and Middendorp (1978), as well as Meloen and Middendorp (1985) and Meloen et al. (1988).

Authoritarianism as Cognitive Simplicity

Rigidity of thought, closed-mindedness, and other concepts related to cognitive complexity have been used to characterize the thought processes of authoritarians. Harold Schroder and his colleagues developed a scoring system for a related variable called *integrative complexity* (Schroder, Driver, & Streufert, 1967). Integrative complexity refers to the combined ability of an individual to both differentiate and to integrate complex information. A person low in integrative complexity will tend to use compartmentalized thinking, make premature closure in situations of conflict, and be prone to misperception or distortion of information. Schroder et al.'s scoring system has been employed to score archival materials such as speeches of revolutionary leaders (Suedfeld & Rank, 1976) and in many other studies. Suedfeld's student Philip Tetlock (1983, 1984) has suggested connections between the black-and-white thinking that is one characteristic of the authoritarian personality and integrative complexity.

Tetlock has used this very simple conception of authoritarianism in a number of studies—of U.S. senators (Tetlock, 1983), of British MPs (Tetlock, 1984), and the like. Because this work is oriented in the main toward the authoritarianism of the left controversy, we have discussed it in chapter 7 of this volume. Here, we simply note this as one of the much-discussed approaches to "authoritarianism" in the 1980s, and criticize the work on integrative complexity as an extreme simplification of authoritarian personality theory. The concept is related to the authoritarian rigidity literature discussed by Christie in chapter 4 of this volume. Ray (1988a) has criticized the use of cognitive style variables, which do not predict "conservatism, authoritarianism or racism."

The Peripatetic John J. Ray

Perhaps the most prolific author of journal articles on authoritarianism living today is John J. Ray, who has been publishing since 1970; in the 1980s alone he published over 40 articles on authoritarianism. Basically, Ray is a critic of *TAP* who attacks from many directions, but whose basically empirical approach seems to have had little cumulative impact. Many of his articles are short and polemical, citing data from his own or previous studies. His work is controversial, partly because his political concerns are so obvious. Nevertheless, his commitments are hard to pin down. He admits to having been a Nazi in Australia (Billig, 1985) but insists that it was for purposes of participant observation. Sometimes he characterizes himself as a conservative and sometimes (Ray, 1985a) as an anarchist. He spends a goodly amount of effort attacking leftists, as indicated by his (1985b) contribution to the Potsdam conference, which was entitled "The Psychopathology of the Political Left."

Ray is not held in great repute by many other researchers in authoritarianism (Billig, 1979). Ray's (1988a) paper in *Political Psychology*, criticizing the work of Jim Sidanius (1985), received pointed replies both from Sidanius (1988) and from Ward (1988). He seems impatient with serious theoretical analysis, and often seems merely interested in making his point of the moment. For example, he wrote in one paper (1982a) that "Rokeach succeeded in producing items that were *just* closed-minded with little other political polarization" (p. 35). In correspondence, I pointed out to him that there is now considerable evidence of a strong relationship between dogmatism and conservatism. He answered that, of course he knew this, but that he had been "simply saying that 'D' was *schematically* unrelated to conservatism" (J.J. Ray, personal communication, December 19, 1982).

One other example showing why Ray's work is often greeted with skepticism is his treatment of a survey that he conducted (1988b) that purported to test Lester Milbrath's (1984) environmental theory. Ray inferred from Milbrath's writings that Australian Labor Party members would show more "altruistic compassion" and less support for materialistic achievement than Nationalist Party members. When the results significantly supported these predictions, he wrote that the support was tenuous because the t values only surpassed the $p < .05$ level by a small margin. No measure of environmental attitudes was taken, despite Milbrath's observations that environmentalism crosses traditional party concerns. Thus, Ray's (1988b) article simply misses the point. This is typical of Ray's casual approach to the interpretation of empirical data.

Three Theories

In a steady output of studies begun in Sweden in the early 1970s, Jim Sidanius has pitted three "theories" about the relationship of political attitudes to ideology. The first studies employed large samples of Swedish secondary school students who took the Swedish Conservatism (S) Scale, a conservatism scale similar to Wilson's (1973) C Scale and Kerlinger's (1984) Referents Scales; these scales ask the respondent to accept or reject concepts named by a single word or phrase, such as *nudity*, or *bible truth*, or *socialism*. Besides the S Scale, Sidanius's subjects were given tests of political interests and affiliations. He reported some support for authoritarian personality theory (less political interest, more rigidity on the right), and also for context theory (subjects at both conservative and liberal ends of the scale read more, had more information). Extremism theory (the hypothesis of similarity of rigidity and closed-mindedness between extreme leftists and extreme rightists) received little support.

In the 1980s, Sidanius's work has been more sophisticated. Besides Swedish samples, he has studied college student samples in the United States. We will discuss one of these studies; our criticism of this approach to authoritarianism is on somewhat the same grounds that we criticized Tetlock's conceptions; it omits much of the richness of authoritarian personality theory. Sidanius and Lau (1989) studied the responses of a large sample ($N = 2,397$) of University of Texas students. The primary variables of interest in the present context were conservatism and political sophistication. (Because conservatism is strongly correlated with authoritarianism, it serves as a stand-in for authoritarianism here.) Political sophistication involved broad political knowledge of candidates and issues. As predicted, there was a curvilinear relationship between conservatism and political sophistication—both low and high conservative scorers had higher sophistication than those in the center. Thus, the context theory was supported. However, political sophistication had a negative linear relationship with racism, supporting authoritarian personality theory.

Sidanius intends to study the entire domain of social-political attitudes and their relationship to personality and cognition. He does not, however, really pit the three theories against one another, because each has a domain of attitudinal functioning in which it is correct. Extremism theory works for certain variables—opinionation, for one thing, as shown by the McCloskey and Chong (1985) study cited in chapter 7 of this volume. Authoritarian personality theory "works"—racism, for example, is always linearly related to authoritarian or conservative scores. Finally, context theory predicts correctly that people with stronger political interests, right or left, will have more sophistication.

The Potsdam Conference on Authoritarianism

The International Conference on Authoritarianism and Dogmatism, organized by Professor Donald J. Hanson of the State University College of the Arts and Sciences at Potsdam, New York, was held at that institution on October 12 and 13, 1984. A worldwide representation of about 100 scholars interested in these issues attended; one attendee called it "a gathering of true believers" (R. Christie, personal communication, April 7, 1991). Of the papers presented, 48 were published in *The High School Journal* in 1985 (Vol. 68, Whole Issues 3 and 4). I mention two of the contributors (Ray, Duckitt) in other contexts in this chapter. Here, I want to give special attention to two of the papers, those by Deborah Browning and Michaela von Freyhold.

Ego Development and Authoritarianism

Jane Loevinger originally suggested a relationship between ego development stage and authoritarianism in the early 1960s. (She is in fact a Berkeley graduate, having studied with Else Frenkel-Brunswik.) In her 1976 book, Loevinger suggested parallels between her nine ego development levels and the "Types and Syndromes" described by Adorno in chapter 19 of *TAP* (Loevinger, 1976, p. 99). The *impulsive* ego stage corresponds to the high-prejudiced psychopathic rebel described by Adorno. Adorno's "impulsive" low scorer is also seen by Loevinger as belonging at the impulsive stage. The *self-protective* ego stage, a primitive reward/punishment consciousness, corresponds to the high-scoring types labeled by Adorno as crank, manipulator, and authoritarian (most frequent).

Conformist stage individuals are group-oriented and tend to stereotype. Adorno's "surface resentment" and "conventional" (frequent) are the high F types, and what he called the "rigidly unprejudiced" are found among low scorers. The transitional stage *conformist/conscientious* was suggested by Loevinger as the ego level of only the low-scoring "easy-going" type (which, Adorno said, was a frequent type). At the *conscientious* ego stage is found the low-scoring "protester" (another frequent type). Loevinger suggests that the "genuine liberal's" ego development would lie between the transitional *individualistic* stage and the *autonomous* stage.

These speculative correspondences with the Adorno's types want empirical confirmation. A step in that direction was taken by Deborah Browning (1983, 1985, 1987). In her Potsdam paper Browning (1985) reported on her analysis of data from a 1973 survey study of the moral values of young people by Daniel Yankelovich. The survey included a 12-item form of Loevinger's (1976) Sentence Completion Test (SCT)—her test for assessing levels of ego development. The SCT was given following a long interview that contained standard questions reflecting many different attitudes and values. The nine scales developed by Browning (1985) from Yankelovich's items included the Moralistic Attitudes Scale and the Law and Order Orientation Scale, both seen as related to authoritarian aggression.

Browning (1985) found that authoritarian attitudes were strongest at the *conformist* stage of development. Authoritarianism scores (aggression) were found to peak at this stage, whereas related scale scores, for example the Masculine Roles score, showed linear relationships: Women at the lower stages of ego development held the most stereotyped sex-role views. For men, there was an inverse relationship for the Masculine Roles Scale (preconformists endorsed the strong male role more than post-conformists), and there was a linear growth in the Feminist Attitudes score with higher stages of ego development for the men. Thus, at the self-protective stage, both women and men endorsed strong assertive male behavior, whereas women but not men also endorsed the women's liberation values set forth in the Feminist Attitudes Scale. Browning's (1985) findings of high authoritarianism in the conformist stage tie in nicely with Duckitt's theory of authoritarianism as group orientation, to be discussed below.

German Research in the 1960s

In her paper on authoritarianism in Germany, Michaela von Freyhold (1985) described the German A Scale, whose development she began in

TABLE 8.1. The A Scale.

1. Politics is corrupt, a decent person keeps out of it.
2. Only through work one can become really happy.
3. Most young people today are leading a too easy life, it's high time they learned strict discipline again.
4. There will always be wars, that's how people are.
5. There is in our parties too much talk and discussions, this will never lead us anywhere.
6. We should draw a final line under our past. Others have committed equally bad things.
7. Germany is and always will be the bulwark against bolshevism.
8. The way our prisons work these days, punishment almost becomes a reward.
9. Many reports about concentration camps are exaggerated.
10. Americans may be ever so civilized, but they lack real culture.
11. Trade unions are selfish interest groups who do not care for the general welfare of the population.
12. Hitler's methods of extermination were brutal but it would be good if one could get rid of incurable criminals in a more humane fashion.
13. Human nature can not be changed. Man remains what he is.

Source: von Freyhold, 1985, p. 246 (her translations, for illustration only).

1960 and used in a study (von Freyhold, 1971) that she called "the last major study in the classical manner on authoritarianism" (1985, p. 241). This study was conducted under Teodor Adorno while he was director of the Frankfurt Institute for Social Research. The A Scale was difficult to devise, because it was to be administered to Germans not long after the war. It seemed important to do, however, for two reasons:

First in order to reintroduce the issue of authoritarianism in the German debate when too many people were trying to reduce the problem of the recent German past to one of "having been misled by Hitler." Secondly, given the heavy taboo on overt fascist utterances in postwar Germany, it appeared interesting to measure this potential indirectly. (von Freyhold, 1985, p. 242)

Von Freyhold found it impossible to construct usable reversed items. The final scale consists of 13 items, plus four buffer items. Because the scale has seldom appeared in English, it seems appropriate to reproduce it here (Table 8.1).

Surveys conducted in Germany during the 1960s contributed evidence of the A Scale's validity. High scorers showed sympathy with the Nazi regime, were anti-Semitic, and were generally ethnocentric—these were real authoritarian tendencies rather than educational bias, von Freyhold (1985) maintained. The classical authoritarian character—"the rigid 'anal' character with the typical preoccupation with cleanliness, order and parsimony" (von Freyhold, 1985, p. 242)—was evident among high scorers in the 1960s. In the 1980s, however, von Freyhold (1985) suggested, the more common authoritarian among the middle classes in Germany is the "conventional authoritarian" (Klages & Herbert, 1983), who is anxious not to stand out from others, but whose support of democratic institutions is superficial. Above all, authoritarians of the mid-1980s were apathetic, she argued. This apathy was not just a neutral attitude, but an actual alienation from politics and a resentment among older Germans of democratic political processes in general. Low scorers more often evidence interest in politics; paradoxically, the most convinced activist low scorers tend to endorse Item 2 on the A Scale.

All in all, concluded von Freyhold (1985), authoritarians (particularly the conventionals) are still to be found in Germany, but low authoritarians are relatively more frequent in the 1980s. These lows are people described by Inglehart (1977) as postmaterialists and by Klages and Herbert (1983) as nonconventionals. These modern German types tend to be suspicious of both left and right political remedies, and are more likely to find sympathy with the Green party.

Current Research in Germany

With new and sophisticated methods of data analysis, beginning in the late 1980s in Germany there has been a surge of interest in the variable of authoritarianism. In particular, there has been wide use of a new general authoritarianism miniscale. Derived from the New General Authoritarianism Scale (NGAS) (Lederer, 1981), it consists of four (sometimes only three) items and has been used in research where authoritarianism is an important part of the theory being examined. The scale items are shown in Table 8.2; they were chosen within the context of international authoritarianism research with the New General Authoritarianism Scale. The items composing the miniscale showed high internal consistency and high factor loadings in several applications in different countries.

In particular, the NGAS miniscale has been used successfully as a predictor of party preference in a representative study of German voters ($N = 2,017$) (see Braehler et al., 1991). As expected, authoritarianism was correlated with the left–right scale (.41)—the higher the authoritarianism score, the greater the preference for the right-wing parties. Members of

TABLE 8.2. The New General Authoritarianism Mini-Scale as currently used in Germany (translated by G. Lederer).[1]

1. Among the most important qualities that a person can have is disciplined obedience to authority.
2. The facts on crime and sexual immorality suggest that we will have to crack down harder on some people if we are going to save our moral standards.
3. We should be grateful for leaders who tell us exactly what to do and how to do it.
4. It usually helps the child in later years if he is forced to conform to his parents' ideals.

1. The authoritarianism mini-scale as well as the original New General Authoritarianism Scale are documented in the *ZUMA Skalen Handbuch* (*ZUMA Handbook of Scales*) 1991.

the CDU and CSU had high authoritarianism scores, the Greens the lowest scores. The miniscale was also used in a study of 1,201 students at the University of Giessen on the subject of AIDS and its prevention; a correlation of .40 was found between authoritarianism and the tendency to discriminate against HIV-positive individuals (Bardeleben, Reimann, & Schmidt, 1989).

The three-item version of the miniscale was used in an effort to predict sympathy among a representative sample of German voters for the extreme right-wing party known as *Republikaner*. Of all the indicators, this scale turned out to be the best predictor; authoritarianism correlated .62 with sympathy for the Republikaner (Rippl et al., 1991). As in previous studies, authoritarianism was positively correlated with age (.48) and negatively with education (−.34). In contrast to prior findings, no link was found to exist between authoritarianism and feelings of political efficacy.

Authoritarianism as Group Orientation

Whereas the classical definitions of authoritarianism have emphasized the rejection of outgroups, a recent attempt at reconceptualization emphasizes the other side of the coin, loyalty to the ingroup. John Duckitt (1989) conceptualizes authoritarianism as "the normatively held conception of the appropriate relationship between group and individual member, determined primarily by the intensity of group identification and consequent strain towards cohesion" (p. 63).

In essence, Duckitt (1989) suggests that we jettison the complicated personality conceptualization of authoritarianism in favor of one emphasizing one's beliefs about one's group and the obedience that should be accorded to group norms and leaders. He suggests that the F Scale's validity in predicting social behavior derives from the many questions that deal with these beliefs. In actuality, he finds, F-Scale authoritarianism predicts behavior such as prejudice and hostility toward outgroups but does not do very well in predicting interpersonal behavior within the group. The RWA Scale dispensed with much of the theoretical rationale of the F Scale but still retains, in the trait clusters (conventionality, authoritarian submission, and authoritarian aggression), a basically personological approach. The more reliable correlations to behavior found with the RWA Scale are due, in Duckitt's eyes, to the structure of the RWA Scale, which even more than the F Scale taps beliefs about the ingroup.

Another problem diagnosed by Duckitt (1989) is the lack of theoretical specification of the underlying dimension. Authoritarianism is clearly one end of the scale, but what is its opposite? Early thinking in the Frankfurt Institute dealt with the revolutionary personality; transmuted to the milieu of the United States, the opposite end of the authoritarianism dimension became the democratic personality. However, Duckitt points out that authoritarian rebellion is common: Witness the fascist takeovers in Germany, Italy, and Spain in the 1930s, and the numerous military coups throughout the world since World War II. The anchoring concept that Duckitt (1989) finds most compatible with his views is libertarianism; he explains the reconceptualized dimension as follows:

At one extreme would be the belief that the purely personal needs, inclinations, and values of group members should be subordinated as completely as possible to the cohesion of the group and its requirements. At the other extreme would be the belief that the requirements of group cohesion should be subordinated as completely as possible to the autonomy and self-regulation of the individual member. These two extreme positions would be labeled authoritarianism and libertarianism, respectively. (p. 70)

The implications of this group-centered conception of authoritarianism are manifold. Generally, differences between people who hold authoritarian beliefs and those who are libertarian would be found only when group membership is salient. Ethnic prejudice, for example, is usually a matter of "us" and "them"—of ingroup versus outgroup. Likewise, the reason that patriotism and authoritarianism commonly cohere is that patriotism is an ingroup–outgroup matter. Although the idea of authoritarianism as an individual difference variable is retained, the theater in which these differences play is changed:

Thus, individuals' conceptions of the appropriate relationship that should exist between group and individual should only come into play to influence thought and action within group contexts and when group matters and categorizations become salient and relevant. In purely interpersonal situations on the other hand, when group matters are completely irrelevant, the construct would generally have relatively little significance for the explanation of behavior. (Duckitt, 1989, p. 80)

Duckitt's thesis is generally well-grounded in the research conducted by the late Henri Tajfel and his colleagues (Tajfel & Turner, 1986) on the "minimal group." Their theory of social identity states that groups provide a frame of reference for self-definition. A "positive" social identity is "based to a large extent on favorable comparisons that can be made between the in-group and some relevant out-groups" (Tajfel & Turner, p. 16). Authoritarians, it seems, exaggerate the differences between ingroup and outgroup. In a study whose outcome illustrated this process, Downing and Monaco (1986) conducted a field experiment on a New England ski slope. The subjects were 227 ski-school students, who judged the performances of their own group and outgroup members after a period of instruction in basic ski maneuvers. For identification, outgroup members wore blue racing ties; ingroup members green ties. Subjects scoring high on the F Scale rated the performance of the ingroup members higher, and the performance of the outgroup members lower, than did the low authoritarian subjects. In fact, the low authoritarians did not differentiate between ingroup and outgroup members in their assessment of the skill shown by the novice skiers.

Situational Causes of Authoritarian Behavior

The German response to Hitler supports the hypothesis that environmental stressors increase authoritarian tendencies, as well as the hypothesis that the German character was particularly susceptible. Authoritarianism research has focused on personality rather than on situational or environmental causation. However, the basic behavioral clusters seen by *TAP* as characteristic of the high F-Scale scorer are, arguably, also stimulated by threatening social conditions—crime waves, high unemployment, and economic depression. These factors were all present in the Germany of the early 1930s, when the Nazis took power with the consent of a large plurality of the German people. Added to these stressful circumstances was the national humiliation of loss of the First World War and the imposition of reparations by the victors.

Stephen Sales

An important series of studies into environmental stimulation of authoritarian responses was conducted by Stephen Sales (1972), who first studied conversion rates to authoritarian and nonauthoritarian churches in the Seattle, Washington, area. He compared rates for periods before and during major environmental threats (the Great Depression, the social and economic upheaval of the late 1960s). Authority-oriented churches (Roman Catholic and others) showed greater percentage increases in membership during threat periods than did the more liberal churches (United Church of Christ and others). The opposite was true during periods of affluence.

In a laboratory experiment, Sales and Friend (1973) assessed the F-scale scores of student volunteer subjects who had performed poorly in an experimental task. These subjects showed increased F-Scale scores as compared with successful subjects, whose scores actually decreased. Subjects threatened by failure in the experiment also showed greater conformity to an authority figure. The finding that threat increases authoritarian responses had also been reported by Dittes (1961), Zander and Havelin (1960), Berkowitz and Knurek (1969), and Jorgensen (1975).

In a study employing archival data, Sales (1973) found that economic stress produced by the Great Depression increased authoritarian behaviors in the U.S. population at large. People became more admiring of power and toughness, as evidenced in popular culture by the emergence of comic strips featuring powerful protagonists (*Superman*, *Dick Tracy*, and

The Lone Ranger). Tough leaders are preferred by authoritarians, and the public seems to become more authoritarian in the face of threat. The power motives of the U.S. presidents elected between 1924 and 1980 were assessed by David Winter (1987). Evidently, more powerful leaders were preferred by the voters in times of social stress: McCann and Stewin (1987) found a correlation of .56 between the degree of threat (as rated by a group of historians) and the power motivation (Winter's scores) of the president elected that year.

Sales (1973) also found greater societal cynicism (another authoritarian characteristic stressed by Adorno et al., 1950) during hard times. American magazine articles of the 1930s were clearly more cynical or pessimistic than those from the previous decade, suggesting a more "authoritarian" audience. Superstition, anti-intraception, and concern with overt sexuality—all marks of the authoritarian personality—also showed increases during the depression. Superstition was indicated by significantly more articles on astrology; Sales's (1973) findings on superstition were replicated using German data by Padgett and Jorgensen (1982), who did a time-series analysis of German popular literature and economic conditions from 1918 to 1940. McCann and Stewin (1984) found that the number of parapsychology articles in the psychological literature also varied directly with indices of threat such as the unemployment rate. Sales also found that anti-intraception (opposition to probing into one's psychological motives) and authoritarian aggression increased during the depression. These findings regarding changes in authoritarian behaviors from pre- to mid-depression years were essentially replicated in a second study reported in the same article utilizing data from the relatively serene early 1960s and from the stressful late 1960s. Meloen's (1983) extensive review of F-Scale research also supported Sales's (1973) hypothesis that environmental stressors increase authoritarianism in a society.

Sales's research points to the conclusion that many authoritarian behaviors are situationally induced. These findings support our earlier remarks about the effects of social strife on the German people's response to Hitler. They say nothing about individual differences in response to environmental stress. The focus of most authoritarianism research, however, has been on these individual differences, that is, on personality explanations of the authoritarian response. This personality focus has occupied most scholars of authoritarian phenomena in the last 40 years.

Authoritarianism and Jury Behavior

Social psychologists have conducted considerable research on the psychology of the jury. The work on scientific jury selection (Schulman, Shaver, Colman, Emrich, & Christie, 1973); the study of mock juries (Kassin, 1984); and posttrial interviews with jurors (Moran & Comfort, 1982) all suggest that authoritarianism plays a role in the jury's decision. Many of the early studies were cited by Christie in chapter 5 of this volume. This work has continued through the 1980s, as illustrated by Kassin and Wrightsman's (1988) *The American Jury on Trial: Psychological Perspectives*. These authors note that authoritarians seem to have a bias toward convictions; they point out, however, that while high authoritarians tend to vote to convict the accused, there are exceptions:

When faced with a defendant who commits a "crime of obedience" (e.g., a young Marine who commits murder in response to a superior's order or a parent accused of child abuse in the course of disciplining a son or daughter), or when the defendant *is* an authority figure like a policeman, authoritarian jurors become *less* punitive in their judgments. (p. 35)

Authoritarianism, Militarism, and Humanism

Peace researcher William Eckhardt (1991) has reviewed much of the early work on radicalism-conservatism, nationalism, militarism, dogmatism, religiosity, and toughmindedness as they overlap with authoritarianism. His treatment of these concepts demonstrates the ideological subjectivity involved in the various emphases. What we seem to have is a *family* of concepts with considerable commonality. According to Eckhardt, the commonality, in terms of correlation, is mild to moderate, but nevertheless persistent:

One fairly reliable finding seems to be the basic psychological pattern running through all these personalities . . . inner conflicts or self-contradiction, denial or repression of these conflicts, projection of denied or disliked concepts of the self, and justification of the return of the repressed. Another [reliable finding] seems to be the origin of these personalities in frustrating childhood disciplines (anxious, directive, hypocritical, inconsistent and punitive). (p. 118)

Eckhardt classifies the various approaches according to their emphasis on affect, cognition, ideology, behavior, or morality. The pattern of relationships holds up quite well in most of these areas, with the exception of the affective variables that compose "the weakest link in the chain of correlations" (Eckhardt, p. 120). Eckhardt wrote, "What we have to deal with here are basic ideas and philosophies rather than human feelings" (p. 121).

One author mentioned by Eckhardt (1991) *had* dealt with the affective realm. This author, Silvan Tomkins (1962, 1965, 1991) is renowned for his study of human affect. Tomkins's (1963) ideas on affect and ideology were quoted by Eckhardt (1991, p. 102), who directly cited the theoretical gist of Tomkins's theory: "In summary, we believe that how positively or how negatively a human being learns to feel about himself and about other human beings will also determine his general posture toward the entire ideological domain" (Tomkins, 1965, p. 97). Eckhardt did not follow up on this insight, however, because he had little to go on in terms of correlations between Tomkins's (1964) *Polarity Scale*, which operationalized Tomkins's theory of the relationship between affect and ideology, and the variables of authoritarianism, militarism, and so forth. References to the *Polarity Scale* had been very limited during the time the major research covered by Eckhardt's review was conducted (1930–1980). Recently, however, there has been a resurgence of interest in Tomkins's theory and method (Stone, 1986; Stone & Schaffner, 1988).

Tomkins's (1964, 1965, 1991) polarity theory, now referred to as script theory, in its general form, emphasizes the important connection between positive affects (joy, interest); negative affects (fear, shame, contempt); and ideology. The pattern of affects important to the psychic economy of "humanistic" individuals is different from that of "normative" individuals. To simplify, humanistic individuals experience a higher ratio of positive to negative affect than do normative individuals.

Normative and humanistic ideologies are measured by Tomkins's (1964) *Polarity Scale*; updated versions are to be found in Stone and Schaffner (1988), and in Knight (1992). The scale measures normative and humanistic tendencies in various domains of ideology ranging from child rearing to philosophies of science to theories of human nature. The format is the "polarity" item: two statements that may or may not seem diametrically opposed to the testee, who is told that he or she can agree with one or the other, both, or neither. In the realm of human nature, for example, the respondents seldom use their option to choose both when presented with the following polarity:

Human beings are basically good/Human beings are basically evil.

However, many people choose both statements in the polarity relative to child rearing:

Children should be taught how to act so that they can grow up to be fine adults/Children must be loved so that they can grow up to be fine adults.

Humanistic or left-wing personality scripts are related to liberal or low-authoritarian personal tendencies. Normative scripts seem to be related more strongly to authoritarian personalities, and to a lesser extent to conservatism. Recent evidence supports Tomkins's (1965) contention that these tendencies are independent—a person can be both normative and humanistic! A recent study (Stone, 1991) of the relationship between these variables and authoritarianism as measured by the RWA Scale showed the following:

1. Normative and humanistic scores correlated only $-.23$ ($p < .05$), supporting the notion that these are relatively independent variables.
2. Normative scores correlate highly with RWA ($r = +.54; p < .01$).
3. Humanism correlated only $-.23$ ($p < .05$) with RWA scores.

These results suggest that the normative score is quite close to author-itarianism, whereas humanism measures liberalism but not libertarianism (or whatever the low end of the RWA Scale is called).

The importance of these findings is that the Polarity Scale, based as it is in an explicit theory about the relationship of affective scripts to ideology, may provide a breakthrough in the study of the origins and dynamics of the authoritarian personality. It also adds to the current movement for greater attention to ideology by social psychologists (Billig, 1982).

Conclusion

The present author participated in a graduate seminar in social psychology taught by Dr. Jack M. Wright.[1] One of the topics reviewed in that seminar was *The Authoritarian Personality* and the subsequent research (through 1960). Students left that seminar with the clear impression that the end of the road had been reached in research on authoritarianism. Twenty-five years later, one of the participants in the Potsdam Conference, Dr. Detlef Oesterreich (1985), reached pretty much the same conclusion, although for different reasons:

Authoritarianism seems to be a very delicate concept. Although it is a scientific concept conceived to explain human behavior, it is immediately concerned with politics. This close connection led, in some respects, to a development of the concept which cannot be fully understood in a purely scientific context but which requires political understanding too. I think that the concept changed in accordance with international affairs, declaring, after fascism had been defeated, communism to be the major enemy of western societies. The consequences for the concept were, as I pointed out, first its development into a psychological construct which abandoned its historical and socio-economic roots, second the revision of the F Scale with the intention of identifying communists as author-itarian too, and third the tendency to evaluate the authoritarian personality as abnormal, unhealthy and maladjusted to defend one's own values as normal. (pp. 101–102)

Oesterreich was pessimistic: He predicted the end of authoritarianism as a concept in social science unless it could "again be used for the explana-

---

[1] University of Florida. Dr. Wright, whose career was cut short by an untimely death, was the author of one of the hundreds of classic studies of authoritarianism that we are unable to mention (Wright & Harvey, 1965). It confirms the idea that social psychologists were turning away from authoritarianism research that the handbook on attitude scales coauthored by Shaw and Wright (1967) omitted mention of the F Scale. However, Marvin Shaw denies this: "It was just that the F Scale seemed more of a personality scale than an attitude scale" (M. E. Shaw, personal communication, June 5, 1991).

tion of average behavior in the tradition of Fromm and Reich"
(p. 102).

The present review of current authoritarianism research gives some
reason for hope. The continued interest spurred by Altemeyer's example,
the increased research in Europe, and new theoretical insights such as
those provided by Browning's work and Duckitt's theory are grounds
for optimism. Certainly the work by Sales and his successors helps to
reconnect authoritarianism to the sociopolitical context. All in all, these
are exciting times for renewal in this field.

Much needs to be done, however, along the lines of Oesterreich's
criticism. More attention needs to be given to theory, and to alternatives
to *TAP* theory. More programmatic research needs to be undertaken,
after Altemeyer's example. And the *origins* of authoritarian impulses will
never be fully understood until long-term longitudinal research becomes
more commonplace. This research seems more vital in the long run to
human survival than research on military security measures. A small
portion of the star-wars research budget would go a long way toward
furthering our understanding of ourselves and our destructive impulses.

9
Authoritarianism in German Adolescents: Trends and Cross-Cultural Comparisons

Gerda Lederer

As a mathematics teacher from a suburban New York high school I found myself in Hamburg, West Germany, in the summer of 1973. I had come to have a closer look at a methodology that produced mathematics achievements in West Germany superior to those of the United States (Husen, 1967). I was given the opportunity to do so, along with two dozen German-speaking American colleagues, because the Federal Republic of Germany faced a serious shortage of mathematics and science teachers at the time.

I had the first inkling of the unexpected that awaited us during a series of preparatory seminars. The American teachers were cautioned not to engage in any frontal teaching. They were instructed *not* to admonish the students to be quiet, and to refrain from the imposition of discipline in the classroom.

In practice, teaching under these circumstances assumed a certain Alice-in-Wonderland quality. Shortly after my arrival in Hamburg, I was to accompany a German teacher on a class outing with 32 twelve-year-olds. I was told that we could not assemble our charges with a whistle when it was time to return; we could not even ask them to line up and be counted. In the school building, teachers were not to stop the youngsters from running, a customary safety measure in my American school. On one occasion, I was kept from separating two boys who were engaged in a violent fight. A German colleague explained to me that it was the aim of the educational system to teach the students *not* to obey authority, either that of the teachers or of the parents.

This period in the early 1970s marked the height of the antiauthoritarian movement in German education. Some student protesters of the late 1960s had tried to anticipate the liberation of the individual from society's "economic and technological oppression" by emancipating the small child. They established kindergartens with the aim of producing "growing individuals . . . who will consistently try to remove barriers, coercions and institutionalized oppression that inhibit them in the realization of their identity" (Zimmer, 1972, pp. 191–192). Though accepted by only a small portion of the population, this radical departure from classical educational practices left its mark on the educational system and led to a reexamination of customary practices. In a psychological examination of adolescents in West German society that received wide recognition, Ziehe (1975) saw a dilemma in the teacher's psychological need to be loved by the students while teaching them to be critical of authority. He found that "the teacher's sole meaningful achievement can be found in the student's learning occasionally to reject him" (p. 254). To the foreign observer it was striking that classroom management, teacher expectations, and cultural values were all out of step with the traditional values of German society. Although rarely made explicit, it was generally assumed that the traditional emphasis on obedience that had prevailed in German schools and homes had paved the way for fascism and the Holocaust. German youngsters were less compliant than their opposite numbers in America and far less obedient than I remembered from the German schools of my childhood. I found myself more interested in this pervasive phenomenon than in the methods of mathematics instruction I had come to study. What, exactly, had changed? Had others also observed this change?

I began my inquiry by distributing a semistructured questionnaire to my American colleagues. The replies confirmed my own observations as to the attitudes and behavior of German teachers and students. Thus, I was led to spend the year observing and recording countless manifestations of a culture involved in a very self-conscious process of change. Upon my return to the United States, I was determined first to formulate and then to answer the questions relating to this antiauthority behavior that I had observed.

The Research Questions

The focus of the German reforms was, first of all, to change attitudes about the exercise of authority: Adults must refrain from the imposition of authority and children must learn to question it. A second ingrained German attitude that was earmarked for change was the assumption of German superiority, together with its devaluation of all things non-German. This attitude had reached a pinnacle during national socialism; it was accompanied by stress on self-sacrificing obedience for the glorification of the fatherland. At least these seemed to be the targets of the reform movement. To examine the movement and its results more carefully, I formulated four questions:

1. What, precisely, were the variables in German society that seemed to be destined for change?

2. Had the efforts at change been effective? That is, could a change in specific attitudes of German adolescents between 1945 and 1975 be documented?
3. Could a similar assessment of these variables among adolescents during the same time span be made in the United States so that an intercultural comparison could be carried out?
4. If changes were documented, how fundamental were they? Could a nation change its values and norms, its very national character, in less than three decades?

This chapter reviews the research undertaken to answer these questions, including comparisons based on subsequent data collection in Austria and East Germany. The findings will then be discussed in the light of evidence from other social scientific investigations.

The Background

The origins of the obedient and nationalistic attitudes of the German people have been traced historically by many writers (e.g., Craig, 1982). Indeed, the failure of the German republic following the First World War has been attributed to the lack of democratic orientation in the populace.

The image of the authoritarian German has also been the subject of German literature. An eloquent example is Heinrich Mann's (1918/1982) satirical portrait of the German of the Wilhelminian era, *Der Untertan* (literally, *The Underling*, published in English 1945 as *Little Superman*). Begun in 1906, Mann completed this work in 1913 but for political reasons was unable to publish it until 1918. In this novel Mann described in his characters many of the personality characteristics associated forty years later with *The Authoritarian Personality* (*TAP*; Adorno et al., 1950). He foresaw the inevitability of the First World War and anticipated the characteristics of the Nazis of Hitler's Germany.

Der Untertan is the story of Diedrich Hessling, son of an authoritarian paper manufacturer, who learns the meaning of authority in childhood. He fears his father yet feels compelled to love him. From an early age, he serves his superiors passionately and acts as a secret informer. Encouraged by his contemporaries, he excels in the brutal treatment of the only Jewish student in his class.

As a university student, Diedrich perfects his dual desire to submit and dominate in fraternal organizations. Upon his father's death, he follows in his father's footsteps. Mann traces Diedrich's successful career as despot of his factory, representative of his village, and passionate vassal of his emperor.

Prophetically, Mann has one of his characters comment on power gone mad: "And so it can happen that a new type [of person] will populate the land, one who does not see cruelty and oppression merely as means on the road to the betterment of the human condition but instead as the essence of life itself" (pp. 182–183).

Attempts to make a social-psychological study of these attitudes began in Germany in the 1930s and came to fruition in the publication of *The Authoritarian Personality* in 1950 (see chapters 1 & 2, this volume). Many of the characteristics identified by Adorno and his colleagues as authoritarian (Adorno et al., 1950, p. 228ff.) seemed to me to describe the attributes German society was trying to change in the 1970s.

Although the subjects of Adorno et al.'s (1950) study had been Americans, research by Michaela von Freyhold (1971) carried out in 1960 using representative samples of West Germans supported key findings of *TAP* (see chap. 1, this volume).

The Design of the Study

If my questions were to be answered, data on former levels of authoritarianism would have to be located and new data collected. I was able to find the results of a study by the Harvard psychologist D. McGranahan in 1945 on adolescent authoritarianism in the United States and Germany. He asked 16-year-old subjects questions about obedience, patriotism, and ethnocentrism.

The American portion of a cross-cultural study of social norms and authoritarianism by Kagiticibasi (1967), who compared Turkish and American 16-year-olds, also proved useful. She had employed some of McGranahan's items in her surveys. Kagitcibasi had taken great care to make her questionnaire as culture-free as possible, so it proved suitable for cross-cultural comparisons. A German study from the mid-1960s yielded a further data point (see Waldman, 1963). My own youth surveys, undertaken in 1978–79 in the United States and in West Germany, used the Kagiticibasi instrument. These multiple observations allowed me to make a trend analysis in each country, together with current cross-cultural comparisons.

The Variables of Authoritarianism

The survey instrument first used in 1966 and again in 1978–79 employed questionnaire items organized into seven distinct scales reflecting different aspects of attitudes to authority and to outgroups (Kagitcibasi, 1967; Lederer, 1983). Among the scales were general authoritarianism, state authoritarianism, parental authoritarianism, and dogmatism. Item–whole correlations and Cronbach alpha coefficients were determined for each subscale, and interscale correlations calculated. However, the unidimensionality of the survey instrument could not be taken for

TABLE 9.1 New General Authoritarianism Scale (Factor 1); factor loadings for four data sets.

Item	U.S. 1966	U.S. 1978	FRG 1979	AUS 1980
34. In this complicated world of ours the only way we can know what is going on is to rely on leaders or experts who can be trusted.	.376	.454	.407	.433
35. Among the most important qualities that a person can have is disciplined obedience to authority.	.485	.648	.639	.562
37. The main thing in life is for a person to want to do something important for his country.	.379	.436	.531	.355
38. Patriotism and loyalty are the first and most important requirements of a good citizen.	.383	.551	.621	.466
51. The moral standards of the American (German) people are higher than the moral standards of foreign people.	.363	.507	.600	.388
80. A child should feel a deep sense of obligation to act in accord with the wishes of his parents.	.432	.437	.602	.581
81. Children should always be loyal to their parents.	.675	.554	.425	.485
82. Children should do nothing without the consent of their parents.	.428	.523	.512	.494
83. Every person should feel a great love, gratitude, and respect for his parents.	.665	.509	.527	.483
93. It usually helps the child in later years if he is forced to conform to his parent's ideas.	.439	.619	.542	.422
94. People today are in general more violent and immoral than people of previous generations.	.376	.527	.324	.410
95. The facts on crime and sexual immorality suggest that we will have to crack down harder on some people if we are going to save our moral standards.	.490	.464	.592	.546
114. There is a divine purpose in the operations of the universe.	.377	.420	.317	.300
115. What the youth need most is strict discipline, rugged determination, and the will to work and fight for family and country.	.487	.487	.588	.570
116. The minds of today's youth are being hopelessly corrupted by the wrong kind of literature.	.487	.497	.553	.524
117. It is only natural and right for each person to think that his family is better than any other.	.393	.382	.520	.483
118. The worst danger to real Americanism (to the German culture) during the last 50 years has come from foreign ideas and agitators.	.372	.576	.483	.465
119. We should be grateful for leaders who tell us exactly what to do and how to do it.	.416	.484	.569	.464

granted. Thus, each of the data sets collected using the modern question-naires (Kagitcibasi in the United States, 1966; Lederer in the United States, 1978; Lederer in West Germany, 1979) was subjected to Varimax factor analysis. It was found that a traditional authoritarianism factor was indeed the strongest, first factor of each analysis. There was a high communality among items of all three data sets for the first factor of a four-factor solution.

Eighteen items meeting the criterion of high loading on Factor 1 for each of the three data sets were then combined to make up the New General Authoritarianism Scale (NGAS). No "reversed" items were among these eighteen, even though nearly 50% of the original scale items had been stated in the nonauthoritarian direction to avoid acquiescent response set. Reversed items were shown once more to be less effective measures of authoritarianism than items stated in the authoritarian direction. The NGAS was used as a basis of comparison between countries over time. The items and factor loadings for each data set are shown in Table 9.1.

The McGranahan (1946) survey provides an independent comparison, using some items that were quite different from F-scale statements. However, some of the responses of McGranahan's American and German subjects anticipated the dimensions of authoritarianism elaborated in *TAP*. For example, the respondents were asked to indicate whom they considered to be "the greatest man in the history of the world." The 10 most frequently mentioned names in both groups, comprising more than 90% of the total references in each case, showed significant differences. McGranahan wrote about the 10 most frequently mentioned names in each group as follows:

All the individuals in the . . . German list are symbols of great political or military power, rulers of states or armies or both. Of the first American ten, four men are distinguished for contritutions to history that did not involve the wielding of great military or political power (Christ, Columbus, Edison, Franklin). . . . [These findings are evidence of the] German admiration for power and authority . . . presumably an important psychological element in the well-known German tendency toward political and social organizations in which, as in the feudal system, each individual has a superior toward whom he is submissive, and inferiors over whom he can wield power (McGranahan, 1946, pp. 252, 253).

It is also interesting to note that the most frequently mentioned name on both lists was Roosevelt and that, "in their subservience to American authority, the German youth have curiously rated Eisenhower and Truman higher than have the American youth. (In a similar test done on . . . German children in the French zone . . . Eisenhower and Truman did not appear and Roosevelt dropped in popularity, leaving Bismarck and Frederick the Great to head the list . . .)" (McGranahan, p. 253). Table 9.2 shows some of the items of the McGranahan survey with the responses given in 1945 and 33 years later.

TABLE 9.2 Responses to eight items of the McGranahan study from four surveys of adolescents (percentage choosing the authoritarian response).

Items	West German		United States	
	1945[1]	1979[2]	1945[1]	1978[2]
1. A soldier who refuses, during a war, to obey an order to shoot an innocent prisoner is justified. ("no" answers)	44	7	29	12
2. A boy who beats up smaller children is worse than a boy who disobeys his elders. ("no" answers)	30	12	29	16
3. A boy is justified in running away from home if his father is cruel to him. ("no" answers)	50	16	30	25
4. In the families I know, older brothers are expected to have the right to give orders to younger brothers and obtain obedience. ("yes" answers)	23	13	9	36
5–8. In your opinion, are members of your own nation better than the following? ("yes" answers)				
Italians	70	15	43	19
Poles	71	10	38	24
French	57	3	40	13
Germans			41	24
Americans	27	4		

1. Data from McGranahan study (1646).
2. Data from Lederer study (1983).

Results and Interpretations

Table 9.3 shows the item means and standard deviations for each item of the New General Authoritarianism Scale for the Kagitcibasi survey (1967) and the surveys carried out in the United States in 1978 and in the Federal Republic of Germany in 1979. In this table, the higher values indicate greater support for democracy (low authoritarianism) and the lower values less support for democratic values (high authoritarianism). The differences between the scale means and the individual item means of the three surveys are also shown. The decline of authoritarianism in the United States from 1966 to 1978 is evident from the significant difference in scale means between these surveys ($p < .01$). In addition, statistically significant differences are also shown for these two surveys for 15 of the 18 items of the scale.

The difference in authoritarianism between American and German adolescents in 1978–79 is similarly evident. The scale means lie close together, with $M = 3.24$ ($SD = .59$) for the United States and $M = 3.55$ ($SD = .55$) for West Germany. However, the difference is statistically significant ($p < .01$), with the German adolescents scoring higher in their support of democratic values (lower on authoritarianism). Significant differences in the same direction were shown for 14 of the 18 scale items.

TABLE 9.3 New General Authoritarianism Scale (NGAS) data for U.S. 1966, U.S. 1978, and FRG 1979 studies (item means, standard deviations, and differences between groups on item means; high scores represent support for democratic values, i.e., low authoritarianism).

Item	U.S. 1966 (N = 294, Cronbach-alpha .81, scale mean 2.899, sd .528)		Difference between U.S. 1978 and U.S. 1966	U.S. 1978 (N = 661, Cronbach-alpha .87, scale mean 3.239, sd .586)		Difference between FRG 1979 and U.S. 1978	FRG 1979 (N = 919, Cronbach-alpha .87, scale mean 3.554, sd .546)	
	Mean	sd		Mean	sd		Mean	sd
34	3.02	1.24	.35**	3.37	1.16	.10	3.27	1.05
35	2.59	1.17	.65**	3.24	1.19	.50**	3.74	1.01
37	3.15	1.10	.54**	3.69	1.01	.21**	3.90	.94
38	2.22	1.04	.93**	3.15	1.13	.69**	3.84	.94
51	3.13	1.10	.46**	3.59	.99	.27**	3.86	.97
80	2.34	1.00	.43**	2.77	1.04	.53**	3.30	.93
81	2.25	.99	.21**	2.46	1.07	.29**	2.75	1.04
82	3.51	1.14	.19*	3.70	1.02	-.23**	3.47	.97
83	2.13	1.06	.25**	2.38	1.12	.39**	2.77	1.00
93	3.77	1.06	.13	3.90	1.00	.16**	4.06	.83
94	3.17	1.26	-.08	3.09	1.19	.07	3.16	1.08
95	2.41	.96	.34**	2.75	1.07	.47**	3.22	1.05
114	2.48	.99	.37**	2.85	.94	1.12**	3.97	.92
115	2.76	1.01	.58**	3.34	1.05	.75**	4.09	.93
116	3.52	1.12	.11	3.63	1.06	.28**	3.91	.85
117	2.97	1.12	.21**	3.18	1.07	.24**	3.42	1.00
118	3.09	.98	.40**	3.49	.86	-.07	3.42	.93
119	3.63	1.03	.15*	3.78	1.01	.00	3.78	.91

* sig. level < .05
** sig. level < .01

Difference between scale means U.S. 1978 and U.S. 1966 .340**
Difference between scale means FRG 1979 and U.S. 1978 .315**

Socioeconomic class has been shown in past research to be a significant factor in determining authoritarian attitudes; because social classes were not represented equally in the two samples, a comparison was made of scale means by social class. This comparison showed statistically significant differences to exist at every social class level, in the expected direction (Lederer 1981, p. 97).

The responses shown in Table 9.2 illustrate the decline in authoritarian attitudes in West Germany among adolescents between 1945 and 1979 and a similar decline in the United States during the same time span. They also show that authoritarianism was more prevalent in Germany than in the United States in 1945 and that the opposite was true in 1979. A separate analysis of dogmatism items from surveys in the Federal Republic of Germany and the United States in the 1960s and repeated in the 1978–79 surveys yielded similar results (see Lederer, 1981, p. 99).

In summary, on the basis of the authoritarianism studies discussed, it was evident that authoritarianism had declined among adolescents in the period between 1945 and 1978 in both the United States and West Germany. It was further shown that whereas the German youths had been substantially more authoritarian than the Americans in 1945, the West German subjects were somewhat less authoritarian than their American cohorts in 1979. Given the limitations imposed by sampling errors, the decline of authoritarianism still appears to have been more substantial in West Germany than in the United States (Lederer 1981, 1982, 1983).

The Trend Continues

Further research on political attitudes of German and American adolescents was carried out in the mid-1980s. In a joint research project of the University of Georgia and the Bundeszentrale für politische Bildung of West Germany, 522 German and 483 American 16- to 18-year-olds were surveyed with an 80-item questionnaire probing confidence in political institutions and leadership and political participation (Hepburn et al., 1987). The American students had significantly more confidence and were more supportive of Congress, whereas German students were more critical of judges and showed more commitment to supporting candidates from minority parties. In a comparison of attitudes toward constitutional principles of equality and individual rights, the West German students expressed stronger commitment to these principles and showed greater opposition to compromising them. In addition, they showed greater independence and critical perspective. The authors concluded that the trend reported by the IEA study in the mid-1970s and by Lederer in 1979 continued in the mid-1980s.

The Case of Austria

In 1980, the questionnaire previously employed with West German and American adolescents was administered to adolescents in Austria. These data were also subjected to factor analysis. Again the first factor of a four-factor solution was an authoritarianism factor; the same 18 NGAS items showed high loadings on this factor.

A comparison of the scale scores for the NGAS for Austria (1980), the Federal Republic of Germany (1979), and the United States (1978) shows surprisingly little difference. On a scale of 1 (most authoritarian) to 5 (least authoritarian), with 3 denoting the neutral position, Austria's scale mean was 3.34, West Germany's 3.55, and America's 3.24. The 16-year-olds of each country tended to disagree with the authoritarian positions stated, and between-country differences were remarkably small. An item-by-item comparison shows that Austrian youngsters were slightly but consistently more authoritarian than West German youngsters.

Authoritarianism Among Adolescents in the 1990s: A Look Ahead

With the opening of the borders of East Germany, followed by the demise of the German Democratic Republic, as we enter the last decade of the 20th century, the question is being asked, How authoritarian are the "other" Germans? What is the legacy of 40 years of state authoritarianism? How do children raised in that society differ from those across the former border to the West?

As soon as circumstances permitted, after East Germany's borders were opened but before unification took place, in the spring of 1990 we carried out a survey of adolescents in the then-DDR, with the same instrument used in the prior surveys in West Germany, the United States, and Austria. Subsequently, it was decided to update the surveys in West Germany, the United States, and Austria, and lately social scientists from Moscow and China have shown interest in conducting such surveys of adolescents in their countries. Of these, only the East German data collection has so far been completed and analyzed.

As expected, the data show that East German adolescents are significantly more authoritarian than their West German contemporaries—but they show also that most differences are unexpectedly small. Startling differences were recorded in ethnocentrism, with East Germans showing themselves to be more subject to prejudice than West German subjects. Dissimilarities in factor structure and organization point to different types of authoritarians in the East and in the West.

TABLE 9.4 Eigenvalue and percentage of the variance explained by Factor 1 (Authoritarianism) of the four-factor analysis.

Data set	Eigenvalue	% of variance
U.S. 1966	6.5	42.7
U.S. 1978	9.7	54.8
FGR 1979	10.2	53.9
AUS 1980	7.8	44.3

Discussion

One result of this survey is that it demonstrates the robustness of the authoritarianism concept. A strong and distinctive authoritarianism factor emerged in each of the four data sets (U.S., 1966; U.S., 1978; FRG, 1979; AUS, 1980); the same questionnaire items were indicators of authoritarianism across time and cultures. Although items from many sources had been included in the questionnaire, over half of the best items were based on F-scale items formulated by Adorno et al. (1950).

Of the four surveys on which such comparable data were available, the eigenvalue of the authoritarianism factor was highest for West Germany and lowest for the United States in 1966 (see Table 9.4).

Item 35 ("One of the most important qualities that a person can have is disciplined obedience to authority") was the highest loading and thus the most important item of the authoritarianism factor of the entire questionnaire in the U.S. (1978) and the West German (1979) surveys, third highest in the Austrian (1980) survey, and fifth highest in the U.S. (1966) survey. For the Austrian data, the three lowest loading items of the NGAS were Item 114 dealing with religion (.30), Item 37 dealing with patriotism (.36), and Item 51 dealing with ethnocentrism (.39). In contrast, Item 51 had a loading of .60 in the German data and .51 in the U.S. (1978) data (but only .36 for the U.S., 1966, data).

Our survey results show young Austrians to be no more authoritarian than young Germans or young Americans. However, national loyalty and ethnocentrism, which are integral parts of the authoritarianism syndrome in the United States and Germany, are not reserved for the authoritarians in Austria; on the subscales concerned with "respect for state authority" and "rejection of foreigners," Austrians were significantly more authoritarian than Germans. There were no differences on these scales between Americans and Austrians (see Lederer, 1988).

Adolescent Authoritarianism Over Time: A Summary

The hypotheses formulated at the beginning of the chapter have been operationalized and tested. On the basis of data collected cross-nationally over time it was shown that West German 16-year-olds have substantially changed their attitude to authority over the span of 3½ decades. This change is substantial not only relative to the Germans' former views, but their attitudes have become very similar to those of their American contemporaries. In fact, small but statistically significant differences in scale scores consistently show the West German subjects to be less authoritarian than the Americans.

Data collected in Austria with the same instrument reveal authoritarian scale scores of Austrian youth to be very similar to those of the two other national groups. A more detailed analysis shows the Austrian 16-year-olds to share with their elders a pervasive and protective affection for their country, uncritical patriotism, and ethnocentrism.

Numerous studies by sociologists, psychologists, and political scientists bear out the findings relating to the changes in values and attitudes in West Germany. In the following pages, some of these studies will be drawn on to paint a picture of the authoritarianism embedded in the values and attitudes of German society following the Second World War and of the slow road to democracy during the subsequent four decades.

An Authoritarian Culture? Germany After World War II

In *Father Land*, Bertrand Schaffner (1948) presented an anthropological and psychiatric study of authoritarianism in the German family. A descendant of German parents, Schaffner lived in a German-American community and spent several years in his youth in the Germany of the 1920s. His study focuses on the German family. Such study is crucial because of "the remarkable parallel between the rules that govern [the family] and the credos of national, political life" (Schaffner, 1948, p. 4). His research had its origins at a screening center set up by the Information Control Division (ICD) of the American military government in Germany in 1945. Through interviews, surveys, sentence completion tests, and examinations Schaffner studied people ranging in age from 19 to 70 and representing family constellations existing in the first German Empire, the First World War, the Weimar Republic, and under National Socialism. "From these data," he concluded, "it would appear that the basic premises of German family life show no significant differences during these seventy-six years" (p. 13).

The following excerpts from *Father Land* (Schaffner, 1948) create a vivid picture of the authoritarianism within the German family and the values and principles inculcated early in life:

Family life revolves around the figure of the father. He is omnipotent, omniscient, and omnipresent . . . the source of all the authority, all the security, and all the wisdom. . . . Every other member of the family has lower status and lesser rights. . . . The father . . . judges and decides . . . the issues [and] serves as a model for his children. . . . (p. 15)

In case of rebellion or disobedience, the father believes in punishing promptly, vigorously, and justly. . . . It is the goal of family life to have trained one's children to implicit obedience by the age of five. . . . He rarely embraces or fondles his children. . . . (p. 21, 23)

The German mother . . . is completely dependent on her husband. . . . The German woman is not a pacifist, but believes that combat is glorious, and that without war a nation becomes decadent. This is to be expected from the fact that women derive their political views from men. . . . (p. 40)

It is important to understand the atmosphere in which German children are raised, because the psychological trends induced in children become a permanent part of the adult personality . . . From infancy on, the child learns that he is part of a system in which he is of inferior rank and that he must obey his superiors. (p. 41, 42)

Schaffner's (1948) focus was on readying Germany and the Germans for democracy, and all that he discovered in his investigation made him skeptical of the possibility of success of the American mission:

National Socialism was not a revolution in German life but a continuation and intensification of the traditional approach to life. . . . The word "denazification" . . . is basically dangerous because it fails to point out the fundamental organic relationship between Nazism and Germanism, and the fact that National Socialism was a sequential growth out of German culture. (p. 80)

Adorno (1960) disagreed with Schaffner's thesis that the triumph of fascism in Germany was related to the "supposedly patriarchal-authoritarian structure of German society" (p. 376). This theory is based on a social structure, Adorno wrote, that had already changed at the time of the Weimar Republic and that "has completely disappeared today." Adorno thought Paul Federn's psychoanalytic theory more relevant. Federn (1919) related the Hitler cult to the fall of the monarchy and saw in it a substitute for the nonexistent father figure and not a fatherly likeness. Here, Hitler is seen as an infinitely enlarged projection of the weak ego and not of the traditional fatherly authority.

In a thoughtful study entitled *Society and Democracy in Germany*, Ralf Dahrendorf (1965/1967) presented a critical historical, political, and philosophical analysis of Germany and the Germans in the 20th century. In a chapter dealing with political culture, Dahrendorf reported that participation in elections was notoriously high in Germany during all political periods, ranging between 76% and 88% for the years from 1903 to 1961. Nevertheless, examining the quality of political behavior Dahrendorf concluded on the basis of surveys carried out between 1952 and 1962 that Germans in their majority are unpolitical (p. 314) because the political is deeply unimportant for them and they would really much prefer not to be drawn out of the "freedom" of their four walls (p. 327):

The political socialization of the German is incomplete . . . Democratic behavior becomes ritualized, a mere observance of external demands, a "duty" of citizenship. If one scratches this ritualism but a little, there often appears one of the many versions of active and passive authoritarianism, or a complete lack of orientation, the political effect of which is probably no less authoritarian. (p. 326)

Like Schaffner (1948), Dahrendorf (1965/1967) is pessimistic about the growth of democracy in Germany. He doubts that the democracy that has been decreed will really take root. His slim hope is the existence of a democratic and highly political minority and the possibility that it is growing. He writes:

We should not exclude the possibility that what was stuck on does at last grow on and that ritual adaptation becomes intelligent and independent practice at last. (p. 326)

If there is hope for Germany, writes Dahrendorf (1965/1967), it must involve a strengthening of political commitment. Schaffner, writing in 1948 shortly after the end of World War II, attempted to explain the nature of German society to an American audience. Dahrendorf, a German with a social democratic family tradition and himself a victim of the Nazis, addressed his book, written 15 years later, to a German audience. Both believe that the susceptibility to fascism is embedded in the traditional values of German society and both find it hard to believe in fundamental change. Ten years after Dahrendorf's negative assessment was published, definite signals connoting widespread changes in West German society were reported by observers of the West German scene.

West Germany in the Process of Change

In 1975, the International Association for the Evaluation of Educational Achievement (IEA) published the results of a large-scale study dealing with civic education in 10 countries (Torney, Oppenheim, & Farnen, 1975). An instrument was developed for the surveys that included areas of cognitive, affective, and behavioral content (Oppenheim & Torney, 1974). The researchers found the samples of adolescents from the Federal Republic of Germany to score higher on democratic values and lower on a factor of authoritarianism than those of any of the other nations tested (Torney et al., p. 220ff.).

A survey of writings on political culture in the Federal Republic of Germany by Merelman and Foster (1980) enumerated a large number of studies that led the authors to a similar conclusion. They found that there has been an increase in support for democratic values such as tolerance, freedom of expression, interest in political events, and so on, over time. Merelman and Foster further remarked:

Since the 1960s about 15,000 different grassroots groups have emerged to try to influence political decisions, particularly concerning the environment, atomic energy, consumer and neighborhood issues. (p. 453)

Another source of information on the political changes in the Federal Republic of Germany is the two-volume comparison of political attitudes in five nations by Almond and Verba. In the first volume, *The Civic Culture* (1963/1965), the authors developed a profile of the Germans similar to that by Dahrendorf (1963/1965). On the basis of data collected in 1959, they found that basic trademarks of authoritarianism still prevailed. Like Dahrendorf, Almond and Verba (1963/1965) found the German attitude to politics to be passive and formal and the norms favoring active political participation not well developed (p. 312). They concluded:

Weakness of the participant role in Germany, especially the lack of an informal participatory culture, suggests that too much reliance is placed upon hierarchical leadership. Though the formal political institutions of democracy exist in Germany and though there is a well-developed political infrastructure . . . the underlying set of political attitudes that would regulate the operation of these institutions in a democratic direction is missing. (pp. 429, 496)

In the second volume, *The Civic Culture Revisited* (Almond & Verba, 1980), David P. Conradt wrote that significant changes have taken place in the Federal Republic of Germany. By the late 1970s, Conradt reported, "by all measures, the Federal Republic . . . is a model of democratic political stability. Indeed, on some measures that will be discussed, Germany today is closer to the civic culture than Britain or the United States" (p. 221).

Changes Within the West German Family

Because there is ample evidence that the classical authoritarianism that reached its height during National Socialism in Germany has been superseded by a largely democratic civic culture, it seems important to examine the changes in values and patterns of socialization within the family in the Federal Republic of Germany since Schaffner (1948) made the observations quoted earlier.

Conradt (Almond & Verba, 1980) concluded his observations about the changes in West Germany by examining childhood socialization, one of the sources to which such change in political culture is often attributed. He found that public attitudes toward child rearing in the Federal Republic of Germany had become significantly more liberal over the past quarter century (Almond & Verba, p. 252). Another study (Fischer, Fuchs, & Zinnecker, 1985) that comes to the same conclusion was published in the fall of 1985 by the Jugendwerk der Deutschen Shell, a division of the German Shell Oil Company. Shell has regularly sponsored comparative youth studies and in 1985 compared a representative sample of West German 15- to 24-year-olds with a representative sample of 45- to 54-year-olds, that is, with the corresponding parent generation (Fischer et al., 1985). An additional data set was furnished by a Shell study carried out in the early 1950s, when the 45- to 54-year-olds were themselves 15 to 24 years old. Asked to classify the type of upbringing they experienced, 63% of the adults—compared to 35% of the youths—classified their upbringing as strict or very strict. Of the adults, 36% thought their upbringing to have been lenient and kind, compared with 60% of the young group. Equally important, the desirability of a strict upbringing had undergone profound change. Whereas youths who classified their upbringing in 1955 as "strict" expressed the desire to raise their children the same way, equating a strict with a good upbringing, the youths in 1984 who claim to have experienced a strict upbringing plan to raise their children differently. Those who classified their upbringing as "lenient and kind" largely plan to raise their children as they have been raised (Fischer et al., 1985, Vol. 3, p. 164).

The use of corporal punishment has also declined. In a survey of 18- to 22-year-olds carried out in 1950, 86% of the young men and 62% of the young women said that they were punished with severe beatings. In the 1980s, only 9% of those born in 1965 reported being beaten as children (Fischer et al., 1985, pp. 264–265). The main goals of child rearing have also undergone change: In the 1950s, 25% of the population considered "obedience and submission" a very important goal, and 28% named "self-reliance and free will" in that category. In 1983, the goal "obedience and submission" was named by 9%, "self-reliance and free will" by 49%.

There is also evidence that the roles within the German family have changed. The percentage of youngsters who feel that they have a say in family decisions has been rising steadily since 1962, whereas the percentage of parents who never play with their children has fallen from 64% in the 1950s to 10% in the 1980s. When asked whether young people could learn anything from adults, 95% of both the young respondents and the older generation concurred, but only 3% of the youths saw their mother or father as their role model.

Conclusions

How deeply rooted are the changes in Germany? Might attitudes revert to their former positions? Has a true change in personality structure taken place? Are we seeing only the effects of social desirability and group conformity? The profoundly changed attitudes not only in Germany but also, for example, in the American South since the passing of civil rights legislation in the 1960s have raised some questions about the theories underlying *TAP*. They have made the authoritarianism syndrome appear less fixed and durable than the authors of *TAP* had anticipated and have raised questions about the origins of the syndrome. Speaking for many social scientists, Thomas T. Lewis (1990) feels that cognitive social learning theory can best account for the variety of authoritarian phenomena observed:

When people grow up within a particular system, they learn to assume that the system is the expected norm. Learning through observation and imitation, most people internalize the dominant attitudes of the socio-political culture (or at least the subculture which they experience). . . . It would appear that an authoritarian system would tend to promote the development of authoritarian attitudes, but since this is a dialectical relationship, it would also appear that the existence of authoritarian attitudes would be one major component of the infrastructure supporting an authoritarian system. (pp. 163–164)

Sanford (1973) asserts that "freedom from authoritarianism increases with education—not only because of exposure to enlightened culture, not only because of intellectual development, but because personality itself changes under the impact of well-directed education" (p. 162). However, Sanford (1973) does not support a purely cognitive explanation of authoritarianism; instead, he stresses the "interaction of personality and culture, of psychodynamic and cognitive processes" (p. 161).

An examination of the factors that led to the changes reported among West German adolescents over time supports Sanford's (1973) view. Such an analysis must include the many agents of political socialization during the time span, such as the family, the school, the media, the peer group, and the *Zeitgeist* (the intellectual spirit and philosophical outlook characteristic of the country and the era) and in this case can be thought of as an example of Sanford's (1973) "well-directed education" (see Lederer, 1981, pp. 19–24). It leads to the conclusion "that personality structures, even 'deep' or 'central' ones, are sustained by the social system in which the individual lives and can change when that system changes" (Sanford, 1973, p. 166). It does not alter the fact that the authoritarian personality syndrome continues to be relevant within the societal context and that individual psychological factors will be of crucial importance in accounting for individual differences and in determining individual attitudes and behavior.

10
The Authoritarian Personality in the United States and the Former Soviet Union: Comparative Studies

Sam McFarland, Vladimir Ageyev, and Marina Abalakina

Until the spring of 1988, Soviet psychologists had almost no access to Western research on authoritarianism. Adorno, Frenkel-Brunswik, Levinson, and Sanford's (1950) classic, *The Authoritarian Personality*, was found only in special library preserves, and even specialists had great difficulty getting access to this work. Books on related constructs, such as Rokeach's (1960) *The Open and Closed Mind* on dogmatism, were similarly restricted, at least in many areas of the former Soviet Union. While many Soviet psychologists knew these works existed, very few had the opportunity to read and evaluate them first hand.

Marxist-Leninist ideology long dictated the existence of the "New Soviet Man." As a result, the adoption of Western constructs and empirical cross-cultural comparisons with Western countries were disparaged. Constructs such as authoritarianism and its correlates, ethnocentrism and anti-Semitism, were simply not considered, because these concepts could reveal negative traits in Soviet Man. Soviet psychologists for several generations regarded the authoritarian personality and its correlates as descriptive only of Western social reality and assumed that they bore no relation to Soviet socialist society. The concept of the authoritarian personality was used only for the pejorative description of Western culture and did not become a working construct in Soviet social science. Scales measuring anti-Semitism, ethnocentrism, and authoritarianism were not translated into Russian, nor were parallel instruments developed. Not one empirical study was conducted.

Adorno's name and the authoritarian personality were often mentioned in Soviet texts that reviewed Western psychology; see Roshchin (1980); and Shikhirev (1980, 1985). However, these works provided mainly an ideological critique of authoritarianism and offered little description or scientific analysis of the Adorno group's work. Rather, Adorno and his associates and successors were accused of such ideological errors as "bourgeois apologism," "biological reductionism," and "Freudianism."

The term *authoritarian*, however, was used in other ways and contexts by Soviet social scientists. The phrase *authoritarian leadership style*, as coined by Kurt Lewin and his associates (Lewin, Lippitt, & White, 1939), was commonly used, and a number of empirical studies were conducted (Kitov, 1984; Lomov & Zhuravlev, 1978; Zhuravlev, Rubakhin, & Shorin, 1976). As a result, the term *authoritarian* was well known to Soviet authors, but its meaning was restricted to a style of leadership. Soviet work on authoritarian leadership styles did not relate that work, conceptually or empirically, to the problem of the authoritarian personality.

Following 1985 and the coming of perestroika, the term *authoritarian* was used also to describe the management structure of Soviet society and economics. Terms such as *authoritarian bureaucratic system* and *authoritarian methods of management* became widely used by economists, politicians, and the mass media to describe the centralized management system now being dismantled.

Nevertheless, this broader use of the term *authoritarian* did not awaken Soviet psychologists to the issue of the authoritarian personality. Until now, the question of the authoritarian personality has not been formulated either as a scientific issue or as a problem for life in Soviet society.

Our aim was to examine whether the construct of the authoritarian personality was as applicable in the Soviet Union as it is in Western countries. We believed that the construct of authoritarianism was especially relevant for the Soviet Union and that its study there has particular importance. Given the Soviet Union's centuries-old tradition of autocratic government, the study of authoritarianism there could help us to understand the relationships, if any, between political authoritarianism and the authoritarian personality. Of particular importance, we believed that understanding Soviet authoritarianism could help in gauging the readiness of the Russian population for the democratic institutions which were being implemented and for democratic rather than power-oriented solutions to the many ethnic and nationalist issues that confronted the Soviet Union.

Many barriers impeded the social, economic, and political changes that swept through the Soviet Union, but none seemed more important than the psychological ones. As many Western commentators have suggested, Russian political history and culture may have created an authoritarian consciousness in the general population to the degree that this consciousness appeared to be a major obstacle to the democratization of Soviet society (see Shipler, 1990).

Shortly after *The Authoritarian Personality* described the authoritarianism of the political right, others began to ask, "Is there an authoritarianism of the left?" (see Shils, 1954). This issue, now in its fourth decade, is reviewed by Altemeyer (1988a, pp. 258–264). Because communists and other "left-wingers" in Western democracies generally score lower than "right-wingers" on Rokeach's (1960) Dogmatism scale and not significantly different from those in the political middle, Stone (1980) concluded that left-wing authoritarianism is a myth. Eysenck (1981) and Ray (1983a) have challenged Stone's conclusions. This discussion was hindered until the present study by the inability to measure authoritarianism in communist countries.

It seemed likely that while communists in Western countries will be very nonauthoritarian, faith in communism in communist countries should actually be a component of authoritarianism. If, as Altemeyer (1981) has argued, conventionalism, authoritarian submission, and authoritarian aggression are the central defining elements of the authoritarian personality, communists and left-wingers in Western democracies are necessarily nonauthoritarian. They are unconventional almost by definition. They are likely to be unsubmissive to established authorities, and they are likely also to champion free speech, the right to political dissent, and other civil rights. In the Soviet Union, however, where communism itself was the convention, authoritarianism should have *included* adherence to communism, authoritarian submission to the ingroup (i.e., communist) authorities, and repressive attitudes toward nonconventional groups. These nonconventional groups seemed likely to include capitalists and champions of democracy rather than communists. Authoritarianism in the West is associated with strong anticommunism (Altemeyer, 1981), but the authoritarian personality in the Soviet Union seemed likely to correlate with anticapitalism and antidemocracy instead. However, Soviet authoritarianism was expected to correlate positively with ethnic prejudices and sexism, just as in the West (Altemeyer, 1981).

Study I: Comparisons of Soviet and Western Authoritarianism

Study I was planned and conducted in spring 1989. Because the study of Soviet authoritarianism was new, it was important to verify the general insights upon which the notion of the authoritarian personality was initially founded by the Adorno group. In their bootstrap series of studies, the study of anti-Semitism led first to the seminal insight that prejudices against outgroups are highly correlated and reflect a general disposition to reject outgroups that the Adorno group called ethnocentrism. The concept of the authoritarian personality arose only later in an effort to understand the psychological roots of this general ethnocentrism (Sanford, 1956).

Following this original course, Study I was framed to ask the following sequential questions.

1. Are prejudices against outgroups highly correlated among Russians as they are among Western populations? The Soviet Union had different

outgroups than does the West, but a similar pattern of correlations among all prejudices was expected. Communists are an outgroup victim of prejudice among Western authoritarians, and prejudice against communists is highly correlated with other racial, ethnic, and sexual prejudices (see McFarland, 1989a). In the Soviet Union, capitalists, dissidents, and champions of democracy were appropriate outgroups, and negative attitudes toward these groups were expected to be correlated with the common prejudices based on race, sex, and age.

2. Could a general measure of authoritarianism be adopted for studying authoritarianism among Russian-speaking Soviets that was internally consistent and in which all items loaded on a general factor? Altemeyer (1988a) has recently noted that the mean interitem correlation on his Right-Wing Authoritarianism (RWA) scale has fallen for student samples from .25 in 1973 to an average of .15 for the years 1984 through 1987. Both Altemeyer (1988a) and McFarland (1989b) found that the mean interitem correlation on the RWA for adults is now .22. Altemeyer (1988a) has suggested that this "ungluing" of the authoritarianism scale may be due, in part, to the relative social calm in North America at the present time. The authoritarian syndrome may manifest itself most strongly during periods of social unrest, that is, during times when the conventional social order is under attack. Should social unrest arise again, the items may "reglue." Following this suggestive notion, it seemed likely that the average interitem correlation among comparable authoritarianism items in the Soviet Union would be higher than is now found for Western samples. The Soviet conventional order was under siege, and the Soviet Union was experiencing a deep conflict of consciousnesses between those who wanted to continue holding to the Marxist-Leninist beliefs and symbols and those who were anxious for democratic alternatives. In this conflicted social context, the authoritarianism items seemed likely to cohere more tightly than they do for current North American samples.

3. Would the authoritarian personality predict ethnocentrism and specific prejudices among Russian-speaking Soviets as it does among Western populations? The Adorno group found that their original ethnocentrism (E) and authoritarianism (F) scales correlated .75 (Adorno et al., 1950). Altemeyer's (1981) RWA and his own measure of general prejudice were correlated .43, much less than the original F and E scales. Altemeyer attributed the larger correlation to the fact that all items on the original scales were positively worded and that the Adorno group selected and deleted items in developing their two scales with a view to how well each item correlated with the other scale. The current study used essentially balanced scales and did not arbitrarily select items to enhance the ethnocentrism–authoritarianism correlation. Good scales should assure that the correlation between ethnocentrism and authoritarianism accurately reflects the strength of their relationship among Soviets.

4. What demographic variables would predict Soviet authoritarianism? In Western studies, formal education is perhaps the most consistent demographic correlate of authoritarianism; authoritarianism decreases with advances in education. Correlations between the original unbalanced F scale and education level were often in the − .40s and − .50s (see Christie, 1954), but correlations are much lower with balanced authoritarianism scales. Altemeyer (1981) found correlations from − .24 to − .30 between RWA and the formal education level of his students' parents. McFarland (1989b) recently found that education level and the RWA correlated − .24 for a sample of 463 Kentucky adults. Education in North America appears to create individuals who are less authoritarian and who are more tolerant of differences and diversity. Altemeyer (1988a) found that students' RWA scores drop significantly across four years of college. However, open-mindedness toward ideas and respect for diversity of peoples are clear, if implicit, goals of education in North America. In the Soviet Union, by contrast, education was autocratic, aimed at inculcating Marxism-Leninism rather than teaching students to think for themselves. Schools that have nonauthoritarian atmospheres and that emphasize cognitive development appear to reduce authoritarianism far more than those that have authoritarian atmospheres and emphasize rote learning (Simpson, 1972). It was an open question, then, whether Soviet education would weaken or strengthen authoritarianism.

Authoritarianism in the West is also positively related to age in the range of .15 (Altemeyer, 1988a) to .20 (McFarland, 1989b). This correlation was expected to be larger in the Soviet Union, because many surveys have shown that the generation gap in authoritarian-like social attitudes is very strong. For example, one survey (cited in *Moscow News*, March 1989) found that while 57% of Moscow residents over 40 said they feared that anarchy would result from democratization, only 19% of those under 30 shared this fear.

Authoritarianism (RWA) is also correlated − .20 with the size of one's childhood hometown (McFarland, 1989b), and among married persons, it increases with the number of children (Altemeyer, 1988a). Similar relations were expected among Russians.

The Soviet Union was long a closed society, and citizens needed special permission to travel abroad. We expected, however, that either actual travel to foreign countries or the vicarious experience of foreign cultures (measured here by the self-reported knowledge of foreign languages) would contribute to lower authoritarianism, because those who had these experiences had more opportunity to undo their Soviet ethnocentrism. McFarland (1989b) found that the number of foreign countries Kentucky women had visited correlated with their RWA scores, $r = − .30$, but no such relationship was found for men, $r = .13$, ns.

Authoritarianism is negatively related to social class indices such as blue-collar versus white-collar occupations and income. Soviet authoritarianism also seemed likely to relate to occupation and occupation level as in the West, but income seemed less likely to do so; income in the Soviet Union was not related to employment status as it is in the West. Neither the F scale (Adorno et al., 1950) nor the RWA (Altemeyer, 1981; McFarland, 1989b) is significantly related to gender, and no relationship was expected among Russian-speaking Soviets.

We did not expect, however, that these demographic correlates would explain a large portion of the correlation between authoritarianism and ethnocentrism. The authoritarian syndrome is a personality dynamic in its own right, not merely a stand-in for low education and social rank and advanced age. Altemeyer (1988a), for example, found that controlling for education only slightly reduced the relationship between authoritarianism and punitiveness. Similarly, the authoritarianism–ethnocentrism relationship should be reduced only marginally when the demographic correlates are controlled by partial correlation.

Finally, authoritarianism in the West is generally associated with membership in conservative political parties and organizations (see Altemeyer, 1988a). In the 1989 Soviet context, Pamyat was the distinctively right-wing organization, although the Communist party was regarded as conservative as well. National Front groups and the arising democratic and reformist unofficial organizations were distinctively liberal in the 1989 Soviet panorama. Assuming that the Western pattern held, we expected that those who were members of conservative groups would be significantly more authoritarian than those who belong to the latter groups. Comsomol members were expected to be moderate in their authoritarianism, because they were younger, more reformist, and less ideologically committed than their party elders. Also, while Comsomol was the Young Communist League, virtually all youths in previous years joined Comsomol whether or not they shared communist beliefs.

Method

Eight outgroups were selected as appropriate targets of prejudice for Russian-speaking Soviets: capitalists, Jews, the non-Russian nationalities, women, dissidents, youth, advocates of free press, and advocates of democracy. These were selected because our experience suggested that they were often the focus of derogatory comments from those who championed the conventional Soviet Marxist-Leninist political system.

Using Likert (1932) scaling procedures, a series of positive and negative Russian-language statements were written about each group. The negative statements were generally selected from statements made by ultra-nationalistic Russian groups such as Pamyat. Positive statements were written by the authors. The number of statements about each group ranged from 4 (about free press, e.g., "All Russian writers who emigrated from the country, including A.I. Solzhenitsyn, must be openly published in the Soviet Union," negatively scored) to 15 (about Jews, e.g., "Jews have already conquered most of the Western world, and now they are trying to conquer us"). These scales contained approximately the same number of positive and negative statements about each group.[1]

Altemeyer's 30-item RWA scale (Altemeyer, 1988a, pp. 22–23) was selected for translation in preparing a Russian-language scale, because it has both higher internal consistency and consistently stronger validity coefficients than the rival F scale or Lee and Warr's (1969) balanced authoritarianism scale (Altemeyer, 1981, pp. 175–214). An inspection of the RWA's items revealed only five that appeared wedded to Western culture and therefore inappropriate for measuring Russian authoritarianism. Four of these praised religious authorities and condemned apostates. A simple substitution of sacrosanct Soviet authorities appeared sufficient. For example, Altemeyer's (1988a) Item 4 reads, "People should pay less attention to the Bible and the other old traditional forms of religious guidance. . . ." We merely substituted, "People should pay less attention to Marxism-Leninism. . . ." The fifth item (Item 26), "Communism and those who are out to destroy religion . . . ," was replaced with "Capitalists and those who are out to destroy socialism. . . ." For the remaining items, our effort was to retain as closely as possible the meanings of the original items in good Russian grammar and syntax. The items were first translated by Ageyev, then independently compared with the English variant by Abalakina, who offered some refined wordings. The response codes for all prejudice and authoritarianism items were scored on a 6-point scale ranging from 1 (Strongly disagree) to 6 (Strongly agree). No neutral option was provided.

All items from the prejudice scales and from the authoritarianism scale were combined with demographic items, which assessed sex; age; education level; size of childhood residence (from rural to large cities); current residence; general occupation and general level of occupation; marital status; number of children; monthly income; membership in various public organizations (the Communist Party, Pamyat, Comsomol, National Front movements or informal organizations); the number of foreign languages spoken; and the number of foreign countries visited, if any. The final instrument contained 120 items.

In May, 1989 two hundred copies of the questionnaire were administered in person in Moscow by the All-Union Center for the Study of Public Opinion, and 200 more were given in Tallinn, Estonia, by the Computer and Information Center of Estonian Radio and Television. Only persons for whom Russian was their first language received the questionnaire. Both organizations used for this study a quota sampling

---

[1] All scales used in this study are available from Sam McFarland both in Russian and in English.

procedure, which insured equivalent numbers of each sex and distributions of age, education, and occupation levels that approximated those of all Russian speakers in these cities.

Results

One hundred and eighty-five questionnaires were returned in Moscow and 183 in Tallinn. Eighteen questionnaires from Moscow and 4 from Tallinn were dropped from the sample because more than 4 of the 120 questions were unanswered, leaving a final sample of 346. For those with four or fewer missing items, the two most neutral responses (3, 4) were alternately entered for the missing items, a procedure that added insignificant error to the individuals' total scale scores.

With limited refinements, the items selected to measure each prejudice produced internally consistent scales. One item each from the Prejudice Toward Women and Capitalists scales was eliminated because these items lowered the scales' internal consistencies (coefficient alpha). The summary characteristics of each scale are given in Table 10.1. With the exception of the Prejudice Toward Women scale, each scale had an adequate to strong internal consistency.

Table 10.2 presents all correlations between the attitudes toward the various outgroups. With a median correlation of .53, it is clear that a generalized ethnocentrism strongly influenced the responses to the various scales. Principal components analysis of the eight prejudice scales yielded a single robust ethnocentrism factor that accounted for 60% of the variance. Loadings on this factor ranged from .55 (Prejudice Toward Women) to .86 (Antidemocracy Prejudice).

The Russian version of the RWA scale also proved highly successful. Coefficient alpha for the entire scale was .92. The mean interitem correlation was .27, substantially higher than the .22 reported by Altemeyer (1988a) and McFarland (1989b) for the English-language scale for adult North American samples. A t test comparing the interitem correlations for the Russian and Kentucky samples (McFarland, 1989b) was highly significant, $t = 6.36, p < .001$. All items loaded strongly on a first general factor in both samples. However, the Soviet sample first factor accounted for 31.3% of the total variance, contrasting with 25.9% for the Kentucky sample. The psychometric characteristics of the Russians RWA scale are presented in greater detail in Ageyev, Abalakina, and McFarland (1989). These results suggest that, as expected, authoritarianism was a more unified and robust individual difference construct among Soviets than among Americans and Canadians.

Because the authoritarianism scale had such strong internal consistency, it was possible to develop a convenient 12-item short form of the scale for use by other Soviet investigators. The six positively worded items and the six negatively worded items with the highest loadings on the general

TABLE 10.1 Summary statistics for attitude scales measuring negative attitudes toward eight outgroups.

Prejudice toward	Mean	SD	Item mean	Alpha
Capitalists (9 items)	26.78	8.20	2.97	.83
Jews (15 items)	36.76	11.40	2.43	.88
Women (5 items)	14.94	4.14	2.98	.62
Dissidents (6 items)	14.63	5.25	2.43	.72
Youth (8 items)	21.22	6.05	2.65	.77
Democracy (10 items)	23.26	7.72	2.32	.78
Free press (4 items)	7.97	3.68	1.99	.76
Nationalities (13 items)	31.35	7.94	2.41	.72

TABLE 10.2 Correlations between prejudices toward the eight outgroups.

	Cap	Jews	Wom	Dis	Yth	Dem	Prs	Nat
Capitalism	1.0							
Jews	.53	1.0						
Women	.35	.45	1.0					
Dissidents	.71	.57	.38	1.0				
Youth	.62	.45	.42	.61	1.0			
Democracy	.66	.58	.34	.74	.57	1.0		
Free press	.58	.35	.21	.68	.53	.68	1.0	
Nationalities	.54	.73	.44	.60	.52	.70	.47	1.0

Note: All correlations are significant at .01 or greater.

authoritarianism factor were selected. This shortened form had an alpha of .89, yielded a single factor with a eigenvalue of 5.67, and correlated .95 with the full scale.

Table 10.3 shows that Soviet authoritarianism strongly predicted each prejudice. The median correlation between authoritarianism and the prejudices was .68 for the full scale and .65 for the short form. The best index of each individual's general ethnocentrism is that person's factor score on the first unrotated factor of the prejudice scales. These scores correlated .83 with the full Russian authoritarianism scale and .82 with the short form.

Table 10.4 reports the correlations between authoritarianism and those demographic variables that could be considered as linear variables. Authoritarianism among Russians was positively correlated with age, negatively with the size of hometown of one's youth (those who grew up in the smallest villages were most authoritarian), slightly with sex (women were a little more authoritarian), and negatively with the number of foreign languages the respondents knew. Our expectation that the correlation between age and authoritarianism would be stronger among Russians than Americans in the Kentucky sample was marginally sup-

TABLE 10.3 Zero-order and partial correlations between authoritarianism and each prejudice controlling for all demographic variables.

Prejudice toward	Full scale	Short form
Capitalism	.71 (.65)	.72 (.67)
Jews	.55 (.54)	.56 (.55)
Women	.39 (.34)	.34 (.30)
Dissidents	.71 (.69)	.70 (.67)
Youth	.72 (.65)	.68 (.62)
Democracy	.74 (.72)	.74 (.72)
Free press	.65 (.60)	.63 (.59)
Nationalities	.63 (.62)	.63 (.62)

Note: Partial correlations controlling for demographic variables (sex, age, education, size of childhood home, number of children, languages known, foreign travel, and level of employment) are in parentheses.

TABLE 10.4 Demographic correlates of Russian authoritarianism (full scale and short form).

	All respondents		Men		Women	
	Full	Short	Full	Short	Full	Short
Sex	.11	.12*				
Age	.30**	.26**	.33**	.28**	.28**	.27**
Education (age 24+)	−.23**	−.19*	−.08	−.01	−.40**	−.38**
Income	−.01	−.02	.01	.00	.01	.02
Size of childhood home	−.28**	−.26**	−.38**	−.37**	−.18*	−.15
Number of children (singles excluded)	.22**	.22**	.25*	.25*	.24*	.26*
Number of languages known	−.21**	−.19*	−.19*	−.15*	−.24*	−.26*
Foreign travel	−.05	−.08	.03	.01	−.23*	−.20*

*$p < .01$. **$p < .001$.

ported, $r = .30$ versus $r = .20$, $p < .10$, using r to z transformations. Education was not related to authoritarianism for men but significantly correlated with authoritarianism for women (more educated women were less authoritarian). In contrast, the size of one's childhood home had greater effects upon males' level of authoritarianism. Among those persons who were or had been married, authoritarianism was positively related to the number of children in the family.

Stepwise regressions were used to discover which of these variables contributed unique variance in predicting authoritarianism. Because the

TABLE 10.5 Stepwise regression of the demographic variables predicting authoritarianism.

Variable	Full scale			Short form		
	R	Beta	F (to enter)	R	Beta	F (to enter)
Male sample						
Size of hometown	.38	−.30	<.001	.37	−.33	<.001
Age	.46	.27	<.001	.42	.21	<.001
Languages known	.49	−.17	<.01	.44	—	<.08
Female sample						
Age	.28	.36	<.001	.27	.34	<.001
Education	.42	−.28	<.001	.40	−.27	<.001
Foreign travel	.46	−.18	<.01	.43	−.16	<.01

patterns of correlations were different for the males and females, separate regression analyses were conducted. As Table 10.5 shows, the weighted sum of hometown size, age, and knowledge of foreign languages produced a multiple correlation of .49 with authoritarianism for males. No other variable contributed significant variance. For women, age, education, and the amount of foreign travel each contributed uniquely to authoritarianism, with a multiple correlation of .46.

One-way ANOVAs were used to examine the relations between authoritarianism and the remaining demographic variables. Authoritarianism was not significantly related to marital status or to current residence (Tallinn vs. Moscow). However, Table 10.6 shows that individuals in cultural work, education, and science had the lowest authoritarianism scores; those working in heavy or light industries or in the service sphere had the highest scores. Considering level of work, retired persons had the highest scores, followed by manual workers, with leaders registering the lowest scores.

However, taken together, these demographic variables explained very little of the ethnocentrism–authoritarianism correlations. With all of these variables controlled, the correlation between ethnocentrism and authoritarianism was reduced only from .83 to .80. For the short form, the comparable reduction was from .82 to .75. Table 10.3 shows that the correlations between authoritarianism and each prejudice were also reduced only slightly.

As expected, Table 10.6 also shows that Party members' scores were significantly higher than those of Consomol members or of members of national front or other informal organizations. Although Party members' scores were not high in the absolute sense, the other liberal groups were distinctively low. Also as we expected, the Pamyat members in our sample had the highest mean authoritarianism scores, but because of the very small n they were not included in the one-way ANOVA.

TABLE 10.6 Group means of authoritarianism by area of work, level of work, and organizational membership.

	N	Full scale		Short form	
		Mean	sd	Mean	sd
Area of work					
In heavy or light factories	84	93.67[b]	22.4	33.19[b]	9.3
In the service sphere	59	93.10[b]	19.4	35.07[b]	10.1
In education or science	72	83.60[a]	22.7	29.92[a]	11.3
In cultural work	36	76.79[a]	24.9	26.53[a]	10.9
In party, soviet, or Comsomol work	15	86.67[a]	18.7	30.53[a]	9.4
University students	47	90.53[ab]	17.9	32.91[ab]	8.3
Full scale: $F = 5.138, df = 5, p < .001$.					
Short form: $F = 4.257, df = 5, p < .001$.					
Level of work					
Workers	63	94.14[b]	18.8	34.06[b]	10.3
Students	69	84.77[a]	18.2	30.41[a]	8.9
Specialists	161	87.66[a]	21.9	31.43[a]	11.0
Leaders	35	83.06[a]	16.9	29.23[a]	8.2
Retired persons	11	104.36[b]	23.2	39.27[b]	12.3
Full scale: $F = 4.233, df = 4, p < .002$.					
Short form: $F = 3.150, df = 4, p < .01$.					
Membership in organizations					
Communist party	84	95.31[b]	20.8	34.46[b]	10.9
Comsomol	91	84.58[a]	18.4	30.24[a]	8.6
National Fronts and other informal organizations	29	81.29[a]	20.5	27.52[a]	10.4
Pamyat	2	124.50	19.1	49.50	3.5
Full scale: $F = 8.72, df = 2, p < .001$.					
Short form: $F = 6.877, df = 2, p < .001$.					

Note: Groups that do not share a superscript differ at 0.05 using Duncan's multiple range test.

Although none of the Soviet and Western samples were totally comparable or fully random, the available data indicate that Russians are on average *less* authoritarian than North Americans. The authoritarianism scores ($M = 88.67$, $SD = 20.76$) were virtually identical in Moscow and Tallinn, where both means were between 88 and 89, but were significantly *lower* than that of the Kentucky sample ($M = 118.50$, $SD = 22.34$), $t = 22.30$, $p < .001$. Altemeyer's (1988a) Canadian students' parents' RWA scores "average around 175" (p. 30) on his 9-point scale, which translated to a 6-point scale is approximately 120, very similar to the Kentucky sample and about 31 points higher than both Soviet samples on the Russian version.

The lower levels of Soviet than Western authoritarianism could be dismissed if the translated RWA scale were systematically more stringent, requiring greater authoritarianism in order to receive a high score. However, we are confident of the accuracy and cultural appropriateness of our translations and new items. Although a few items may be inadvertently more stringent or lenient, it is clear to us that the Russian scale is not consistently more stringent, certainly not enough so to account for the magnitude of differences between Russian and North American samples.

Nor were these differences caused by differing demographic characteristics of the samples. The mean ages of the Russian and Kentucky samples did not differ significantly, (34.6 and 36.8 respectively, $t = .62$, ns), nor did the means of other demographics. Further, subgroup comparisons with Kentuckians consistently revealed lower Soviet authoritarianism: Soviets were less authoritarian if they were under 30 ($Ms = 82.2$ vs. 116.1) or over 60 (104.6 vs. 132.9), college educated (87.2 vs. 116.7) or had only finished high school (90.0 vs. 129.7).

A small sample collected in Irkutsk ($N = 112$) took the short-form RWA scale about 5 months after the original study. The comparisons suggest that the low Moscow and Tallinn authoritarianism scores were similar to other regions of the Soviet Union. The mean short-form scores for the Moscow, Tallinn, and Irkutsk samples were 32.0, 31.8, and 28.9, respectively; the Irkutsk sample was significantly *less* authoritarian than the other two groups, $F (1,457) = 3.78$, $p < .02$. Subgroups of the three cities divided by age and education typically did not differ from one another, whether under 30 ($Ms = 30.0$, 28.9, and 27.9, ns) or having completed only a high school education ($Ms = 31.7$, 34.0, and 33.6, ns).

The Soviet–North American differences could have been caused by different sampling procedures. Whereas the Moscow and Tallinn samples were quota samples, the Manitoba and Kentucky samples were more haphazard. Altemeyer (1988a) surveyed his students' parents. In Kentucky, student surveyors were instructed to select equal numbers of male and female adults, and to select respondents who varied in age from 21 through old age and in education from less than high school through advanced degrees. However, volunteers, whose authoritarianism scores are typically lower than nonvolunteers, were used in all samples. We have difficulty envisioning how these differing sample selection processes could have produced differences as great as those between the Soviet and North American samples, particularly because the Kentucky and Soviet samples had comparable demographic characteristics.

A recent student sample ($N = 231$) at Moscow State University (Altemeyer, 1990) also found unusually low authoritarianism scores in comparison to North American student samples. Altemeyer reported that "mean student scores have varied from 148 to 157" (1988a, p. 29). On a separate but strikingly similar Russian translation of the RWA, Moscow students' mean was only 123. Altemeyer commented, "I find the Russian data quite amazing. They are quite low in RWA (only Harvard's compares, among all the samples I have seen from North America so far)" (Altemeyer, personal communication, February 7, 1990).

Still, it may also be that Kentuckians (and Manitobian adults) are higher in authoritarianism than other North Americans. A 1990 Kentucky student sample ($N = 128$) collected by McFarland averaged 165. In short, the array of data suggests that Kentucky students are higher than average in authoritarianism but that both Soviet adults and students are unusually low. Still, without fully random samples, the Soviet–North American differences in authoritarianism must be viewed with caution.

We find it particularly interesting that virtually the same authoritarianism scale that correlates strongly with anticommunism among Western samples correlated strongly with anticapitalist attitudes among the Soviets. Altemeyer (1988a, p. 181) reported a correlation of .55 between the RWA scale and a six-item anticommunism measure. Our Russian version correlated .71 with anticapitalism. However, the inclusion of anticommunist and anticapitalist items in the authoritarianism scales may have exacerbated the strength of these correlations: One item in the RWA refers specifically to communism as an evil, and our substitute item addressed capitalism in the same way. Three other items in our Russian scale condemned threats to socialism. However plausible, this confounding was not responsible for our high correlations. The sum of the remaining 26 items (deleting the four confounding items) correlated .69 with anticapitalism, a drop of only .02. Further, the sum of these 26 items also correlated .69 with the sum of the four deleted items and .83 with general ethnocentrism, and none of the other authoritarianism–prejudice correlations reported in Table 10.3 dropped by more than .02. The relative ranking of groups on authoritarianism reported in Table 10.6 was unchanged when these four items were removed.

We conclude that authoritarianism, in whatever culture it is found, produces strong condemnation of the culturally defined enemies. Authoritarianism in America and Canada leads to an especially strong anticommunism; the same authoritarianism in the Soviet Union led to an especially strong anticapitalism (at least when these data were collected in 1989). The authoritarian personality and its effects, it seems, are not the special property of either the capitalist or communist worlds.

To summarize, our first study showed that the authoritarianism syndrome is alive and well in the Soviet Union. Despite the fact that we used different, sometimes opposite, outgroups than those used in the Western studies, the various prejudices were all significantly intercorrelated and yielded a general ethnocentrism factor. With minimal changes in content, our adaptation and translation of Altemeyer's (1988a) RWA scale had a stronger internal consistency than is now generally found in the West. And as in Western studies, the adapted RWA scale (and the 12-item short form) strongly predicted each particular prejudice and general ethnocentrism.

The demographic correlates of authoritarianism in the Soviet Union were very similar to those found in the West. As in Western studies,

Soviet authoritarianism was positively related to age, occupational status, and to the number of children among married persons, and negatively related to the size of hometown of one's youth and to indices of trans-cultural experience. Education predicted lower authoritarianism only for women in the Russian sample. In the Kentucky sample, education tended to correlate more strongly with authoritarianism among females than males ($-.30$ and $-.18$, respectively), although both correlations were significant and differed only marginally from each other, $p < .10$. In both countries, foreign travel correlated with lower authoritarianism only for women. Finally, Soviet authoritarianism, like its Western form, predicted membership in culturally conservative as opposed to progressive political parties and organizations.

Study II: Personal Experiences Leading to Authoritarianism in the Soviet Union and the United States

Whereas Study I found that education and the other demographic cor-relates of authoritarianism were similar for the former Soviet Union and the West, these correlates accounted for at best less than 25% of the variance in authoritarianism in either country. Further, the correlation between authoritarianism and ethnocentrism was only slightly reduced when these demographic variables were controlled. Clearly, other personal factors or social factors induce and reduce authoritarianism. For a next step, it was reasonable to examine whether the personal ex-periences that induced authoritarianism in the Soviet Union are similar to or different from those in the West.

Method

Across several years, Altemeyer (1988a) refined a measure of self-reported personal experiences that cumulatively are correlated in the low .70s with authoritarianism among college students. His final 24-item Experiences Survey (1988a, pp. 343–349) includes a variety of personal experiences that plausibly could induce authoritarianism, such as acquaintance with and reactions to homosexual persons, unconventional families, abusive authorities, physical punishment, adolescent sexual intercourse, and use of marijuana. The instructions to the scale tell respondents to select "0" for any item if they have had no *personal* experience with the question issue (physical punishment, etc.). If they have had a personal experience, they are asked to rate from -4 to $+4$ whether they agree or disagree with a statement about the impact of the experience (e.g., "It has been my experience that physical punishment is an effective way to make people behave"). The 24 statements are balanced in proauthoritarian and antiauthoritarian directions.

In Study II, we collected comparable Soviet and American data on the correlations between the Experiences Survey and authoritarianism. In May and June 1990, one hundred and sixty-six questionnaires containing the short-form Russian RWA scale and a precise translation of the Experiences Survey were administered by 4th-year Moscow State University psychology students,[2] and 124 questionnaires containing the English RWA scale and the Experiences Survey were administered by upperclass psychology students at Western Kentucky University. The students in both cases were instructed to select approximately equal numbers of male and female adults who were diverse in education, age, and occupation. Because only Moscow residents were used in this study, we refer to this sample as a *Russian* sample rather than as a Soviet sample.

Results

The Experiences Survey and RWA correlated for our American sample .78 (.74 when the 12 items from the Russian short form were summed for a comparable American short form),[3] quite similar to Altemeyer's (1988a) results with college students. However, the comparable correlation for the Russian sample was only .43. However these experiences cause or reinforce authoritarianism among Western college students applies strongly also to Western adults but applied only weakly to Russian adults. The 61% common variance between the two scales for the American sample is more than three times as large as the 18% for the Russian sample.

These differences are largely attributable to the very weak internal consistency of the Experiences Survey for Russian sample (mean interitem correlation = .03, alpha = .39) in contrast to the American sample (mean interitem correlation = .14, alpha = .80). Our American scale characteristics are almost identical to those reported by Altemeyer (1988a). Paradoxically, authoritarianism cohered as a personality construct more strongly among Russians than Americans, but the self-reported experi-

---

[2] N. Zakharova, M. Tokareva, and T. Fedorenko are sincerely thanked for translating the Experiences Survey into Russian, and for printing and administering the questionnaires.

[3] The 12 identical English items contained in the Russian short form correlated .96 with the full English RWA. Because of that high correlation, analyses using a 12-item English short form yield virtually identical results to those attained using the full scale. Because of this near identity, English-language results using the full scale can be properly compared with Russian results using the short form.

ences that cohere strongly and may cause authoritarianism in the West did not cohere at all for our Russian respondents.

Importantly, our Russian sample reported averaging far fewer of the experiences that produce authoritarianism than did the Americans. Across all items, our Russian sample had not had the relevant experiences 28% of the time, whereas the Americans had failed to have such experiences only 18% of the time.

For both samples, having had such experiences generally *decreased* authoritarianism. The number of such experiences a person reported was correlated with authoritarianism $-.46$ for the Russian sample and $-.40$ for the American sample. Although Altemeyer (1988a) did not report this statistic, his analyses of a few individual items showed similar results. Altemeyer's (1988a) conclusion appears valid for both our samples: "A large part of the reason Highs remain Highs is that, through self-selection, self-denial, and self-exclusion, they do not have the range of experiences that could have lowered their authoritarianism" (p. 89).

The form of the Experiences Survey allows separating the impact of *having* the experiences from that of *evaluating* the experiences. Point-biserial correlations of the zero versus nonzero responses with authoritarianism indicate the impact of merely having the relevant experience on authoritarianism. The impact of the evaluation of the experiences on authoritarianism can be judged by correlating the evaluations for each item (-4 to $+4$), with authoritarianism only for those persons who report having had each experience. Across all items, the number of the experiences one had and the evaluation of these experiences were correlated only $-.18$ and $-.24$ for the Russian and American samples, respectively. Altemeyer (1988a) did not separate these two components in this way.

Because *having* the experiences and *evaluating* the experiences are conceptually distinct and almost independent, regression analyses were used to determine the influence of the two components on authoritarianism for each sample. Table 10.7 shows that for the American sample, the evaluation of the experiences and failure to have the such experiences contributed to a multiple R of .81 ($R^2 = .65$). For the Russian sample, both components were also significant, but yielded a multiple R of only .56 ($R^2 = .30$). Education and age further contributed to the prediction of authoritarianism for the Russian sample but not for the Americans.

Although these personal experiences and reactions as a whole are more than twice as predictive of American authoritarianism than they were of Russian authoritarianism, comparisons of the responses of American and Russian to individual items still yielded considerable insight into the different roots of authoritarianism in the two cultures. Table 10.8 first presents the proportion of zero responses for each item. In particular, Russians were far less likely than Americans to report personal experiences with physical punishment (Item 1), homosexuals (Item 3), marijuana (Item 18), rebellious ideas (Item 22), and troublemakers who break the

TABLE 10.7 Final regression equations predicting Russian and American authoritarianism from the number and evaluation of the experiences on the Experiences Survey.

Variable	R	R2	Final beta	Significance (to enter)
Russian sample				
Number of experiences	.46	.22	−.36	<.0001
Evaluation of experiences	.56	.30	.33	<.0001
Education	.57	.32	−.20	<.005
Age	.59	.35	.19	<.02
American sample				
Number of experiences	.78	.63	−.72	<.0001
Evaluation of experiences	.81	.66	.23	<.0001

law (Item 24). On the other hand, the Americans were surprisingly less likely to report experience with egalitarian families (Item 19).

These differences in reported experiences are probably partly real and partly due to differing interpretations of the items by Russians and Americans. Russians in 1990, we are sure, had much less experience with homosexuals, marijuana, analyses of religious beliefs, and rebellious ideas. Lower Russian experiences on several other items (Items 2, 11, 12, and 24) in our view reflect the more limited lines of communication among Russians—Russians simply did not know or communicate with as many different people as do Americans. Although we lack scientific data, our experience suggests that Russians were more likely to communicate mainly with others who are similar to themselves than are Americans. Russians' lower experience with authorities who use their power unjustly (Item 34) and with people with rebellious ideas may reflect an actual greater obedience of Russians, which was one of the most common stereotypes of Russians held by Russians and non-Russians alike.

The fact that fewer Russians had experienced physical punishment or done things their parents warned them against reflect, in our view, a more laissez-faire approach to child rearing among Russians than Americans. Although we again lack supportive data, we suggest that American parents in general try to direct and influence their children in more ways and with clearer sets of family values than do Russian parents. As a result, American parents are more likely both to give warnings and to use physical punishment.

Table 10.8 reports (middle two columns) the point-biserial correlations between having had the particular experiences and authoritarianism for the two samples. For the Russians, 10 of the 24 experiences were significantly correlated with lower authoritarianism; for the Americans, 8 of 24. However, only four of these experiences were related to lower authoritarianism for both groups. Both Americans and Russians who has "met lots of different kinds of people" (Item 11); "broken rules at times" (Item

TABLE 10.8 Percent "no experience" and relations between experiences and authoritarianism for each item.

	No experience		Correlation (no experience–RWA)		Correlation (experience–RWA)	
	Russian	American	Russian	American	Russian	American
1. Physical punishment.	38	11	−.12	−.04	.02	.11
2. Know persons with "poor manners."	22	10	−.14	.03	−.02	.09
3. Know homosexuals.	87	37	−.09	−.26*	−.14	.37**
4. Know people disrespectful toward authority.	16	25	−.32**	−.03	.38**	.49**
5. Know both religious and nonreligious.	21	4	−.01	−.12	−.15	.30**
6. Know families with father as head.	22	14	.08	−.18	−.04	.55**
7. Know persons who had sex in last year of high school.	27	19	−.38**	−.20	.29**	.38**
8. Have not received or accepted parents advice.	25	1	−.36**	−.08	.11	.30**
9. Seen pornography.	17	27	−.15	−.23*	.20	.49**
10. Know young who "take advantage of today's greater freedoms."	31	23	−.42**	.04	.14	.51
11. Know different kinds of people.	18	8	−.25**	−.17	.20	.48**
12. Have broken rules.	13	3	−.31**	−.23*	.18	.28**
13. Studied rebellions, engaged in protests, know those who have engaged in protests.	31	24	−.20	−.31**	.22*	.22
14. Know someone who has fallen away from family traditions.	19	23	−.10	−.20	.11	.60**
15. Have done things parents warned against.	16	5	−.34**	.02	.03	.35
16. Know people with rebellious or sharply critical outlook.	16	17	−.38**	−.07	.27**	.49**
17. All authorities have "treated me honestly."	6	1	−.18	.04	.29**	.33**
18. Know those who smoke marijuana.	67	32	−.14	−.19	.11	.34*
19. Know nontraditional families where all are more equal than usual.	30	49	−.16	−.38**	−.20	.21

TABLE 10.8 *Continued*

	No experience		Correlation (no experience–RWA)		Correlation (experience–RWA)	
	Russian	American	Russian	American	Russian	American
20. Know people who are unconventional.	16	21	−.28**	−.23*	.29**	.16
21. Thought critically about traditional religious beliefs.	31	20	−.14	−.26*	−.14	.37**
22. Had rebellious ideas earlier in life.	49	16	−.28**	−.10	.18	.53**
23. Witnessed authorities use power unjustly.	34	19	−.11	−.27*	−.05	.06
24. Know troublemakers or those who break law.	28	16	−.09	−.04	.33**	.57**

*p < .05 **p < .01.

12); "studied rebellions in history, engaged in protests yourself, or know others who did" (Item 13); or have "done unconventional things or known people who are unconventional" (Item 20) were less authoritarian than those who had not. Americans who "know homosexuals" (Item 3), have "encountered material that might be considered pornographic" (Item 9), know "nontraditional families" (Item 19), have "thought critically about traditional religious beliefs" (Item 21) or have "seen times when authorities used their power unjustly or excessively..." (Item 23) are less authoritarian than those who have not had such experiences, but these experiences were not significantly related to authoritarianism for Russians. On the other hand, Russians who knew people "disrespectful toward authority and unpatriotic" (Item 4), who engaged in sexual intercourse by their last year of high school (Item 7), who did not receive or listen to parental instruction (Item 8), who knew "young people who have taken advantage of today's greater freedom" (Item 10), had done things that their parents warned them against (Item 15), knew people with a rebellious or sharply critical outlook on life (Item 16), or who "have had rebellious ideas" themselves (Item 23) were less authoritarian than Russians who had not had these experiences, but these experiences did not predict authoritarianism for Americans.

The last two columns of Table 10.8 show that, in general, whether Americans evaluated these experiences in an authoritarian or nonauthoritarian manner strongly influenced their authoritarianism, since 18 of the 24 correlations were significant. However, the manner in which Russians evaluated these experiences were far less likely to influence their authoritarianism; only 8 of the 24 correlations were significant.

Seven of the eight evaluations that influenced the Russians' authoritarianism were common also to Americans: Both Russians and Americans were less authoritarian to the extent that their experiences indicated that those who are disrespectful are not ignorant troublemakers (Item 4), sexual intercourse is alright in the last year of high school (Item 7), pornography is harmless (Item 9), protest and rebellion may be necessary to end injustice (Item 13), persons with rebellious or sharply critical ideas are impressive (Item 16), authorities have not always been honest (Item 17), and "cracking down" is not the best way to handle troublemakers (Item 24). Russian evaluations that it's better to be unconventional than to be normal (Item 20) led to lower authoritarianism, whereas American evaluations of that experience did not.

Still, 10 of the American evaluations of the experiences that predicted authoritarianism had no such effect on the Russians: Americans were less authoritarian to the extent that their experiences indicated that homosexuals are generally normal—a rare experience for Russians (Item 3), decency is not related to religion (Item 5), egalitarian families are better than those headed by fathers (Item 6), their parents were not always right (Item 8), young people who take advantage of their freedoms *don't* usually mess up their lives (Item 10), no one group has all "the truth" or the "one right way to live," (Item 11), breaking rules can be exciting or fun at times (Item 12), life is not meaningless without family religion or tradition (Item 14), violating parents' warnings was not a mistake (Item 15), earlier rebellious ideas were not foolish (Item 22), and authorities have used their power unjustly (Item 23); but these comparable experiences had no effects on Russian authoritarianism.

This long array of differences can simply be summarized as follows: For Americans, experiences with unconventional sexual practices (homosexuality and pornography), witnessing unjust authorities, and thinking critically about religion and traditions led to lower authoritarianism. For Russians, experiences with political rebellion and rebellion against parents were more critical. For both Russians and Americans, positive attitudes toward sexual liberty and political protest led to lower authoritarianism. For Americans only, critical judgments about religion and positive evaluations of nonauthoritarian families led to lower authoritarianism. And all of these factors predicted authoritarianism more strongly for Americans than for Russians.

Clearly, experiences and reactions that strongly induce authoritarianism in America generally had much weaker influences on Russian authoritarianism. The specific Russian experiences that strongly induced authoritarianism in that culture are not known.

General Discussion

It seemed plausible that the population of the Soviet Union, with its long history of authoritarian politics, would have higher levels of the authoritarian personality than found in democratic North America, but our

Study I results suggest the Soviet levels were in fact lower. Although this result must be interpreted with caution, neither the demographic characteristics of the samples, regional variations within the Soviet Union and North America, nor the sampling procedures appear adequate as explanations. Yet at the least, our simplistic assumption that more authoritarian political systems inculcate higher levels of the authoritarian personality appears simply wrong.

Assuming that the lower Soviet authoritarianism was real, we have no firm explanation for it. We tentatively suggest three possibilities. First, "democratization" was the new social ideal in the Soviet Union, championed by Gorbachev and even more vigorously by populist leaders such as Boris Yeltsin. The popularly elected Congress of People's Deputies held its first session, which was nationally televised and broadcast, just as the data for our first study were being collected. The lower authoritarianism scores may simply have expressed conformity to this new, vigorously pursued political norm. For example, one RWA item reads, "It is best to treat dissenters with leniency and an open mind, since new ideas are the lifeblood of progressive change." Prior to glasnost, the political authorities did not support this idea; in 1989 they virtually championed it. Previously, authoritarian conformity would lead one to disagree with this item; in 1989, a political conformist may have agreed with it. We can discern, post hoc, that conforming to the social norm in 1989 would require less authoritarian responses to many RWA items than would have been required prior to glasnost. If this reasoning is correct, the lower Soviet authoritarianism scores may actually represent an authoritarian conformity to the new social norm. If so, the lower Soviet authoritarianism scores were, in reality, an artifact of the vigorous new (in 1989) political norms in the Soviet Union, and could even be due to a *greater* authoritarian conformity in Soviet society. This post hoc reasoning is clearly circuitous, but our long knowledge of Soviet culture suggests its plausibility.

Second, we suggest that for Soviet society it may be possible to draw a distinction between the authoritarian personality and "totalitarian political thought." Although political totalitarianism did not make Soviets higher than Westerners on the authoritarian personality, it may have made Soviet political thinking more "totalitarian" in our sense. As we mean it, totalitarian political thought includes the assumption that a great leader is needed to solve our problems, as opposed to the belief that there are many persons in the society capable of political leadership, or that problems can be solved by parliamentary means. However, this totalitarian thinking may not assume, unlike most of the RWA items, that this leader must be punitive or repressive. He or she is merely rare or unique. In addition, totalitarian political thought assumes that there is a "right" solution to political and social problems that all clear-minded persons can recognize and accept rather than a plethora of partial and imperfect ones, and it assumes that government properly has the power to bring these solutions into reality. As a corollary, when government does not see the right solution and act on it, revolution is needed. Until very recently, Soviet political thought embodied this tradition. Again, this right solution may not be punitive or repressive in the authoritarian sense, but its validity is nonetheless unambiguous, and its application to society requires only proper decisions and the power and will to implement them. We suggest that this mode of thought is not identical to the authoritarian personality, may still be quite strong in the former Soviet Union, and may change only slowly with the long experience of democracy.

Finally, it may be that Soviets were simply lower in authoritarianism than North Americans. The democratic revolutions throughout Eastern Europe in 1989 showed that decades of political authoritarianism did not destroy the longing for freedom. Perhaps the lower authoritarianism scores among Soviets expressed their rejection of their own history of political authoritarianism.

Our results from Study II suggest that the Soviet totalitarian political system may have actually subverted the authoritarian family structures that induce authoritarianism in the West, thereby producing lower personal authoritarianism. Soviet political totalitarianism removed from parents their Western role as the primary source of values and beliefs for children. Living under such a system, some true-believing and compliant parents reinforced the totalitarian values. A few brave ones, at considerable risk, tried to instill alternative values in their children. However, under such a system many parents—likely, the majority—neither internalized the system's values nor were able to profess alternative ones. As a result, they adopted the safe laissez-faire, value-free approach to child rearing we noted earlier. By its own totalitarianism, the Soviet political system thus undermined the authoritarian family dynamics that promote personal authoritarianism in the West.

This study of Soviet authoritarianism enlightens both right-wing authoritarianism and "left-wing authoritarianism." Right-wing authoritarians in both countries have championed the conventional political norms, rejected all outgroups and displayed general ethnocentrism, and have been drawn toward reactionary and conventional political groups. If left-wingers are defined as communists and their fellow travelers, left-wingers in the West are low in authoritarianism, whereas those in the Soviet Union were high. On the other hand, if left-wingers are simply those who reject the conventional political norms and champion nonconventional ones, in both North America and the Soviet Union left-wingers have been low in authoritarianism. In both cultures, however, authoritarianism has been nondemocratic in the sense that authoritarian persons have been more prone to censure dissent and deny to outgroups full participation in the society.

The terms *left-wing* and *right-wing* must be applied cautiously, particularly when referring to the Soviet situation. As Stone (1980) has argued, the psychological dynamics of the Western far left may be quite different from that of right-wing authoritarians. Still, Russian political history appears to support the view that Russian prerevolutionary left-wing extremists had many similarities to right-wing authoritarians. Dostoyevsky's *The Possessed* (1914) described the hate, violent prejudices, and authoritarian obedience to the revolutionary party among the Russian revolutionaries in the late 19th century. Far-left political movements in Russian history, as perhaps elsewhere, often proclaimed a fight for freedom that disguised a struggle for power.

The Soviet communists became the political right almost as quickly as they achieved power. Communists in North America, who are small minorities and distinctly unpopular, may be left-wing and quite different psychologically from their right-wing counterparts, yet the Soviet case would lead us to expect that they might quickly display right-wing characteristics if they suddenly found themselves with total political power. In the Soviet Union, the postrevolutionary communist authorities immediately established a strict social stratification and very strong barriers between themselves and the general public, even though their program had proclaimed social equality. As Orwell (1946) proclaimed, alluding to this Soviet stratification, "All animals are equal, but some animals are more equal than others" (p. 148). The Party leaders created a structure of special privileges for themselves in almost every area, including access to housing, recreation, health care, food, consumer goods, and even information. They quickly impeded the free flow of these to the general public. As the 1990 Party Congress showed, many communists continued to oppose relinquishing any real power to the popularly elected Soviet bodies and still struggled to retain control over the real vehicles of power such as the press, the military, and the KGB. The Soviet people generally perceived their proclamations of socialism and of concern for the people as hypocrisy, as last-ditch efforts to retain power and privilege.

As our scale results show, Soviet communists clearly held the attitudes of right-wing authoritarians, not their opposite. The true left-wingers in the late Soviet Union were those who championed causes typically championed by the political right in the West: a free-market economy and economic liberty. The political left in the Soviet Union, rather than in the West, combined the struggle for these freedoms with the traditional struggles of the Western political left for human rights and against all forms of totalitarianism. It is not surprising to us that the true "right wing" in the Soviet Union in its last days included the communists, the Russian nationalists, and those with fascist beliefs—groups who are traditionally enemies. In 1990, these groups in fact joined forces in opposition to the democratic transformation of the Soviet Union. These groups were all authoritarian and antidemocratic.

The lower experience–authoritarianism correlations among Russians found in Study II can be fully understood only by referring to another general cultural difference between the Soviet Union and the West. We suggest a new theory, which we shall call Mentality–Experience Split Theory (MEST). In our view, Soviet culture and society created an isolation of experience and behavior, on the one hand, from thought, on the other. This separation has been deeper than found in the West. (Mikheyev, 1987, presents a similar analysis of the split between the private and public spheres in Soviet life.) We believe that lower experience–authoritarianism correlations among Russians in our study merely illustrated this phenomenon and that this split probably could have been replicated in many domains. For our immediate issue, we suggest that any scale of self-reported experiences would have correlated modestly at best with authoritarianism. Although the world of experience and behavior (combined under the term *activity* in Soviet psychology; see Kozulin, 1986) and that of thought may each have its own inner consistency, these worlds have been generally separate and isolated from mutual influence. In the Soviet Union, thought was less shaped by experience, and activity by thought, than has occurred in the West.

This split was neither mere political conformity nor the "double thinking" described so brilliantly in *1984* (Orwell, 1948). It has deep roots in the Russian tradition, long predating the Soviet period. Pushkin's (1964) *Eugene Onegin* and Lermontov's (1966) Petchorin in *A Hero of Our Time* illustrate the "lost personality," a central figure in 19th-century Russian literature. These characters, like many others, harbored profound thoughts and felt intense responsibilities but were utterly passive. They were unable to turn their thought and will into constructive activity, to apply their inner spirituality to useful ends, or to act on their intentions.

The split described by Pushkin and Lermontov was no doubt accentuated by the enormous ideological pressure and political control of the Soviet period. The split has been expressed in many ways. Soviets in our experience have developed the characteristic of more prolonged, difficult, and hesitant decision making than do Westerners, as well as longer delays between decision and action. Their intentions and activities have been often contradictory.

This split in the recent past was sometimes overcome by fully accepting communist ideology and practice. But in this case the division between thought and action was annihilated by conformity, loyalty to power, depersonification, and the loss of individuality. This is the path that led to the creation of the "New Soviet Man" or, as he was pejoratively called, "Homo Sovieticus."

Understanding the Soviet separation of thought from behavior and experience is probably essential for fully understanding our Study II data. We were not surprised by the low correlations. It is our view, based on our long experiences with Soviet culture, that authoritarian attitudes belonged to the mental realm and that personal experiences of both authoritarian and nonauthoritarian types belonged to the separate realm of activity. Because these were separate realities, personal experiences in the behavioral sphere have had little influence on the sphere of authoritarian attitudes. For Americans, by contrast, the split between experience and thought is not so deep, and the stronger correlations between the experiences and authoritarianism are a natural result.

General Conclusions

The study of Russian authoritarianism began just as the Soviet period was ending. Despite the similar demographic antecedents of authoritarianism in the Soviet Union and North America, each political system has contributed to the development of authoritarianism in unique ways that are as yet only partially understood.

Parallel scales are now available for continuing to study authoritarianism in Russia and in English-speaking countries. The development of the parallel Russian-language scale is our main methodological contribution.

The substantive contributions of our studies may be summarized as follows: First, ethnocentrism and the authoritarian personality were found to be valid individual difference constructs in the Soviet Union, as they are in the West. In 1989, in fact, authoritarianism was more internally consistent in the Soviet Union than in North America, perhaps due to the great political upheaval in the Soviet Union at that time. Second, we have shown that Soviet ethnocentrism, like its Western counterpart, was strongly rooted in the authoritarian personality. As in the West, authoritarian ethnocentrism included all culturally condemned outgroups. Just as Western authoritarians are hostile toward communists, Soviet authoritarians expressed hostility toward capitalists. Third, the demographic correlates of authoritarianism and the political allegiances that follow from it are strikingly similar across East and West. Yet fourth, the personal experiences that appear to produce authoritarianism in the West had far less influence on authoritarianism in the Soviet Union. Surprisingly, we have found that, for whatever reason, Soviets were seemingly less authoritarian than are North Americans.

At a theoretical level, we have proposed a Mentality–Experience Split Theory (MEST), suggesting that the low correlations between personal experiences and authoritarianism in the Soviet Union were due largely to the generally greater separation of experience and mentality in the Soviet Union than in the West: Experience had less influence upon thought, and thought has less upon activity, in the Soviet Union than in the West.

At a practical level, we admit that our goal was political as well as scientific. The great political conflict in the Soviet Union in 1989–91 was mainly between authoritarian and democratic forces, and we were deeply concerned about the outcome of that conflict. We feared the totalitarianism could return to the Soviet Union and bring with it a full array of horrifying results—as almost occurred in the August 1991 coup. We hoped that introducing the concepts of authoritarianism and ethnocentrism as working constructs in Soviet social science and demonstrating their relevance could advance the democratization of Soviet society. Public understanding of these constructs can still help in preventing a return to more authoritarian policies.

Acknowledgements. This research was financed by the Soviet Academy of Sciences as a portion of a grant to Vladimir Ageyev entitled "The Soviet Man as the Subject of International Relations: New Political Thinking in 'People's Diplomacy' and International Contacts" and by a Western Kentucky University Faculty Research Grant to Sam McFarland. A special indebtedness is owed to the late Heino Liimets, head of the Department of Pedagogy and Psychology, Tallinn Pedagogical Institute, whose invitation to McFarland to spend a semester there as a Fulbright Senior Lecturer made this work possible.

Part IV
Conclusions

11
The Status of Authoritarianism

WILLIAM F. STONE, GERDA LEDERER, AND RICHARD CHRISTIE

In a book that seemed fantastic at the time, Sinclair Lewis (1935) laid out a possible scenario whereby the United States became a fascist dictatorship. In *It Can't Happen Here*, Lewis described the complacency with which the citizens of the United States of America allowed their freedoms to be taken from them. Fear of the appeals of fascism spurred the efforts of the authors of *The Authoritarian Personality* (Adorno, Frenkel-Brunswik, Levinson, & Sanford, 1950) as it has the efforts of the author of *Enemies of Freedom* (Altemeyer, 1988a). Their theses were that personality is an important element in the rise of fascism. Investigation of the connection between authoritarianism and destructive obedience remains a central concern of our effort.

The present work has attempted to assay the current state of research and theory, 40 years after the publication of *The Authoritarian Personality* (*TAP*). This has not been a simple task, for many reasons. In the first place, in 1950 everyone began talking about *authoritarianism*, whereas during the research process the focus had been on the makeup of the prefascist personality. In fact, authoritarianism was conceived as one of several variables that made up this personality:

Consideration of E-scale results strongly suggested that underlying several of the prejudiced responses was a general disposition to glorify, to be subservient to and remain uncritical toward authoritative figures of the ingroup and to take an attitude of punishing outgroup figures in the name of some moral authority. Hence *authoritarianism* assumed the proportions of a variable worthy to be investigated in its own right . . . a number of such variables were derived and defined, and they, taken together, made up the basic content of the F scale. (Adorno, et al., 1950, p. 228)

Late in the day, it was decided to name the book based on this research *The Authoritarian Personality*. But for this decision, authoritarianism would have a different meaning today. The concept, almost an afterthought, has been *reified* by some observers and derogated as useless by others. We have tried to take a balanced view of the topic. Nevertheless, it is not an easy task to separate the wheat from the chaff in this area. We begin our assessment with some theoretical considerations and will cite the retrospective views of one of the authors of *TAP*, Nevitt Sanford (1973).

Personality and Ideology

To study authoritarianism is to investigate relationships between personality and ideology. The basic hypothesis underlying this research is that an authoritarian personality predisposes one to accept or be attracted to fascist ideology. *TAP*'s working definition of authoritarianism seems to have been that of a personality syndrome that closely predicts anti-Semitism. The authors also gave a more theoretical definition of the authoritarian based on psychoanalytic theory. This view saw the authoritarian as a person who is dependent on parental and other authority by virtue of inadequate ego strength and the consequent use of various defense mechanisms to deal with hostile and sexual impulses. The simplified approach of Altemeyer (1981, 1988a) defines authoritarian personality as a set of closely interrelated attitudes (conventional, aggressive, submissive) that *could* be taken to reflect the underlying dynamics suggested by *TAP*.

The specification of fascist ideology presents more problems, because social psychologists, adept at dealing with attitudes toward specific issues, objects, or groups, have little understanding of ideologies, which are complex group-level phenomena. As Billig (1984) suggests, " 'ideology' refers to patterns or *gestalts* of attitudes, and as such embraces a number of topics which are usually separated in social psychological analyses." Various authors have pointed out that ideologies are shared ways of conceptualizing reality; in Mannheim's (1960) phrase, ideology is "the whole outlook of a social group" which combines the experiences of individuals: "Every individual participates only in fragments of the thought system, the totality of which is not in the least a mere sum of these fragmentary individual experiences" (Mannheim, 1960, cited by Billig, 1984, p. 446). We will return to this problem of relating authoritarian personality to fascist ideology.

The Meaning of Authoritarianism

One could argue that the investigation that led to *The Authoritarian Personality* was "theory driven," in that the investigators were generally psychoanalytically oriented and were interested in investigating fairly general hypotheses about the relationship of personality to prejudice.

Following publication of the 1950 report, however, critics focused not on the concept of authoritarianism that emerged from the study but on one measure, one "operational definition," if you will, of authoritarianism: The F scale. Nevitt Sanford (1973) suggested that the intense focus on this one scale was a symptom of the general positivist emphasis in psychology that resulted in research funding priorities that placed "a virtual ban . . . on comprehensive inquiries into personality" (p. 163). Thus, most of the 2,000 studies found by Meloen (1983) were of a one-shot nature rather than parts of comprehensive research approaches.

Ironically, Sanford's (1973) complaint reflects the perceived success of the F scale in capturing the essence of the prefascist personality. If authoritarianism can be measured by summing one's agreement or disagreement with 30 F-scale items in a questionnaire that can be answered within a few minutes (a procedure that can assess hosts of individuals if a group administration is used), it is clearly more time and labor efficient than undertaking a depth interview for each and every respondent, in conjunction with giving and laboriously analyzing batteries of clinical instruments. Most of the research reported in this book has used the F scale or variants thereof, with the exception of Hopf's chapter (chap. 6), which espouses an updated psychodynamic approach and advocates more clinically-oriented research.

What can we say about the efficacy of the original F scale as a measure of authoritarianism almost half a century after its construction? Sanford (1973) commented that Max Horkheimer's reference to "a new 'anthropological' species" should be interpreted to mean that we cannot understand authoritarian personalities from the standpoint of an altogether different historical era. Many of the statements that made up the F scale have entirely different meanings today; the anti-intellectualism expressed by authoritarians of the 1940s is not that expressed by contemporary college students:

There is little interest among these students [of the early 1970s] in the old issue of the things of the mind versus the practical, and recourse to authority of some kind as the source of truth and knowledge seems to have been replaced by recourse to feeling and intuition. (Sanford, 1973, p. 165)

The point, says Sanford, is that "personality itself—not just issues and ways of regarding them—changes with the times" (p. 165). The authoritarian described in the pages of *TAP* "now seems a bit quaint" (p. 165). Sanford illustrated by pointing out that the type of hysteric patient treated by Freud in 1900 was rare by the 1930s.

The rightist authoritarian we studied in the 1940s participated in and was shaped by, even as he helped to shape, the life of his times; and we should expect the same of political man today. . . . Personality structures, even "deep" or "central" ones, are sustained by the social system in which the individual lives and can change when the system changes. (p. 166)

This message is well illustrated by McFarland, Ageyev, and Abalakina's (chap. 10, this volume) finding that the most authoritarian people in Russia today are the most dedicated communists.

The F Scale in Perspective

Given the foregoing comments about social and historical change in attitudes and personality, we must ask the following question: Despite the findings cited by Meloen (chap. 3, this volume), many of which were made years ago, does the F scale have any useful purpose today?

The F scale was designed to do two things: first, it was intended as a means of quantifying the fascist potential in order to estimate its strength in various groups of subjects; second, it was to provide an indirect measure of anti-Semitism (and, later, ethnocentrism) without specifically mentioning minority groups. Hyman and Sheatsley (1954) raised questions about the latter procedure, because using scores on various versions of the Ethnocentrism scale as one criterion for the retention of F-scale items might artificially enhance the reported correlations between the F and E scales. However, as the research progressed, *TAP*'s investigators increasingly employed internal consistency as the criterion for selecting items. Thus, those items were retained on the later versions of the F scale that best discriminated between the subjects in the top and bottom quartiles of the total score distribution.

Although the F scale is often referred to as a *personality* scale it differs from most scales of that genre in that the F-scale items were written in the third person and many of them had ideological content. For example, contrast the item

What the youth needs most is strict discipline, rugged determination, and the will to fight for family and country[1]

with the Minnesota Multi-Phasic Personality Inventory item

I often have sweaty palms.

The authors of *TAP* identified nine a priori clusters of items as a theoretical guide in constructing the F scale. The clusters and the number of items in each (some items appear in two or more clusters, so the total exceeds 30) are as follows: Conventionality (4), Authoritarian Submission (7), Authoritarian Aggression (6), Anti-Intraception (4), Superstition and Stereotypy (6), Power and Toughness (7), Destructiveness and Cynicism (3), Projectivity (5), and Sex (3). One Destructiveness and Cynicism item (Item 28, *TAP*, p. 238),

---

[1] All F-scale items cited in this chapter are from Form 40/45 (the final version), found on pp. 255–257 of *TAP* (Adorno et al., 1950).

America is getting so far from the true American way of life that force may be necessary to restore it

was inadvertantly omitted from the table on pp. 255–257 of *TAP*.

Evaluation of the relative discriminatory power of items falling in the clusters is complicated for the following reasons:

1. The use of a score summed over responses to all items means that the total score is more influenced by items falling in the most heavily represented clusters (e.g., the eight Authoritarian Aggression items contribute more to the total score than do the two measuring Destructiveness and Cynicism).
2. Because some items are assigned to more than one category it is difficult to separate the influence of membership in one cluster from membership in the other in evaluation.
3. Some of the items were assigned to clusters without a clear rationale; it requires a bit of empathetic intuition with the authors to understand why individual items were classified as they were.
4. In reexamining the F-scale items written in the mid-1940s, it is apparent that some of them are clearly outdated, for example, Item 22 (classified under Power and Toughness):

It is best to use some prewar authorities in Germany to keep order and prevent chaos.

An item whose interpretation has changed over time is Item 31,

Nowadays more and more people are prying into matters that should remain personal and private

which was classified as measuring Projectivity and Anti-Intraception in 1945 and ranked 12th in discriminatory power. However, less than a decade later, during the heyday of McCarthyism, it was found that in at least some samples of college students the item discriminated negatively (i.e., the lowest scorers on the F scale were more likely to agree than the high scorers on the total scale). One interpretation is that what seemed semiparanoid in middle-class samples in one decade was perceived as social reality in the next. Today, computer technology has given this item added relevance.

One thing *is* clear in examining the items in the final reported version of the F scale (Form 40/45, *TAP*, pp. 255–257, and Table 9, p. 260). The *three most discriminating items* were ones in the Authoritarian Aggression cluster. One of these (Item 25) was classified as tapping Sex as well:

Sex crimes, such as rape and attacks on children, deserve more than mere imprisonment; such criminals ought to be publicly whipped, or worse.

Another (Item 13),

What youth needs most is strict discipline, rugged determination, and the will to work and fight for family and country.

was also seen as measuring Power and Toughness. Among the top 15 in discriminatory power, 4 other items also belonged to the hypothesized Authoritarian Aggression cluster. Only 4 of the 7 Authoritarian Submission items also appeared in the top 15, as do 2 of the 3 Sex items. (Item 25, above, also measured Authoritarian Aggression.)

It should come as no surprise that the authors of *TAP* (Adorno et al., 1950) reported that "the items in any one cluster correlate with one another no better than they do with numerous items from other clusters. We are justified in using these clusters, therefore, only as *a priori* aids to discussion" (p. 262). This statement is based upon results obtained on a sample of 517 women students, which was not used for the item analyses of Form 40/45. Only two groups of college students were among the 17 samples of convenience (1,569 respondents) used for the item analysis (*TAP*, Table 10, VII, p. 263).

Validity of the F Scale

Mantell's (1972) study of Green Berets and conscientious objectors during the Vietnam War (see also chapter 6, this volume) is just one example of a study offering support for the validity of the F scale. Combining in-depth interviews with the results obtained with several measures of authoritarianism, Mantell found impressive differences between the groups in the direction predicted by *TAP*. Despite the criticisms of the F scale and the acceptance of Altemeyer's (1988) RWA scale as a replacement, there is considerable evidence of the F scale's validity as a measure of authoritarianism. The RWA scale has stimulated research by narrowing the focus to authoritarian submission, aggression, and conventionality, but at the cost of abandoning the still fertile theoretical framework of *TAP*. There *is* need for a formalization of *TAP* theory and a broader comparison of the authoritarian personality à la *TAP* with Altemeyer's right-wing autoritarian, since Altemeyer's prolific research is methodologically homogeneous. Meloen's (chap. 3, this volume) survey of the massive literature on the F scale, particularly the work on known groups, provides strong support for the descriptive aspects of authoritarian personality theory.

The discriminatory power of F-scale items initially classified as measuring Authoritarian Aggression is supported by the only known study contrasting hard-core Nazis—a sample of former members of the elite Waffen SS—with one of veterans of the German Wehrmacht (regular armed forces) (Steiner & Fahrenberg, 1970a,b). Their scores, based on 21 items selected from the various versions of the F scale, indicated that there were significant differences ($p < .01$). Of nine items that had been classified by *TAP* in the Authoritarian Aggression cluster or the Power and Toughness cluster, all differentiated the groups at the $p < .01$ level of significance. In each case, the SS veterans agreed more strongly with the authoritarian statement. (Both were fairly high F, of course: $M = 5.23$ ($n = 229$) for the SS, $M = 4.52$ ($n = 201$) for the Wehrmacht.) Differences on only three other items reached the $p < .01$ level of significance: one Submission item (of three so classified), one of three Destructiveness and Cynicism items, and one of three items from the Projectivity cluster. Anti-Intraception fared particularly badly; only one item of five discriminated Waffen from Wehrmacht veterans, and that item was cross-classified in the Authoritarian Aggression cluster.

It should be emphasized that various considerations, including those of political sensitivity, played a role in Steiner and Fahrenberg's (1970b) selection of items to be administered to samples of survivors of military service in World War II. The Waffen SS sample was obtained through the cooperation of a former colonel in the organization, and its members were forbidden under German law from belonging to any formal association of veterans. If this did not create enough of a sampling problem, the fact that SS storm troopers had an extremely high casualty rate in combat means—other things being equal—that it is hazardous to make any post hoc generalizations about the level of differences that might have been found if some German psychologist had invented the equivalent of the F scale and administered it to representative samples of the two organizations during World War II.

Caveats aside, we regard Steiner and Fahrenberg's (1970a,b) findings as striking confirmation of *TAP*, given that the scale developed to measure "pre-Fascist" ideology (based on California students and a miscellany of available adult groups) clearly differentiated the surviving members of the Wehrmacht from the hard-core fascists of the Waffen SS, some 20 years after World War II.

The ratio of discriminating to nondiscriminating items in the F scale appears to be highest among those measuring Authoritarian Aggression, the two Sex items that tap it in combination with Authoritarian Submission, and Authoritarian Submission. The depth-psychological items such as Projectivity and Anti-Intraception have not fared as well. Rereading them, almost half a century after they were written, suggests two possiblities: (a) Their wording was too much in the 1940s idiom, or more crucially, (b) it is harder to word items that capture the essence of the hypothetical psychoanalytic mechanisms.

There is a further point which relates to the a priori assignment of items to hypothetical clusters. The F scale has been given to untold thousands of samples and resulted in the publication of hundreds of articles, some of which reported factor analyses of the F scale. Most such analyses violated currently recommended procedures. For example, the number of items per subject ratio considered acceptable for factor analysis has often been ignored; relevant data on the samples tested have often not been reported. Unrepresentative samples of college students have been employed. Given these caveats, it is not surprising that no known report has produced factors or clusters that fit the hypothetical clusters suggested in *TAP*.

When one looks at the *content* of the items that have emerged with the highest loadings on the one or two main factors from the factor analytic studies, two major classifications of discriminating items emerge. The first deals with aggression and sex, e.g., the *sex crimes* item (Item 25) previously cited. A second grouping that has also emerged strongly, and sometimes overlaps with the first, has to do with the constellation of items revolving around youth (e.g., Item 1):

Obedience and respect for authority are the most important virtues children should learn.

This item was initially classified as fitting under the rubrics of Conventionalism and Authoritarian Submission.

The Reinvigoration of Authoritarianism Research

Renewed interest in authoritarianism has been stimulated by world events: There has been a resurgence of fascism during the decades of the 1970s and 80s—in the Netherlands, in Great Britain, and in the two reunited parts of Germany—and the question of authoritarianism in the former Eastern block nations. In the forefront of the current renewal of research interest is the work of Bob Altemeyer (1981, 1988a) of the University of Manitoba. His books represent a comprehensive research program—they report 20 years of systematic study that has drawn a considerable amount of favorable review. Other investigators, such as John Ray (1976, 1988a, 1988b) have published prolifically but have failed to stimulate much interest. Perhaps Altemeyer's fame results from the care with which he secures his conclusions: His first publication on authoritarianism summarized more than 10 years of systematic research and thinking. Altemeyer's thoughtful approach resulted in the development of a widely acclaimed balanced scale, the Right-Wing Authoritarianism (RWA) scale (1981, 1988a). Together with this scale, a parsimonious theory has developed that includes just three variables as defining authoritarianism. Thus, the RWA scale, rather than the F scale, has become the new lightning rod for criticism and discussion, and an impetus to further research.

Some Comments on the RWA Scale

Interest in the measurement and reinterpretation of authoritarianism and its social psychological concomitants has been spurred by Altemeyer's approach to the problem of authoritarianism, from a learning perspective rather than a psychodynamic one. Altemeyer was committed to psychometric purity in obtaining a measure of right-wing authoritarianism (RWA) designed to have the highest possible reliability while counterbalanced to control for response set—the methodological bugaboo that led to the credibility crisis with the original F scale in the 1950s. For an account of the way Altemeyer's research fit into and took off from earlier studies, see Christie (1991).

In the laborious process of revising and rewriting items from the F scale, and others correlated with it, Altemeyer (1981) found that items originally classified under the hypothetical rubrics of Authoritarian Aggression, Authoritarian Submission, and Conventionality survived his rigorous criteria in repeated revisions of both the protrait (worded in the authoritarian direction) and contrait (worded in the antiauthoritarian direction) items.

It is interesting to compare original F-scale items with those developed by Altemeyer for the RWA scale. (The RWA items discussed are from the 1982 version of the RWA scale, Altemeyer, 1988, pp. 22–23.) For example, the classic F-scale statement about *obedience* (Item 1, cited above) appears as Item 12 of the RWA scale. Another identical item is numbered 21 on the F scale and 19 on the RWA scale:

Young people sometimes get rebellious ideas, but as they grow up they ought to get over them and settle down.

As mentioned above, Altemeyer balanced the RWA scale with contrait items. He added new items and revised F scale items to simplify complex thoughts in the interest of eliminating double-barreled (ambiguous) items that were prevalent in the F scale. To gain internal consistency, he eliminated the theoretically significant but psychometrically poor items that dealt with projectivity and obsessive concern with sex. There are items concerned with sex, but they are straightforward approve-or-disapprove statements like the following contrait item (RWA Item 10):

There is nothing immoral or sick in somebody's being a homosexual.

In addition to simplification and balancing, Altemeyer's (1981, 1988a) RWA scale dispensed with ideas that seem irrelevant to modern ideology. It seems an important task to explore historical changes of meaning as indicated by F scale items that did not work in Altemeyer's research. There are no references, in the RWA scale, to issues that were among the best discriminators on the F scale, like the item on "supernatural power" (F Item 8) or the item that denies ambivalence toward parents (F Item 27):

There is hardly anything lower than a person who does not feel great love, gratitude, and respect for his parents.

Both of these statements were ranked among the five best items in the last two versions of the F scale. As Samelson pointed out in chapter 2 of this volume, these changes from the F scale to the RWA scale are theoretically important. We need to gain a better understanding of the changes that Altemeyer has made, because such changes reflect evolution in social thought.

Ideology

Christie (chap. 1, this volume) and Samelson (chap. 2, this volume) have argued (a) that changes in ideology affect the content of authoritarian attitudes, and (b) that ideology itself has influenced research goals, methods, and perspectives. The literature on left-wing authoritarianism discussed by Stone and Smith (chap. 7, this volume) leads us to similar conclusions. It should be noted that most of the research on the authoritarian personality has been generated by politically liberal social scientists, whereas the insistence on the existence of left-wing authoritarians has been by neoconservatives such as Edward Shils. The recent findings on right-wing authoritarianism among Soviet communists (chap. 10, this volume) is bound to revive this controversy. However, Altemeyer (1988a) anticipated these findings of high authoritarianism among Russian communists, remarking that support for the status quo is right wing, even if the prevailing system would have been thought left-wing prior to its establishment and entrenchment.

Authoritarians and Groups

A new theory that has begun to receive attention is Duckitt's (1989) interpretation of authoritarianism as an intense orientation to the ingroup. This idea builds on the analysis of the importance of in- and out-groups to understanding the nature of prejudice (Allport, 1954, pp. 29–65) and taps into the extensive research on group attachment by Tajfel (1981) and his students. An important field experiment by Downing and Monaco (1986) provides support for the idea that authoritarians are particularly attached to their groups. In their discussion of a convention paper report of this study, Horowitz and Rabbie (1982) pointed out a series of findings of greater group orientation among men than women:

The pattern of these findings resembles that reported by Downing and Monaco ... for authoritarians and non-authoritarians. One might say that, like authoritarians, males are relatively predisposed to perceive aggregates of individuals as groups; conversely, that females, like non-authoritarians, are predisposed to perceive aggregates of individuals as separate persons. Being disposed to view others as members, males rate ingroup members higher than outgroup members regardless of winning or losing.

Such group research points out the pervasiveness of ingroup–outgroup distinctions, and the plausibility of interpreting authoritarianism at least in part as group orientation. It is also important to note that in more permanent groups these effects are magnified. Also, groups have shared ideologies, and the authoritarian responds both as a group member and as one who has been attracted to the particular ideology that is embedded in that group.

Cross-Cultural Research

A new wave of cross-cultural research on authoritarianism has emerged during the 1980s and early 1990s and has given rise to some promising new theories of authoritarianism. Oesterreich (1974, 1992), active in authoritarianism research in West Germany since the early 1970s, has developed a theoretical concept of authoritarianism as a basic pattern of human response: a flight into security on the part of anxious, insecure subjects, especially under circumstances of stress. According to Oesterreich's theory, the process of successful socialization is the replacement of deference to authority with other conflict solving strategies.

In the Netherlands, Meloen and others (chap. 3, this volume) have participated in research driven by the researchers' concerns about the rising tide of neo-Nazi activity in their country. There is also increasing interest in the research that has been carried out in Germany, research which has hitherto received little attention. Lederer (1981; chap. 9, this volume) found a decline in authoritarianism among German youth from 1945 to 1978 that could be due to changes in child-rearing practices in (the former) West Germany (although the patterns she describes sound more *permissive* than the ideal authoritative pattern described by Baumrind, 1971). However, an alternative hypothesis is provided by Sales's (1972, 1973) research showing environmental influences on authoritarian attitudes. Contributing to the decline in authoritarianism found by Lederer could also be the economic resurgence of (the former) West Germany during the period under study. The differences between East and West Germany, the (former) Soviet Union, the United States, and Austria provide plentiful grist for thought and ideas for further research.

Perhaps the most provocative recent inquiry is the research on authoritarianism in the (former) Soviet Union. McFarland and his colleagues (chap. 10, this volume) found that RWA scores are highest among Communist party cadres, but very low (compared to Kentucky samples) in Russian cities. The Russian public opinion researcher Popov (personal communication, July 3, 1991) disagrees with the latter finding; his surveys suggest high levels of authoritarianism in the Soviet Union, particularly outside the major cities. He has not, however, used a standard scale of authoritarianism like the Russian adaptation of the RWA scale used by McFarland. Soviet researchers, now that their society is more open, are collaborating with colleagues from other countries in continuing investigations centered on these questions.

Developmental Issues

We know very little about the origins of authoritarian tendencies; it is only recently that systematic research following the lead of Loevinger's (1976) ego theory and of Baumrind's (1971) work on styles of parenting have been undertaken, for example by Browning (1983, 1985). Likewise, attachment theory has been little examined in relation to authoritarianism; Hopf has begun the analysis of these issues in her chapter in this volume (chap. 6). It seems clear from her work that mothering has been underestimated as a causal factor in the development of authoritarianism.

Even if *The Authoritarian Personality*'s emphasis on the role of the strict punitive father was valid in the 1940s, the changing status of family relations in the Western world might lead to different findings today. In the United States, as in other industrial countries, the intact nuclear family is a rarity. A large proportion of children are now reared by single parents or in families with one stepparent. An example of this phenomenon was furnished by a student of one of the editors of this volume, who reported that his son felt unusual in his second-grade class because he was the only student living with both natural parents. "He thought we ought to get divorced," the graduate student reported.

The role of mothering now seems clearly crucial, as do the early relationships emphasized by attachment theory. An example cited by Hopf (chap. 6, this volume) is that many of Ackerman and Jahoda's (1950) anti-Semitic patients had domineering or rejecting mothers. Further progress is to be found in the developmental literature, as in the follow-ups to Baumrind's (1971) notion of a middle-of-the-road parenting style—"Authoritative" parenting—which seems to result in outcomes which differ from those due to authoritarian or permissive styles. One example is the study by Buri, Louiselle, Misukanis, and Mueller (1988), who found that adolescents' reports of authoritative parenting are related to high self-esteem, whereas those who report authoritarian parents have poorer self-images.

Tomkins's (1991) theory of ideological scripts, which emphasizes the parent's role in children's emotional development, also has implications for the development of authoritarian personalities. The Polarity scale (Knight, 1992), the instrument Tomkins developed for the investigation of ideological orientations, yields two scores, one on humanism and one on normativism; the former is correlated with feminine values, the latter with a masculine orientation and with authoritarianism as measured by the RWA scale (personal communication from W.F. Stone, December 7, 1991). This focus on the emotional make up of authoritarians, together with a fast-growing current literature on affect and emotional learning (e.g., Ekman, 1982) will likely resurrect some of *TAP*'s ideas on the emotional constitution of the authoritarian, in contrast to the cognitive emphasis of Altemeyer's (1981, 1988a) theory.

Authoritarianism and Prejudice

A central finding of *TAP* was the link between authoritarianism and prejudice. Though Altemeyer (1981) did not include ethnocentrism among the attitudinal clusters defining right-wing authoritarianism (p. 148), he cited 16 studies that showed significant positive correlations between ethnocentrism and authoritarianism (Table 2, pp. 34–35). Right-wing authoritarianism will generally be correlated with ethnic and racial prejudice, thought Altemeyer, "because such prejudice is a conventional outlet of aggressive impulses. The authoritarian believes that certain authorities approve of this prejudice, and he may believe that groups such as blacks threaten the established social order." (1981, p. 153). Of course, we realize that authoritarianism is only one of a multitude of factors involved in acts of aggression, but the undeniable fact that it is a constant accompanying factor not only warrants but necessitates the continued study of the origins, correlates, and manifestations of the authoritarian personality today.

Environmental Causation

Sales (1972) related economic threat to greater receptivity to the appeals of authoritarian leaders and institutions. In times of economic insecurity and political uncertainty, an increased need for the affirmation of group identity is manifest along with increasing enmity toward outgroups. (A recent publication by Doty, Peterson, and Winter, 1991, gives support to Sales's formulation.) Enshrouded in the anonymity of a group that reflects one's own fears, values, and feelings (feelings that are shared with family and peers), the individual's smoldering ethnic resentments erupt. These origins of ethnic animosity are compounded in individuals who have suffered emotional neglect or abuse during childhood.

An Assessment

We need to take the long view on authoritarian personality theory, considering both its history and the changing meanings of authoritarianism. The prevailing ideological climate had much to do with the way *TAP* was framed and presented. Likewise, its reception was influenced by the prevailing climate and by the state of social science at the time. The *ideas* did not get a fair hearing because of the focus on technical methodological issues like "response set", a problem that had already been dealt with by the authors of *TAP*. The importance of response sets was exaggerated in the enthusiasm to criticize *TAP*. Attention was lavished almost exclusively on the F scale rather than on the general proclivity to be attracted to fascism. The "network" of relationships was pretty much ignored, as was the theoretical plausibility of an authoritarian personality despite the previous theorizing of Wilhelm Reich (1933); Erich Fromm (1941/1965); Abraham Maslow (1943); Ross Stagner (1936a, 1936b); and Allen Edwards (1941, 1944).

Much of the early experimental research on the behavior of subjects high and low on authoritarianism was inadequately designed and incompletely reported. The conflicting findings regarding "rigidity" of high authoritarians in the Einstellung task exemplifies the state of the art of experimental social psychology as much as it reveals evidence of authoritarian behavior (see Christie, chap. 4, this volume). There is need, still, for careful experimentation using modern methods, controls, and statistics; the literature on punitiveness by jurors reveals more consistent results than some of the previous research, both confirming the existence of authoritarian aggression and supporting the importance of experimental investigation (see Christie, chap. 5, this volume).

Leaders and Followers

Some theorists have asserted that authoritarian dominance and submissive tendencies go together in the same person. For example, Maslow (1943) wrote that these tendencies "have two sides, both of which exist in the same person." He adopted Fromm's terminology: "Every character is both sadistic and masochistic" (Maslow, p. 408). This may or may not be true, since there has been relatively little research on authoritarian dominance behavior.

Dillehay (1978) noted that the focus of authoritarian research is on the followers rather than the leader of an autocratic group or regime:

Research on authoritarianism applies less to superleaders of social and political movements than to the broad spectrum of participants in those movements, such as the lower middle class in Germany of the 1930s. Fromm, remember, was trying to account for German national character rather than explain how Hitler got to be the person he was, although Fromm did that, too (Fromm, 1941, pp. 221ff.). Research since has applied the concept to broad populations, or at least intended that it be applied in that way. (p. 87)

We find the same tendency in subsequent research, despite the common assumption made by the novice. There is very little evidence, one way or the other, for designating certain leaders as authoritarian, as opposed to Machiavellian or narcissistic. This point, that virtually the entire research literature on authoritarianism has dealt with followership, cannot be overemphasized. The number of studies of the leadership behavior of authoritarians is extremely small.

Fascism and Authoritarianism

We return to the question of the relationship of the authoritarian personality to fascist ideology. Authoritarianism has been presented as a personality syndrome that predisposes one to accept fascist ideology. A crucial question pertaining to our review of the research is, Has this linkage been demonstrated? It seems clear that with few exceptions it has not. Research results suggest, however, that authoritarianism is but one of several factors predisposing people to accept fascist ideology. Other plausible factors are low intelligence, low education, lack of political sophistication, and external threats of specific kinds.

Among possible approaches to explore the nature of the linkage between the authoritarian personality and fascist ideology more closely, the following might be suggested:

1. By Meloen's (chap. 3, this volume) logic, neofascist groups should have more, and democratic and antifascist groups fewer, authoritarians in their midst than general population samples. Meloen found support for these predictions. But, we might ask, given a relatively high RWA or F-scale score, what is the probability that the individual might join a fascist group?

2. Adoption of an ideology generally presupposes adherence to a particular reference group. The somewhat scanty evidence that high Fs are more ingroup-oriented would lead to the following more complex psychosocial hypotheses for their attraction to fascism: (a) *If* the person exists in a particular social climate (economic threat coupled with the presence of a viable fascistic ideology), in which he or she feels particularly threatened, and (b) *if* the person finds that people he or she identifies with are profascist, and (c) *if* the person has a strongly authoritarian personality, *then* he or she will be likely to adopt fascist ideology.

Strength and Weakness

The title of our book, *Strength and Weakness*, still seems apt because of its reference to the primary authoritarian characteristic of admiration for strength and contempt for weakness. This was a key idea that was reflected in an F scale item (Item 26) that read

People can be divided into two distinct classes: the weak and the strong.

Mock jury studies do show that authoritarians blame weak (low-status) victims more readily than strong (high-status) ones. We thought that we would find male authoritarians endeavoring to be manly, trying to avoid being the least bit feminine, which is equated with weakness. This line of thought suggests that there should be a relationship between authoritarianism and the ideology of machismo, which includes belief in (a) violence as manly, (b) entitlement to callous sex, and (c) danger as exciting (Mosher & Tomkins, 1988). One thinks particularly of the recent cases of fundamentalist preachers who espouse authoritarian attitudes yet have on a number of occasions been discovered in flagrant displays of callous and exploitative sex. However, it seems likely that machismo applies only to a subset of authoritarians. The macho syndrome is male-oriented and thus neglects female authoritarians. A high-authoritarian woman might either be very feminine (conventionality) or very masculine to demonstrate her own contempt for weakness.

If indeed an obsession with strength and weakness anchors authoritarian orientations, we would expect sex differences. Because women are less concerned about either being seen as strong or about hiding their weaknesses, it seems logical that women would have lower scores even on an imperfect instrument such as the F scale. Overall, the groups tested by Adorno and colleagues (1950) did show lower scores for women, but the authors felt that these were sample and not population differences. Altemeyer (personal communication, June 15, 1991) reports no sex differences, in extensive but geographically and culturally restricted samples (most of his subjects are Manitoban college students). The lack of sex differences may point to a weakness in the RWA scale's conceptualization. Given that normative scores on Tomkins's Polarity scale (1964) correlate both with RWA and masculinity, and RWA scores fail to correlate with masculinity (W.F. Stone, personal communication, December 5, 1991), we should give more thought to alternative conceptualizations of authoritarianism.

Conclusions

Despite the flaws in the research, the theoretical and methodological controversies, and, at times, a decline of interest in the subject, the concept of authoritarianism remains vital. Certainly, the revival of interest in the concept of the authoritarian personality has been profoundly affected by the political context (e.g., Reagan and the Iran-Contra affaire; the civil rights movement; Vietnam; and more recently, events in Eastern Europe and the Persian Gulf). Also, the viability of TAP has been enhanced by the demonstration of its relevance in such diverse areas as the decision-making process of juries and the prediction of voting behavior or the attitude toward AIDS.

The concepts of authoritarian aggression, authoritarian submission, and conventionalism *are* basic; authoritarians are still ubiquitous and the authoritarian syndrome remains cohesive: The authoritarian sees the world as a hierarchy of stronger and weaker. We hope that this review will stimulate the expansion of authoritarianism research and inspire theoretical inquiry into these issues.

References

A. Reviews of the Literature on Authoritarianism

Altemeyer, B. (1981). *Right-wing authoritarianism*. Winnepeg: University of Manitoba Press.

Bhushan, L.I. (1982). Validity of California F-Scale: A review of studies. *Indian Psychological Review*, *23*(1), 1–11.

Byrne, D., & Kelley, K. (1981). Authoritarianism. In *An Introduction to Personality* (3rd ed.,). Chap. 5 Englewood Cliffs, NJ: Prentice Hall.

Cherry, R., & Byrne, D. (1977). Authoritarianism. In T. Blass (Ed.), *Personality variables in social behavior*. Hillsdale, NJ: Erlbaum.

Christie, R. (1991). Authoritarianism and related constructs. In J.P. Robinson, P.R. Shaver, & L.S. Wrightsman (Eds.), *Measures of personality and social psychological attitudes* (Vol. 1, 2nd ed., pp. 501–569). New York: Academic.

Christie, R., & Cook, P. (1958). A guide to published literature relating to the authoritarian personality through 1956. *Journal of Psychology*, *45*, 171–199.

Christie, R., & Jahoda, M. (Eds.). (1954). *Studies in the scope method of the authoritarian personality*. Glencoe, IL: Free Press.

Dillehay, R.C. (1978). Authoritarianism. In H. London, & J.E. Exner (Eds.), *Dimensions of Personality* (pp. 85–127). New York: Wiley.

Eckhardt, W. (1991). Authoritarianism. *Political Psychology*, *12*, 97–124.

Eysenck, H.J., & Wilson, G.D. (Eds.). (1978). *The psychological basis of ideology*. Lancaster, England: MTP Press. (Baltimore: University Park Press, 1978).

Kelman, H.C., & Hamilton, V.L. (1989). *Crimes of obedience: Toward a social psychology of authority and responsibility*. New Haven, CT: Yale University Press.

Kirscht, J.P., & Dillehay, R.C. (1967). *Dimensions of authoritarianism*. Lexington, KY: University of Kentucky Press.

Meloen, J.D. (1983). De autoritaire reaktie in tijden van welvaart en krisis [The authoritarian response in times of prosperity and crisis]. Unpublished doctoral dissertation, University of Amsterdam (English abstract).

B. Literature Cited

Ackerman, N.W., & Jahoda, M. (1950). *Anti-Semitism and emotional disorder: A psychoanalytic interpretation*. New York: Harper.

Adelson, J. (1953). A study of minority group authoritarianism. *Journal of Abnormal and Social Psychology*, 48, 477–485.

Adorno, T.W. (1960). "Starrheit und Integration," Soziologische Schriften II, pp. 376–377.

Adorno, T.W. (1961). *Minima Moralia*. Frankfurt am Main: Suhrkamp. (London and New York: Schocken Books, 1978).

Adorno, T.W. (1969). *Stichworte*. Frankfurt am Main: Suhrkamp.

Adorno, T.W. (1973). *Studien zum autoritaren Charakter*. [Studies about the authoritarian character]. Frankfurt am Main: Suhrkamp.

Adorno, T.W., Bettelheim, B., Frenkel-Brunswik, E., Guterman, N., Janowitz, M., Levinson, D., & Sanford, R.N. (1968). *Der autoritare Charakter. Studien über Autorität und Vorurteil* (Vol. 2). [Abridged German version of Volumes I, II, III, and V of *Studies in Prejudice*. Translated and edited by Institut für Sozialforschung, Frankfurt am Main]. Amsterdam: de Munter.

Adorno, T.W., Frenkel-Brunswik, E., Levinson, D.J., & Sanford, R.N. (1950). *The Authoritarian Personality*. New York: Harper and Row.

Ageyev, V.S. (1990). *Intergroup interaction: Social psychological problems* (in Russian). Moscow: Moscow University Press.

Ageyev, V.S., Abalakina, M., & McFarland, S. (1989). The study of authoritarianism in Russia (in Russian). *Sociology Institute Information Bulletin*, (No.) 5, 65–91.

Ainsworth, M.D. (1967). *Infancy in Uganda: Infant care and the growth of love*. Baltimore, MD: John Hopkins Press.

Ainsworth, M.D., Belhar, M.C., Waters, E., & Wall, S. (1978). *Patterns of attachment: A psychological study of the strange situation*. Hillsdale, NJ: Erlbaum.

Allport, G.W. (1954/1988). *The nature of prejudice*. Reading, MAss; Addison-Weseley.

Allport, G.W. (1958). *The nature of prejudice* (abridged edition). Garden City, NY: Doubleday Anchor. (Originally published by Addison-Wesley in 1954)

Almond, G.A. (1952). *The appeals of communism*. Princeton, NJ: Princeton University Press.

Almond, G.A., & Verba, S. (1965). *The civic culture: Political attitudes and democracy in five nations*. Boston: Little, Brown. (Originally published by Princeton University Press, 1963)

Almond, G., & Verba, S. (1980). *The civic culture revisited*. Boston: Little, Brown.

Altemeyer, B. (1981). *Right-wing authoritarianism*. Winnipeg: University of Manitoba Press.

Altemeyer, B. (1988a). *Enemies of freedom: Understanding right-wing authoritarianism*. San Francisco: Jossey-Bass.

Altemeyer, B. (1988b, March/April). Marching in step: A psychological examination of state terror. *The Sciences*, 30–38.

Altemeyer, B. (1990, July). *The mirror-image in U.S.–Soviet perceptions: Recent cross-national authoritarianism research*. Paper presented at the International Society for Political Psychology, Washington, DC.

American Jewish Committee Archives (1939–1955). Unpublished archival material, "Institute of Social Research" and "Records of the Scientific Research Department" files. New York: AJC Centralized Files.

Applezweig, D.G. (1954). Some determinants of behavioral rigidity. *Journal of Abnormal and Social Psychology, 49,* 244–248.

Arendt, H. (1951). *The origins of totalitarianism.* New York: Harcourt, Brace.

Bandura, A. (1977). *Social learning theory.* Englewood Cliffs, NJ: Prentice-Hall.

Bandura, A. (1986). *Social foundations of thought and action.* Englewood Cliffs, NJ: Prentice-Hall.

Bardeleben, H., Reimann, B.W., & Schmidt, P. (1989). AIDS und das Problem der Prävention: Fakten und Fiktonen. [AIDS and the problem of prevention: Fact and fiction]. *Zeitschrift für Sozialforschung, 29*(1), 97–128.

Barnes, S.H. et al. (1979). *Political action.* Beverly Hills, CA: Sage.

Bass, B.M. (1955). Authoritarianism or acquiescence? *Journal of Abnormal and Social Psychology, 51,* 616–623.

Baumrind, D. (1971). Current patterns of parental authority. *Developmental Psychological Monographs, 4*(2, part 2), 1–103.

Baumrind, D. (1973). An exploratory study of socialization effects on black children: Some black-white comparisons. *Child Development, 43,* 261–267.

Baumrind, D. (1989). Rearing competent children. In W. Damon (Ed.), *Child Development Today and Tomorrow* (pp. 343–378). San Francisco: Jossey-Bass.

Berg, K.S., & Vidmar, N. (1975). Authoritarianism and recall of evidence about criminal behavior. *Journal of Research in Personality, 9,* 147–157.

Berkowitz, L., & Knurek, D.A. (1969). Label-mediated hostility generalization. *Journal of Personality and Social Psychology, 13,* 200–206.

Berlin, I. (1990). *The twisted timber of humanity.* Knopf: New York.

Berting, J. (1968). *In het brede maatschappelijke midden.* [In the Wide Middle Section of Society]. Unpublished doctoral dissertation, University of Amsterdam.

Billig, M. (1978). *Fascists: A social psychological view of the National Front.* London: Academic.

Billig, M. (1979). *Psychology, racism and fascism.* Birmingham, England: A.F. and R. Publications (a *Searchlight* pamphlet).

Billig, M. (1982). *Ideology and social psychology.* Oxford: Blackwell.

Billig, M. (1984). Political ideology: Social psychological aspects. In H. Tajfel (Ed.), *The social dimension: European developments in social psychology* (Vol. 2, pp. 446–470). Cambridge, England: Cambridge University Press.

Billig, M. (1985). The unobservant participator: Nazism, anti-Semitism and Ray's reply. *Ethnic & Racial Studies, 8,* 444–449.

Block, J. (1955). Personality characteristics associated with fathers' attitudes toward child rearing. *Child Development, 26,* 41–48.

Bock, M. et al. (1991). "Sozialpsychologische Aspekte von AIDS unter besonderer Berücksichtigung von Diskriminierungs- und Stigmatisierungs- prozessen" (Social psychological aspects of AIDS in the face of processes of discrimination and sigmatisation. Justus-Liebig-Universität, Gießen, un- published report.

Boehm, V.R. (1968). Mr. Prejudice, Miss Sympathy, and the authoritarian personality. *Wisconsin Law Review,* 734–750.

Bonss, W. (1983). Kritische Theorie und empirische Sozialforschung: Anmerkungen zu einem Fallbeispiel. In E. Fromm (Ed.), *Arbeiter und Angestellte am Vorabend des Dritten Reiches.* Munich: Deutscher Taschenbuch Verlag.

Bowlby, J. (1969). *Attachment and loss: Vol. 1. Attachment*. New York: Basic Books.

Bowlby, J. (1973). *Attachment and loss: Vol. 2. Separation, anxiety and anger*. New York: Basic Books.

Bowlby, J. (1980). *Attachment and loss: Vol. 3. loss sadness and depression*. New York: Basic Books.

Bowlby, J. (1988). *A secure base: Clinical applications of attachment theory*. London: Routledge.

Braehler, E., Schuerhoff, R., & Richter, H.E. (1991). [Results of a sample survey of the political and economic situation, and union sentiment in West Germany]. Unpublished ms.

Brant, W.D., Larsen, K.S., & Langenberg, D. (1978). Authoritarian traits as predictors of candidate presference in the 1976 presidential election. *Psychological Reports, 43*, 313–314.

Bray, R.M., & Noble, A.M. (1978). Authoritarianism and decisions of mock juries: Evidence of jury bias and group polarization. *Journal of Personality and Social Psychology, 36*, 1424–1430.

Brehm, S.S., & Kassin, S.M. (1990). *Social psychology*. Boston: Houghton Mifflin.

Bretherton, I. (1985). Attachment theory: Retrospect and prospect. In I. Bretherton & E. Waters (Eds., *Growing points of attachment: Theory and research* (pp. 3–35). *Monographs of the Society for Research in Child Development, 50*(1–2, Serial No. 209) Chicago: University of Chicago Press.

Bringmann, W.G. (1967). Re-examination of ethnocentrism and problem solving rigidity. *Psychological Reports, 20*, 1069–1070.

Brown, J.F. (1940). *The psychodynamics of abnormal behavior* (with Karl A. Menninger). New York: McGraw-Hill.

Brown, J.F. (1942). The origin of the anti-Semitic attitude. In I. Graeber & S.H. Britt (Eds.), *Jews in a gentile world* (pp. 124–148). New York: Macmillan.

Brown, R.W. (1953). A determinant of the relationship between rigidity and authoritarianism. *Journal of Abnormal and Social Psychology, 48*, 469–476.

Brown, R. (1965). *Social psychology*. New York: Free Press.

Browning, D.L. (1983). Aspects of authoritarian attitudes in ego development. *Journal of Personality and Social Psychology, 45*, 137–144.

Browning, D.L. (1985). Developmental aspects of authoritarian attitudes and sex role conceptions in men and women. *High School Journal, 68*, 177–182.

Browning, D. (1987). Ego development, authoritarianism, and social status: An investigation of the incremental validity of Loevinger's Sentence Completion Test (short form). *Journal of Personality and Social Psychology, 53*, 113–118.

Buck-Morss, S. (1977). *The origin of negative dialectics*. New York: Free Press.

Budner, S. (1962). Intolerance of ambiguity as a personality variable. *Journal of Personality, 30*, 29–50.

Buri, J.R., Louiselle, P.A., Misukanis, T.M., & Mueller, R.A. (1988). Effects of parental authoritarianism and authoritativeness on self-esteem. *Personality and Social Psychology Bulletin, 14*, 271–282.

Bushan, L.I. (1969). Comparison of four Indian political groups on a measure of authoritarianism. *Journal of Social Psychology, 79*, 141–142.

Byrne, D. (1965). Parental antecedents of authoritarianism. *Journal of Personality and Social Psychology, 1,* 369–373.

Byrne, D. (1974). *An introduction to personality.* Englewood Cliffs, NJ: Prentice Hall.

Byrne, D., & Kelley, K. (1981). Authoritarianism. In *An Introduction to Personality* (3rd ed., Chap. 5). Englewood Cliffs, NJ: Prentice Hall.

Byrne, D., & Lamberth, J. (1971). The effect of erotic stimuli on sex arousal, evaluative responses, and subsequent behavior. In *Technical report of the Commission on Obsecenity and Pornography* (Vol. 8). Washington, DC: U.S. Government Printing Office.

Campbell, D.T. (1989). Honoring Nevitt Sanford [Review of M.B. Freedman (Ed.), *Social change and personality*]. *Contemporary Psychology, 34,* 944–945.

Centers, R., Shomer, R.W., & Rodrigues, A. (1970). A field experiment in interpersonal persuasion using authoritative influence. *Journal of Personality, 38,* 392–403.

Cherry, F., & Byrne, D. (1977). Authoritarianism. In T. Blass, (Ed.), *Personality variables in social behavior* (pp. 109–133). Hillsdale, NJ: Erlbaum.

Chesler, M., & Schmuck, R. (1973). Participant observation in a super-patriot group. In R.I. Evans & R.M. Rozelle (Eds.), *Social psychology in life* (pp. 191–206). Boston: Allyn and Bacon.

Christie, R. (1954). Authoritarianism re-examined. In R. Christie & M. Jahoda (Eds.), *Studies in the scope and method of "The Authoritarian Personality"* (pp. 123–196). Glencoe, IL: Free Press.

Christie, R. (1955). [Review of H.J. Eysenck, *The psychology of politics*]. *American Journal of Psychology, 68,* 702–704.

Christie, R. (1956a). Eysenck's treatment of the personality of Communists. *Psychological Bulletin, 53,* 411–430.

Christie, R. (1956b). Some abuses of psychology. *Psychological Bulletin, 53,* 439–451.

Christie, R. (1984). [Review of *Right-wing authoritarianism*]. *Contemporary Sociology, 13,* 518–519.

Christie, R. (1991). Authoritarianism and related constructs. In J.P. Robinson et al. (Eds.), *Measures of Social Psychological Attitudes* (2nd ed., Vol. 1, pp. 501–569). New York: Academic Press.

Christie, R., & Cook, P. (1958). A guide to published literature relating to the authoritarian personality through 1956. *Journal of Psychology, 45,* 171–199.

Christie, R., & Garcia, J. (1951). Subcultural variation in the Authoritarian Personality. *Journal of Abnormal and Social Psychology, 46,* 457–469.

Christie, R., & Geis, F. (1970). *Studies in Machiavellism.* New York: Academic Press.

Christie, R., Havel, J., & Seidenberg, B. (1958). Is the F Scale irreversible? *Journal of Abnormal and Social Psychology, 56,* 143–159.

Christie, R., & Jahoda, M. (Eds.). (1954). *Studies in the scope and method of "The Authoritarian Personality."* Glencoe, IL: Free Press.

Cohn, T.S. (1953). The relation of the F scale to a response set to answer positively. (Abstract). *American Psychologist, 8,* 335.

Cook, S.W. (1986). Research on anticipatory ideological compliance. *Journal of Social Issues, 42*(1), 69–73.

Coulter, T.T. (1953). *An experimental and statistical study of the relationship of prejudice and certain variables.* Unpublished doctoral dissertation, University of London.

Cowan E.L., Wiener, M., & Hess, J. (1953). Generalization of problem-solving rigidity. *Journal of Consulting Psychology, 17,* 100-103.

Craig, G.A. (1982). *The Germans.* New York: Putnam.

Dahrendorf, R. (1967). *Society and democracy in Germany.* Garden City, NY: Doubleday. (Original work published 1965).

Devereux, E.C., Jr., Bronfenbrenner, U., & Suci, G.J. (1962). Patterns of parent behavior in the United States of America and the Federal Republic of Germany: A cross-national comparison. *International Social Science Journal, 14,* 488-506.

Dicks, H.V. (1950). Personality traits and National Socialist ideology. *Human Relations, 3,* 111-154.

Dillehay, R.C. (1978). Authoritarianism. In H. London & J. E. Exner (Eds.), *Dimensions of Personality* (pp. 85-127). New York: Wiley.

DiRenzo, G.J. (1967a). Professional politicians and personality structures. *American Journal of Sociology, 73,* 217-225.

DiRenzo, G.J. (1967b). *Personality, power and politics.* Notre Dame, IN: University of Notre Dame Press.

Dittberner, J.L. (1979). *The end of ideology and American social thought: 1930- . 1960.* Ann Arbor, MI: UMI Research Press.

Dittes, J.E. (1961). Impulsive closure as a reaction to failure-induced threat. *Journal of Personality and Social Psychology, 63,* 562-569.

Dostoyevsky, F.M. (1914). *The Possessed.* (C. Garnett, Trans.). London: William Heinemann. (Original work published 1872)

Doty, R.M., Peterson, B.E., & Winter, D.G. (1991). Threat and authoritarianism in the United States, 1978-1987. *Journal of Personality and Social Psychology, 61,* 629-640.

Downing, L.L., & Monaco, N.R. (1986). In-group/out-group bias as a function of differential contact and authoritarian personality. *Journal of Social Psychology, 126,* 445-452.

Dubiel, H. (1985). *Theory and politics.* (B. Gregg, Trans.). Cambridge, MA: MIT Press. (Original work, *Wissenschafts organisation and politische Erfahrung,* published 1978; Frankfurt am Main: Suhrkamp.)

Duckitt, J. (1983). Culture, class, personality and authoritarianism among white South Africans. *Journal of Social Psychology, 121,* 191-199.

Duckitt, J. (1984). Reply to Ray's "Directiveness and authoritarianism: A rejoinder to Duckitt." *South African Journal of Psychology, 14*(2), 65-66.

Duckitt, J. (1985). Social class and F scale authoritarianism: A reconsideration. *High School Journal, 68,* 279-286.

Duckitt, J. (1989). Authoritarianism and group identification: A new view of an old construct. *Political Psychology, 10,* 63-84.

Eckhardt, W. (1991). Authoritarianism. *Political Psychology, 12,* 97-124.

Edwards, A.L. (1941). Unlabeled fascist attitudes. *Journal of Abnormal and Social Psychology, 36,* 575-582.

Edwards, A.L. (1944). The signs of incipient fascism. *Journal of Abnormal and Social Psychology, 39,* 301-316.

Eriksen, C.W., & Eisenstein, D. (1953). Personality rigidity and the Rorschach. *Journal of Personality, 21,* 386-391.

Ex–U.S. Agents (1983, July 6). Ex–U.S. agents tell of efforts to help Barbie. *New York Times*, p. A3.

Eysenck, H.J. (1953). *Uses and abuses of psychology*. Baltimore, MD: Penguin.

Eysenck, H.J. (1954). *The psychology of politics*. London: Routledge and Kegan Paul.

Eysenck, H.J. (1981–82). Left-wing authoritarianism: Myth or reality? *Political Psychology*, *3*, 234–238.

Eysenck, H.J. (1982). [Review of *Right-wing authoritarianism*]. *Personality and Individual Differences*, *3*, 352–353.

Eysenck, H.J., & Coulter, T.T. (1972). The personality and attitudes of working-class British communists and fascists. *Journal of Social Psychology*, *87*, 59–73.

Eysenck, H.J., & Wilson, G.D. (1978). *The psychological basis of ideology*. Lancaster, England: MTP Press.

Federn, P. (1919). Zur Psychologie der Revolution: Die vaterlose Gesellschaft. *Der Österrcichische Volkswirt II*, pp. 571–574.

Fenichel, O. (1931). Review of W. Reich. Geschlechtsreife, Enthaltsamkeit, Ehemoral. *Internationale Zeitschrift für Psychoanalyse*, *17*, 404–408.

Fenichel, O. (1940). The Psychoanalysis of Anti-Semitism. *American Imago*, *1*, 24–39.

Finison, L.J. (1983). The Society for the Psychological Study of Social Issues, peace action, and theories of conflict 1936–1950. *American Psychologist*, *38*, 1250–1252.

Fischer, A., Fuchs, W., & Zinneker, J. (1985). *Jungendliche und Erwachsene '85: Generationen im Vergleich* [Youth and adults '85: generations in comparison] Vol. 3: *Jugend der fünfziger Jahre—Heute* [Youth of the 150s—today]. Opladen, Germany: Leske & Budrich.

Fisher, E.H. (1970). Authoritarianism and agreement response style in predicting altruistic attitudes: Tests of a newly balanced F scale. *Proceedings of the 78th Annual Convention of the A.P.A.*, 327–328.

Flacks, R. (1967). The liberated generation: An exploration of the roots of student protest. *Journal of Social Issues*, *23*(3), 52–75.

Flacks, R. (1984). [Review of *Roots of Radicalism: Jews, Christians, and the new left*]. *Society*, *21*, 89–92.

Freedman, M.B. (Ed.). (1987). *Social change and personality: Essays in honor of Nevitt Sanford*. New York: Springer-Verlag.

French, E.G. (1955). Interrelation among some measures of rigidity under stress and nonstress conditions. *Journal of Abnormal and Social Psychology*, *51*, 114–118.

Frenkel-Brunswik, E. (1948a). Dynamic and cognitive categorization of qualitative material: 2. Application to interviews of the ethnically prejudiced. *Journal of Psychology*, *25*, 261–277.

Frenkel-Brunswik, E. (1948b). A study of prejudice in children. *Human Relations*, *1*, 295–306.

Frenkel-Brunswik, E. (1954). Further explorations by a contributor to *The Authoritarian Personality*. In R. Christie and M. Jahoda (Eds.), *Studies in the scope and method of "The Authoritarian Personality"* (pp. 226–275). Glencoe, IL: Free Press.

Frenkel-Brunswik, E., & Sanford, R.N. (1945). Some personality factors in anti-Semitism. *Journal of Psychology*, *20*, 271–291.

Freud, A. (1946). *The ego and the machanisms of defense* (C. Baines, Trans.). New York: International Universities Press. (Original work published 1936)

Freud, S. (1939). *Moses and monotheism*. New York: Knopf.

Freyhold, M. von (1971). *Autoritarismus und politische Apatie*. Frankfurt am Main: Europaische Verlagsanstalt.

Freyhold, M. von (1985). Old and new dimensions of authoritarianism and its opposite. *High School Journal, 68*, 241–246.

Friend, R.M., & Vinson, M. (1974). Leaning over backwards: Jurors' responses to defendants' attractiveness. *Journal of Communication, 24*, 124–129.

Fromm, E. (1929). Psychoanalyse und Soziologie. *Zeitschrift für Psychoanalytische Paedagogik, 3*, 268–270.

Fromm, E. (1930). Die Entwicklung des Christusdogmas. *Imago, 16*, 305–375.

Fromm, E. (1932a). Über Methode und Aufgabe einer analytischen Sozialpsychologie. *Zeitschrift für Sozialforschung, 1*, 28–54.

Fromm, E. (1932b). Die psychoanalytische Charakterologie und ihre Bedeutung für die Sozialpsychologie. *Zeitschrift für Sozialforschung, 1*, 253–277.

Fromm, E. (1933). [Review of W. Reich, *Der Einbruch der Sexualmoral*]. *Zeitschrift fuer Sozialforschung, 2*, 119–124.

Fromm, E. (1936). Sozialpsychologischer Teil. In M. Horkheimer (Ed.), *Studien über Autorität und Familie* (pp. 77–135). Paris: Alcan.

Fromm, E. (1941/1965). *Escape from freedom*. New York: Avon Books. (Original work published 1941 by Rinehart, New York.)

Fromm, E. (1943). *Fear of freedom*. London: K. Paul, Trench, Trubner. (British edition of *Escape from freedom*)

Fromm, E. (1963). The revolutionary character. In E. Fromm, *The dogma of Christ* (pp. 147–166). New York: Holt.

Fromm, E. (1980). *Gesamtausgabe. Bd. 1. Analytische Sozialpsychologie*. Stuttgart: Deutsche Verlags-Anstalt.

Fromm, E. (1983). *Arbeiter und Angestellte am Vorabend des Dritten Reiches*. (W. Bonss, Ed. and Trans.). Munich: Deutscher Taschenbuch Verlag. (Posthumous translation of Fromm's unfinished English manuscript)

Fromm, E. (1984). *The working class in Weimar Germany*. (B. Weinberger, Trans.). Leamington Spa, England: Berg. (Retranslation of Fromm's 1983 work)

Fromm, E., & Maccoby, M. (1970). *Social character in a Mexican village*. Englewood Cliffs, NJ: Prentice Hall.

Garcia, L., & Griffitt, W. (1978a).

Garcia, L., & Griffitt, W. (1978b). Evaluation and recall of evidence in the Patty Hearst case. *Journal of Research in Personality, 12*, 57–67.

Gergen, K.J. (1973). Social psychology as history. *Journal of Personality and Social Psychology, 26*, 309–320.

Gergen, K.J., & Gergen, M.M. (1986). *Social psychology* (2nd ed.). New York: Springer-Verlag.

Gieser, M.T. (1980). "The Authoritarian Personality" revisited. Unpublished doctoral dissertation, Wright Institute. Ann Arbor: University Microfilms International, No. 8024942.

Ginneken, J. van (June, 1984). *Reich's "Mass psychology of fascism" in Marxist perspective*. Paper presented at the Annual Cheiron Meeting, Vassar College, Poughkeepsie, NY.

Gladstone, R. (1969). Authoritarianism, social status, transgression, and punitiveness. *Proceedings, 77th Annual Convention, American Psychological Association*, 287–288.

Gmünder, U. (1985). *Kritische Theorie* [Critical Theory]. Stuttgart: Metzlersche Verlagsbuchhandlung.

Gold, A.R., Christie, R., & Friedman, L.N. (1976). *Fists and flowers: A social psychological interpretation of student dissent*. New York: Academic Press.

Goldstein, K.M., & Blackman, S. (1978). *Cognitive style*. New York: Wiley.

Gordon, S. (1984). *Hitler, Germans, and the "Jewish question."* Princeton, NJ: Princeton University Press.

Griffitt, W., & Garcia, L. (1979). Reversing authoritarian punitiveness: The impact of verbal conditioning. *Social Psychology Quarterly, 42*, 55–61.

Grossman, K.E. (1984). Die Ontogenese kindlicher Zuwendung gegenuber Bezugspersonen und gegenuber Dingen. In C. Eggers (Ed.), *Bingungen und Besitzdenken beim Kleinkind* (pp. 121–154). Munich: Urban and Schwarzenberg.

Gundlach, R.H., & Riess, B.F. (1954). A criticism of Melby and Smith's "Academic freedom in a climate of insecurity." *Journal of Social Issues, 10*, No. 1, 45–47.

Hagendoorn, A. (1982). *Het Nazisme als ideologie* [Nazism as ideology]. Deventer, Van Loghum Slaterus, The Netherlands.

Hagendoorn, A., & Janssen, J. (1983). *Rechtsomkeer*. [Turn Right]. Ambo: Baarn.

Handlon, B.J., & Squier, L.H. (1955). Attitudes toward special loyalty oaths at the University of California. *American Psychologist, 10*, 121–127.

Hanson, D.J. (1975). Authoritarianism as a variable in political research. *Il Politico, 40*(4), 700–705. (Reprinted in H.J. Eysenck & G.D. Wilson, Eds., 1978, *The psychological basis of ideology*, pp. 137–142. Lancaster, England: MTP Press)

Hart, I. (1957). Maternal child-rearing practices and authoritarian ideology. *Journal of Abnormal and Social Psychology, 55*, 232–237.

Hatton, D.E., & Snortum, J.R. (1971). The effects of biasing information and dogmatism upon witness testimony. *Psychonomic Science, 23*, 425–427.

Hausdorff, D. (1972). *Erich Fromm*. New York: Twayne.

Heintz, P. (1957). Zur Problematik der autoritaren Personlichkeit [The problematic of the authoritarian personality]. *Kölner Zeitschrift für Soziologie und Sozialpsychologie, 9*, 28–49.

Hepburn, M.A., Napier, J.D., & Krieger, R. (1987, November). *Political attitudes of West German and U.S. students: Cross-national and gender differences*. Paper presented at the Annual Meeting of the National Council for Social Studies, Dallas, TX.

Hites, R.W., & Kellogg, E.P. (1964). The F and Social Maturity scales in relation to social attitudes in a deep south sample. *Journal of Social Psychology, 62*, 189–195.

Hoff, E., Lappe, L., & Lempert, W. (1983). Methoden zur Sozialisation junger Facharbeiter (Parts I and II). *Materialien aus der Bildungsforschung, 24*. Berlin: Max-Planck-Institut für Bildungsforschung.

Hoogvelt, A.M.M. (1969). Ethnocentrism, authoritarianism and Powellism. *Race, 11*(1), 1–12.

Hopf, C. (1987). Zur Aktualität der Untersuchungen zur "autoritaren Personlichkeit." *Zeitschrift für Sozialisationsforschung und Erziehungssoziolgie*, 7(3), 162–177.

Horkeimer, M. (Ed.) (1936). *Studien über Autorität und Familie*. Paris: Felix Alcan. (Reprint, Junius-Drucke)

Horkheimer, M. (1939). Die Juden und Europa. *Zeitschrift für Sozialforschung*, 7(1–2).

Horkheimer, M. (1947). *Eclipse of Reason*. New York: Oxford University Press.

Horkheimer, M. (1972a). Die gegenwärtige Lage der Sozialphilosophie und die Aufgaben eines Instituts für Sozialforschung. In M. Horkheimer (Ed.), *Sozialphilosophische Studien* (pp. 33–46). Frankfurt: Fischer. (Original work published 1931)

Horkheimer, M. (1972b). *Critical theory: Selected essays*. New York: Herder and Herder. (Translation of A. Schmidt (Ed.), *Kritische Theory*, 1968).

Horkheimer, M., & Adorno, T.W. *Dialeklik der Aufklarung* [Dialectic of enlightenment], Amsterdam: Querido Verlag N.V.

Horowitz, M., & Rabbie, J.M. (1982). Individuality and membership in the intergroup system. In H. Tajfel (Ed.), *Social identity and intergroup relations* (pp. 241–274). Cambridge, England: Cambridge University Press.

Hoyas, L. de (1985). *Klaus Barbie* (N. Courtin, Trans.). London: Allen.

Husen, T. (Ed.). (1967). *International study of achievement in mathematics* (Vol. 1 & 2). New York: Wiley.

Hyman, H.H., & Sheatsley, P.B. (1954). "The Authoritarian Personality": A methodological critique. In R. Christie & M. Jahoda (Eds.), *Studies in the scope and method of "The Authoritarian Personality"* (pp. 50–122). Glencoe, IL: Free Press.

Inglehart, R. (1977). *The Silent Revolution*. Princeton, NJ: Princeton University Press.

Institute for Social Research. (1941). Research project on anti-Semitism. *Studies in Philosophy and Social Science*, 9, 124–143.

International Institute of Social Research (1939). Research project on anti-Semitism. Unpublished manuscript, stamped 6-29-1939. New York: AJC Archives.

Jackson, D.N., & Messick, S.J. (1957). A note on "Ethnocentrism" and acquiescent response set. *Journal of Abnormal and Social Psychology*, 54, 132–137.

Jackson, D.N., Messick, S.J., & Solley, C.M. (1957). How "rigid" is the "authoritarian"? *Journal of Abnormal and Social Psychology*, 54, 137–140.

Jacoby, R. (1983). *The repression of psychoanlysis*. Basic Books: New York.

Jaensch, E.R. (1938). *Der Gegentypus*. Leipzig: Barth.

Jahoda, M. (1954). Introduction. In R. Christie & M. Jahoda (Eds.), *Studies in the scope and method of "The Authoritarian Personality"* (pp. 11–23). Glencoe, IL: Free Press.

Jarisch, U. (1975). *Sind Arbeiter autoritar?* [Are workers authoritarian?]. Frankfurt am Main: Europaische Verlagsanstalt.

Jay, M. (1973). *The dialectical imagination: A history of the Frankfurt School and the Institute of Social Research, 1923–1950*. Boston: Little, Brown.

Jay, M. (1980). The Jews and the Frankfurt School: Critical theory's analysis of anti-Semitism. *New German Critique*, 7(1), 137–149.

Jensen, A.R. (1957). Authoritarian attitudes and personality malajustment. *Journal of Abnormal and Social Psychology, 54*, 303–311.

Jorgenson, D.O. (1975). Economic threat and authoritarianism in television programs: 1950–1974. *Psychological Reports, 37*, 1153–1154.

Jurow, G.L. (1971). New data on the effect of a "death qualified" jury on the guilt determination process. *Harvard Law Review, 84*, 567–611.

Kagitcibasi, C.C. (1967). *Social norms and authoritarianism: A comparison of Turkish and American adolescents.* Unpublished doctoral dissertation, University of California, Berkeley.

Kassin, S.M. (1984). TV cameras, public self-consciousness, and mock juror performance. *Journal of Experimental Social Psychology, 20*, 336–349.

Kassin, S.M., & Wrightsman, L.S. (1988). *The American jury on trial: Psychological perspectives.* New York: Hemisphere.

Katz, D. (1958). Organizational effectiveness and change: an evaluation of SPSSI by members and former members. *Journal of Social Issues* (Suppl. 11), 1–33.

Kecskemeti, P. (1951). Prejudice in the catastrophic perspective. *Commentary, 11*, 286–292.

Keniston, K. (1971). *Youth and dissent: The rise of a new opposition.* New York: Harcourt, Brace, Jovanovich.

Kerlinger, N. (1984). *Liberalism, conservatism, and the structure of social attitudes.* Hillsdale, NJ: Erlbaum.

Kernberg, O.F. (1980). *Internal world and external reality: Object relations theory applied.* New York: Aronson.

Kirscht, J.P., & Dillehay, R.C. (1967). *Dimensions of authoritarianism: A review of research and theory.* Lexington, KY: University of Kentucky Press.

Kitov, A.I. (1984). *Psychology of economic management* (in Russian). Moscow: Nauka.

Klages, H., & Herbert, W. (1983). *Wertorientierung und Staatsbezug: Untersuchungen zur politischen Kultur in der Bundesrepublik Deutschland.* Frankfurt am Main: Campus.

Kline, P., & Cooper, C. (1984). A factorial analysis of the authoritarian personality. *British Journal of Psychology, 75*, 171–176.

Kluke, P. (1972). *Die Stiftungsuniversität Frankfurt am Main, 1914–1932.* Frankfurt am Main: W. Kramer.

Knight, K. (1992). Measures of liberalism and conservatism. In J.P. Robinson, P.R. Shaver, & L.W. Wrightsman (Eds.), *Measures of personality and social psychological attitudes* (Vol. 2). San Diego, CA: Academic.

Knutson, J.N. (1974). *Psychological variables in political recruitment.* Mimeo. Berkeley, CA: The Wright Institute.

Kohn, P.M. (1972). The Authoritarianism-Rebellion scale: A balanced F scale with left-wing reversals. *Sociometry, 35*(1), 176–189.

Kohn, P.M. (1974). Authoritarianism, rebelliousness, and their correlates among British undergraduates. *British Journal of Social and Clinical Psychology, 13*, 245–255.

Korrespondenzblatt der Internationale Psychoanalytischen Vereinigung. (1931). *Internationale Zeitschrift für Psychoanalyse, 17*, 292–293.

Korrespondenzblatt der Internationale Psychoanalytischen Vereinigung. (1932). *Internationale Zeitschrift für Psychoanalyse, 18*, 559–560.

Kozulin, A. (1986). The concept of activity in Soviet psychology: Vygotsky, his disciples and critics. *American Psychologist, 41*, 264–274.

Kramer, H. (1990), "Die Autoritarianismus-Theorien dis Instituts für Sozialforschung," unpublished ms.

Kutter, P. (1989). *Moderne Psychoanalyse: Eine Einführung in die Psychologie unbewuter Prozesse*. Munich: Verlag Internationale Psychoanalyse.

Lambley, P. (1980). *The psychology of apartheid*. London: Secker & Warburg.

Landauer, K. (1934). [Review of W. Reich, *Massenpsychologie des Faschismus*]. *Zeitschrift für Sozialforschung, 3*, 106–107.

Lazarsfeld, P., & Thielens, W. (1958). *The academic mind: Social scientists in a time of crisis*. Glencoe, IL: Free Press.

Lederer, G. (1981). *Trends in authoritarianism: An attitudinal study of adolescents in two cultures*. Unpublished doctoral Dissertation, Graduate School of Arts and Sciences, Columbia University, New York.

Lederer, G. (1982). Trends in authoritarianism. A study of adolescents in West Germany and the United States since 1945. *Journal of Cross-Cultural Psychology, 13*, 299–314.

Lederer, G. (1983). *Jugend und Autorität: Über den Einstellungswandel zum Autoritarismus in der Bundesrepublik Deutschland und den USA*. Opladen, Germany: Westdeutscher Verlag.

Lederer, G. (1988). Young Austrians and the election of Kurt Waldheim. *Political Psychology, 9*, 633–647.

Lee, R.E., & Warr, P.B. (1969). The development and standardization of a balanced F scale. *Journal of General Psychology, 81*, 109–129.

Lempert, W. (1988). Soziobiographische Bedingungen der Entwicklung moralischer Urteilsfähigkeit. *Kölner Zeitschrift für Soziologie und Sozialpsychologie, 40*, 40–61.

Lermontov, M. (1966). *A hero of our time*. (P. Foote, Trans.). New York: Harcourt, Brace. (Original work published 1840)

Levinson, D.J., & Sanford, R.N. (1944). A scale for the measurement of anti-Semitism. *Journal of Psychology, 17*, 339–370.

Levinson, D.J., & Sanford, R.N. (Eds.). (1982). Preface. In *The Authoritarian Personality* (abridged edition, pp. v–vi.). New York: Norton.

Levinson, D.J., & Huffman, P.E. (1955). Traditional family ideology and its relation to personality. *Journal of Personality, 23*, 251–273.

Levitt, E.E. (1956). The water-jar Einstellung test as a measure of rigidity. *Psychological Bulletin, 53*, 347–370.

Levitt, E.E., & Zelen, S.L. (1953). The validity of the Einstellung test as a measure of rigidity. *Journal of Abnormal and Social Psychology, 48*, 573–580.

Levitt, E.E., & Zelen, S.L. (1955). An investigation of the water-jar extinction problem as a measure of rigidity. *Psychological Reports, 1*, 331–334.

Lewin, K., Lippitt, R., & White, R.K. (1939). Patterns of aggressive behavior in experimentally created social climates. *Journal of Social Psychology, 10*, 271–299.

Lewis, S. (1935). *It can't happen here*. Garden City, NY: Doubleday.

Lewis, T.T. (1990). Authoritarian attitudes and personalities: A psychohistorical perspective. *Psychohistory Review, 18*, 141–167.

Lichter, R.S., & Rothman, S. (1981–1982). Jewish ethnicity and radical culture: A social psychological study of political activists. *Political Psychology, 3*(1–2), 116–157.

Liebhard, E.H. (1970). Socialization im Beruf. *Kölner Zeitschrift für Soziologie und Sozial Psychologie, 22*(4), 715–726.

Likert, R. (1932). A technique for the measurement of attitudes. *Archives of Psychology* (No. 140).

Loevinger, J. (1976). *Ego development: Conceptions and theories.* San Francisco: Jossey-Bass.

Loftus, J. (1982). *The Belarus secret.* New York: Knopf.

Lomov, B.F., & Zhuravlev, A.L. (1978). *Psychology and management* (in Russian). Moscow: Nauka.

Lowenthal, L. (1980). *Mitmachen wollte ich nie.* Frankfurt: Suhrkamp.

Lowenthal, L. (1989). *Critical theory and Frankfurt theorists.* New Brunswik, NJ: Transaction.

Luchins, A.S. (1942). Mechanization in problem solving. *Psychological Monographs, 54* (6, Whole No. 248).

Luchins, A.S. (1949). Rigidity and Ethnocentrism: A critique. *Journal of Personality, 17,* 242–246.

Luck, J.I., & Gruner, C.R. (1970). Another note on political candidate preference and authoritarianism. *Psychological Reports, 26,* 594.

Maccoby, E.E., & Martin, J.A. (1983). Socialization in the context of the family: Parent-child interaction. In P.H. Mussen (Ed.), *Handbook of child psychology* (4th ed., pp. 1–101). New York: Wiley.

Maier, N.R.F. (1930). Reasoning in humans. I. On direction. *Journal of Comparative Psychology, 10,* 115–143.

Main, M., & Goldwyn, R. (1984). Predicting rejection of her infant from mother's representation of her own experience: Implications for the abused-abusing intergenerational cycle. *Child Abuse and Neglect, 8,* 203–217.

Main, M., & Weston, D.K. (1982). Avoidance of the attachment figure in infancy: Descriptions and interpretations. In C.M. Parkes & J. Stevenson-Hinde (Eds.), *The place of attachment in human behavior* (pp. 31–59). New York: Basic Books.

Mann, H. (1982). *Der Untertan* (9th Ed.). Munich: Deutscher Taschenbuch Verlag.

Mannheim, K. (1960). *Ideology and utopia.* London: Routledge and Kegan Paul.

Mantell, D.M. (1972). *Familie und Aggression: Zur Einübung von Gewalt und Gewaltlosigkeit.* Frankfurt am Main: Fischer. (Shorter American version: *True Americans: Green Berets and war resisters.* New York: Teachers College Press, Columbia University, 1974)

Maslow, A.H. (1943). The authoritarian character structure. *Journal of Social Psychology, 18,* 401–411.

McCann, S.J.H., & Stewin, L.L. (1984). Environmental threat and parapsychological contributions to the psychological literature. *Journal of Social Psychology, 122,* 227–235.

McCann, S.J.H., & Stewin, L.L. (1987). Threat, authoritarianism, and the power of United States Presidents. *Journal of Psychology, 121*(2), 149–157.

McCloskey, H., & Chong, D. (1985). Similarities and differences between left-wing and right-wing radicals. *British Journal of Political Science, 15,* 329–363.

McFarland, S. (1989a). Religious orientations and the targets of discrimination. *Journal for the Scientific Study of Religion, 28,* 324–336.

McFarland, S. (1989b). *The current status of authoritarianism in Kentucky.* Unpublished manuscript.

McFarland, S., Ageyev, V., & Abalakina, M. (1990, July). *"The Authoritarian Personality" in the U.S.A. and U.S.S.R.: Comparative studies*. Paper presented at the Meeting of the International Society for Political Psychology, Washington, DC.

McGranahan, D.V. (1946). A comparison of social attitudes among American and German youth. *Journal of Abnormal and Social Psychology, 41*, 245–257.

Melby, E.O. (1953). Cultural freedom and creativity. In M.B. Smith (Ed.), Academic freedom in a climate of insecurity [Special issue]. *Journal of Social Issues, 9*(3), 2–5.

Meloen, J.D. (1983). *De autoritaire reaktie in tijden van welvarrt en krisis.* [The authoritarian response in times of prosperity and crisis]. Unpublished doctoral dissertation, University of Amsterdam. (English abstract).

Meloen, J.D. (1984). *De dynamische sociaal-politieke en ekonomische beinvloeding van potentieel fascisme: de ontwikkeling van een empirisch tijdreeksmodel.* [The dynamic socio-political and economical influence on authoritarianism: The construction of an empirical time-series model]. In *Jaarboek van be Nederlandse vereniging van marktonderzoekers* (pp. 65–84). Harrlem: De Vrieseborgh.

Meloen, J.D. (1990, July). *The authoritarianism concepts of Adorno et. al. and Altemeyer tested*. Paper presented at the meeting of the International Society of Political Psychology, Washington, DC.

Meloen, J.D. (1991a). The fortieth anniversary of "The Authoritarian Personality". *Politics and the Individual, 1*(1), 119–127.

Meloen, J.D. (1991b). De autoritarisme-concepten van Adorno et al. en Altemeyer vergeleken: theoretische analyse en empirische test (The authoritarianism concepts of Adorno et al. and Altemeyer compared: Theoretical analysis and empirical test). In P. Scheepers & R. Eisenga: *Onderdanig en Intolerant* (Submissive and intolerant). Institute of Applied Sociology (ITS), Nijmegen.

Meloen, J.D. (1991c). Een kritische analyse van veertig jaar onderzoek naar de autoritaire persoonlijkheid (A critical analysis of forty years of research into the authoritarian personality). In P. Scheepers & R. Eisenga: *Onderdanig en Intolerant* (Submissive and intolerant). Institute of Applied Sociology (ITS), Nijmegen.

Meloen, J.D., & Middendorp, C.P. (1991). Authoritarianism in the Netherlands: The empirical distribution in the population and its relation to theories on authoritarianism. *Politics and the Individual, 1*(2), 49–71.

Meloen, J.D., Hagendoorn, L., Raaijmakers, Q., & Visser, L. (1988). Authoritarianism and the revival of political racism: Reassessments in the Netherlands of the reliability and validity of the concept of authoritarianism by Adorno et al. *Political Psychology, 9*, 413–429.

Menninger, K.A. (1938). *Man against himself*. New York: Harcourt, Brace.

Merelman, R.M., & Foster, C.R. (1980). Political culture and education in advanced industrial societies: West Germany and the United States. *International Review of Education, 26*, 443–465.

Merton, R.K. (1973). Multiple discoveries as strategic research site. In N.W. Storer (Ed.), *The sociology of science: Theoretical and empirical investigations* (Chap. 17). Chicago: University of Chicago Press.

Metz, G. (1971). *Theoretische und empirische Ansatze einer Untersuchung spezieller Einstellungen.* Unpublished doctoral dissertation, Ludwig-Maximilian-Universität zu München.

Middendorp, C.P. (1978). *Progressiveness and conservatism.* The Hague: Mouton.

Middleton, R. (1976). Regional Differences in Prejudice. *American Sociological Review, 41*, 94–117.

Migdal, U. (1981). *Die Frühgeschichte des Frankfurter Instituts für Sozialforschung.* Frankfurt am Main: Campus.

Mikheyev, D. (1987). The Soviet Mentality. *Political Psychology, 8*, 491–523.

Milbrath, L.W. (1984). *Environmentalists: Vanguard for a new society.* Albany, NY: State University of New York Press.

Milgram, S. (1967). The small world problem. In J.V. McConnell (Ed.), *Readings in social psychology today.* Del Mar, CA: CRM Books.

Milgram, S. (1974). *Obedience to authority: An experimental view.* New York: Harper & Row.

Mitchell, H.E., & Byrne, D. (1973). The defendant's dilemma: Effects of jurors' attitudes and authoritarianism on judicial decisions. *Journal of Personality and Social Psychology, 25*, 123–129.

Mitgliederverzeichnis [membership register]. (1930). Deutsche Psychoanalytische Gesellschaft. *Internationale Zeitschrift für Psychoanalyse, 16.*

Moran, G., & Comfort, J.C. (1982). Scientific juror selection: Sex as a moderator of demographic and personality predictors of empanelled juror behavior. *Journal of Personality and Social Psychology, 43*, 1052–1063.

Mosher, D.L., & Tomkins, S.S. (1988). Scripting the Macho Man: Hypermasculine socialization and enculturation. *The Journal of Sex Research, 25*, 60–84.

Mynhardt, J.C. (1980). Prejudice among Afrikaans- and English-speaking South African students. *Journal of Social Psychology, 110*, 9–17.

Mynhardt, J.C., Plug, C., Tyson, G.A., & Viljoen, H.B. (1979). Ethnocentrism, authoritarianism, and conservatism among South African samples: A two-year follow-up. *South African Journal of Psychology, 9*(1–2), 23–26.

Newman, G.R., Articolo, D.J., & Trilling, C. (1974). Authoritarianism, religiosity and reactions to deviance. *Journal of Criminal Justice, 2*, 249–259.

Oesterreich, D. (1974). *Autoritarismus und Autonomie.* Stuttgart: Ernst Klett Verlag.

Oesterreich, D. (1985). Authoritarianism: The end of a concept? *High School Journal, 68*, 97–102.

Oesterreich, D. (1992). Im Osten nicht rechtsextremer als im Westen [Right-wing extremism—No more prevalent in the East than in the West]. *Erziehung und Wissenschaft,* March, pp. 18–19.

Oppenheim, A.N. (1975, September). *Civic education and participation in democracy: The German case.* Report delivered to the IEEA Symposium, West Berlin, Germany.

Oppenheim, A.N., & Torney, J. (1974). The measurement of children's civic attitudes in different nations. *IEA Monograph Studies No. 2.* New York: Wiley.

Orpen, C. (1970). Authoritarianism in an "authoritarian" culture: The case of Afrikaans-speaking South Africa. *Journal of Social Psychology, 81*, 119–120.

Orwell, G. (1948). *1984.* New York: Harcourt, Brace & World.

Padgett, V.R., & Jorgenson, D.O. (1982). Superstition and economic threat: Germany, 1918–1940. *Personality and Social Psychology Bulletin, 8,* 736–741.

Parrott, G., & Brown, L. (1972). Political bias in the Rokeach Dogmatism Scale. *Psychological Reports, 30,* 805–806.

Peabody, D. (1961). Attitude content and agreement set in scales of authoritarianism, dogmatism, anti-Semitism, and economic conservatism. *Journal of Abnormal and Social Psychology, 63,* 1–11.

Peabody, D. (1966). Authoritarianism scales and response biases. *Psychological Bulletin, 65,* 11–23.

Penrod, S. (May, 1980). *Evaluating social science methods of jury selection.* Paper presented at the Annual Meeting of the Midwestern Psychological Association.

Pettigrew, T.F. (1959). Regional differences in anti-negro prejudices. *Journal of Abnormal and Social Psychology, 59,* 28–36.

Poppelaars, J.L., & Visser, L. (1987). De invloed van een anti-fascisme project: een evaluatie onderzoek naar film "De oplossing" (The influence of an antifascism project: an evaluation of the movie "The Solution"). Research report, Psychological Department, University of Utrecht, The Netherlands.

Psychoanalytische Kurse. (1930). *Psychoanalytische Bewegung, 2,* pp. 303, 605.

Pushkin, A. (1964). *Eugene Onegen.* (V. Nabokov, Trans.) Princeton, NJ: Princeton University Press. (Original work published 1831)

Raaijmakers, Q., Meeus, W., & Vollebergh, W. (1985, April). *Extreme politieke opvattingen bij LBO en MAVO-scholieren.* [Extreme political views of high school students]. Paper presented at the First Dutch Conference of Political Psychology, Nijmegen. The Netherlands.

Raina, T.N. (1974). Comparison of Indian education students belonging to four political parties on a measure of authoritarianism. *Journal of Social Psychology, 92,* 311–312.

Ray, J.J. (1976). Do authoritarians hold authoritarian attitudes? *Human Relations, 29,* 307–325.

Ray, J.J. (1982). Authoritarianism/libertarianism as the second dimension of social attitudes. *Journal of Social Psychology, 117,* 33–44.

Ray, J.J. (1983a). Half of all authoritarians are left-wing: A reply to Eysenck and Stone. *Political Psychology, 4,* 139–143.

Ray, J.J. (1983b). Reviving the problem of acquiescent response bias. *Journal of Social Psychology, 121,* 81–96.

Ray, J.J. (1985a). Racism and rationality: A reply to Billig. *Ethnic & Racial Studies, 8,* 441–443.

Ray, J.J. (1985b). The psychopathology of the political left. *High School Journal, 68,* 413–423.

Ray, J.J. (1988a). Cognitive style as a predictor of authoritarianism, conservatism, and racism: A fantasy in many movements. *Political Psychology, 9,* 303–308.

Ray, J.J. (1988b). Capitalism and compassion: A test of Milbrath's environmental theory. *Personality and Individual Differences, 9,* 431–433.

Reich, I.O. (1969). *Wilhelm Reich; A personal biography.* New York: Avon Books.

Reich, W. (1929). Dialektischer Materialismus und Psychoanalyse. *Unter dem Banner des Marxismus, 3*(5).

Reich, W. (1930). *Geschlechtsreife, Enthaltsamkeit, Ehemoral.* Vienna: Muenster.

Reich, W. (1932). *Der Einbruch der Sexualmoral*. Berlin: Verlag für Sexualpolitik.

Reich, W. (1933). *Massenpsychologie des Faschismus*. Copenhagen: Verlag für Sexualpolitik. [*The mass psychology of fascism*]. [T.P. Wolfe (Trans.). New York: Orgone Institute Press, 1946]. [V.R. Carfagno (Trans.). New York: Farrar, Strauss and Giroux, 1970].

Reich, W. (1966). *Sex-pol: Essays 1929-1934*. L. Baxandall (Ed.), A. Bostock, T. DuBose, & L. Baxandall (Trans.), (pp. 1-74 and 89-249). New York: Random House. (Reprinted from *Unter dem Banner des Marxismus*, 1929, 3, 5; and *Der Einbruch der Sexualmoral*. Berlin: Verlag für Sexualpolitik, 1932).

Reich, W. (1976). *People in Trouble* (P. Smith, Trans.). New York: Farrar, Straus, & Giroux.

Rigaudias-Weiss, H. (1936). *Les enquetes ouvrieres en France entre 1830 et 1849*. Paris: Alcan.

Rigby, K. (1984). Acceptance of authority and directiveness as indicators of authoritarianism: A new framework. *Journal of Social Psychology*, *122*, 171–180.

Rigby, K. (1987). An authority behavior inventory. *Journal of Personality Assessment*, *51*, 615–625.

Rigby, K., & Rump, E.E. (1982). Attitudes toward authority and authoritarian personality characteristics. *Journal of Social Psychology*, *116*, 61–72.

Rippl, S., Schmidt, P., Schürhoff, R., & Seipel, C. (1991). Determinanten der Parteisympathie für die Republikaner: Eine regionale Studie [Determinants of party sympathy for the Republican Party: A regional study]. *Journal für Sozialforschung*, *31*(2), 147–162.

Roe, R.A. (1975). *Links en rechts in empirisch perspectief*. [Left and right wing in an empirical perspective]. Unpublished doctoral dissertation, University of Amsterdam.

Roghmann, K. (1966). *Dogmatismus und Autoritarismus* [Dogmatism and authoritarianism]. Meisenheim am Glan, Germany: Verlag Anton Hein.

Rokeach, M. (1948). Generalized mental rigidity as a factor in ethnocentrism. *Journal of Abnormal and Social Psychology*, *43*, 259–278.

Rokeach, M. (1956). Political and religious dogmatism: An alternative to the authoritarian personality. *Psychological Monographs*, *70*(18).

Rokeach, M. (1960). *The open and closed mind*. New York: Basic Books.

Rokeach, M. (1973). *The nature of human values*. New York: Free Press.

Rokeach, M., & Hanley, C. (1956). Eysenck's tendermindedness dimension: A critique. *Psychological Bulletin*, *53*, 169–176.

Rorer, L.G. (1965). The great response style myth. *Psychological Bulletin*, *63*, 129–156.

Rosenthal, R. (1966). *Experimenter effects in behavioral research*. New York: Appleton-Century-Crofts.

Roshchin, S.K. (1980). *Western psychology as an instrument of ideology and politics* (in Russian). Moscow: Nauka.

Rothman, S., & Lichter, S.R. (1982). *Roots of radicalism*. New York: Oxford University Press.

Rubenstein, R.L. (1975). *The cunning of history: Mass death and the American future*. New York: Harper & Row.

Rubins, J.L. (1978). *Karen Horney: Gentle rebel of psychoanalysis*. New York: Dial Press.

Sales, S.M. (1972). Economic threat as a determinant of conversion rates in authoritarian and nonauthoritarian churches. *Journal of Personality and Social Psychology, 23*, 420–428.

Sales, S.M. (1973). Threat as a factor in authoritarianism: An analysis of archival data. *Journal of Personality and Social Psychology, 28*, 44–57.

Sales, S.M., & Friend, K.E. (1973). Success and failure as determinants of level of authoritarianism. *Behavioral Science, 18*, 163–172.

Salmon, W.C. (1967). *The foundations of scientific inference*. Pittsburgh, PA: University of Pittsburgh Press.

Samelson, F. (1964). Agreement set and anticontent attitudes in the F scale: A reinterpretation. *Journal of Abnormal and Social Psychology, 68*, 338–342.

Samelson, F. (1974). History, origin myth, and ideology: Comte's discovery of social psychology. *Journal for the Theory of Social Behaviour, 4*, 217–231.

Samelson, F. (1978). From "Race Psychology" to "Studies in Prejudice": Some observations on the thematic reversal in social psychology. *Journal of the History of the Behavioral Sciences, 14*, 265–278.

Samelson, F. (1986). Authoritarianism from Berlin to Berkeley: On social psychology and history. *Journal of Social Issues, 42*(1), 191–208.

Samelson, F., & Yates, J.F. (1967). Acquiescence and the F scale: Old assumptions and new data. *Psychological Bulletin, 68*, 91–103.

Sanford, F.H., & Older, H.J. (1950). *Authoritarianism and leadership*. Philadelphia, PA: Stephenson Brothers.

Sanford, N. (1956). The approach of the authoritarian personality. In J.L. McCary (Ed.), *Psychology of personality. Six modern approaches* (pp. 253–319). New York: Logos Press.

Sanford, N. (1973). Authoritarian personality in contemporary perspective. In J.N. Knutson (Ed.), *Handbook of political psychology* (pp. 139–170). San Francisco: Jossey-Bass.

Sargent, S.S., & Brameld, T. (Eds.). (1955). Anti-intellectualism in the United States. *Journal of Social Issues, 11*(3), 54–56.

Sargent, S.S., & Harris B. (1986). Academic freedom, civil liberties, and SPSSI. *Journal of Social Issues, 42*(1), 43–67.

Schaffner, B. (1948). *Father Land*. New York: Columbia University Press.

Schivelbusch, W. (1983). *Intellektuellendämmerung*. Frankfurt am Main: Inselverlag.

Schlenker, B.R. (1974). Social psychology and science. *Journal of Personality and Social Psychology, 29*, 1–15.

Schlesinger, A.J., Jr. (1949). *The vital center*. Boston: Houghton Mifflin.

Schooler, C. (1972). Social Antecedents of Adult Psychological Functioning. *American Journal of Sociology, 78*, 299–322.

Schooler, C. (1976). Serfdom's legacy: An ethnic continuum. *American Journal of Sociology, 81*, 1265–1286.

Schroeder, H.M., Driver, M.J., & Streufert, S. (1967). *Human information processing*. New York: Holt, Rinehart & Winston.

Schulman, J., Shaver, P., Colman, R., Emrich, B., & Christie, R. (1973, May). Recipe for a jury. *Psychology Today*, P. 37ff.

Schumann, S. (1984a). *Rechtsautoritäre (politische) Einstellungen und verschiedene Persönlichkeitsmerkmale ihrer Vertreter*. Munich: Forschungsbericht 84.01, Fachbereich Pädagogik, Hochschule der Bundeswehr.

Seeman, M. (1983). Alienation motifs in contemporary theorizing: The hidden continuity of the classic themes. *Social Psychology Quarterly*, 46, 171–184.

Sellin, T., & Wolfgang, M.E. (1964). *The measurement of delinquency*. New York: Wiley.

Shaw, M.E., & Wright, J.M. (1967). *Scales for the measurement of attitudes*. New York: McGraw-Hill.

Sherman, R.C., & Dowdle, M.D. (1974). The perception of crime and punishment: A multi-dimensional scaling analysis. *Social Science Research*, 3, 109–126.

Sherwood, J.J. (1966a). Authoritarianism and moral realism. *Journal of Clinical Psychology*, 22, 17–21.

Sherwood, J.J. (1966b). Authoritarianism, moral realism, and President Kennedy's death. *British Journal of Social and Clinical Psychology*, 5, 264–269.

Shikhirev, P.N. (1980). *Modern social psychology in the U.S.A.* Moscow: Nauka (In Russian).

Shikhirev, P.N. (1985). *Modern social psychology in Western Europe: Methodological and theoretical problems*. Moscow: Nauka (In Russian).

Shils, E.A. (1948). *The present state of American sociology*. Glencoe, IL: Free Press.

Shils, E.A. (1954). Authoritarianism: "Right" and "left". In R. Christie and M. Jahoda (Eds.). *Studies in the scope and method of "The Authoritarian Personality"*. Glencoe, IL: The Free Press.

Shils, E.A. (1980). *The calling of sociology*. Chicago: University of Chicago Press.

Shipler, D. (1990, June 25). A reporter at large: Between distatorship and anarchy. *New Yorker*, pp. 4–70.

Sidanius, J. (1985). Cognitive functioning and sociopolitical ideology revisited. *Political Psychology*, 6, 637–661.

Sidanius, J. (1988). Intolerance of ambiguity, conservatism, and racism: Whose fantasy, whose reality? A reply to Ray. *Political Psychology*, 9, 309–316.

Sidanius, J., & Lau, R.R. (1989). Political sophistication and political deviance: A matter of context. *Political Psychology*, 10, 85–109.

Simpson, M. (1972). Authoritarianism and education: A comparative approach. *Sociometry*, 35, 223–234.

Smith, M.B. (1950). [Review of *The authoritarian personality*]. *Journal of Abnormal and Social Psychology*, 45, 775–779.

Smith, M.B. (Ed.). (1953). Academic freedom in a climate of insecurity. *Journal of Social Issues*, 9(3), 2–55.

Smith, M.B. (1983). The shaping of American social psychology. *Personality and Social Psychology Bulletin*, 9, 165–180.

Smith, M.B. (1986). McCarthyism: A personal account. *Journal of Social Issues*, 42(4), 71–80.

Smith, M.B., Bruner, J.S., & White, R.W. (1956). *Opinions and personality*. New York: Wiley.

Snortum, J.R., & Ashear, V.H. (1972). Prejudice, punitiveness, and personality. *Journal of Personality Assessment*, 36, 291–296.

Speier, H. (1936). [Review of Max Horkheimer, Ed., *Studien über Autorität und Familie*]. *Social Research*, *3*, 501–504.

Sroufe, L.A. (1983). Infant–caregiver attachment and patterns of adaption in preschool: The roots of maladaption and competence. In *Development and policy concerning children with special needs* (pp. 41–83). The Minnesota Symposia on Child Psychology, Vol. 16. Hillsdale, NJ: Erlbaum.

Sroufe, L.A., & Fleeson, J. (1986). Attachment and the construction of relationships. In W.W. Hartup, & Z. Rubin (Eds.), *Relationships and development* (pp. 51–71). Hillsdale, NJ: Erlbaum.

Sroufe, L.A., & Fleeson, J. (1988). The coherence of family relationships. In R. A. Hinde & J. Stevenson-Hinde. Relationships within families: Mutual influences (pp. 27–47). Oxford: Clarendon.

Stagner, R. (1936). Fascist attitudes: An exploratory study. *Journal of Social Psychology*, *7*, 309–319.

Staub, E. (1989). *The roots of evil: The origins of genocide and other group violence*. Cambridge, England: Cambridge University Press.

Steffensmeier, D.J. (1975). Levels of dogmatism and willingness to report "hippie" and "straight" shoplifters: A field experiment accompanied by home interviews. *Sociometry*, *38*, 282–290.

Steiner, J.M., & Fahrenberg, J. (1970a). Die Ausprägung autoritärer Einstellung bei ehemaligen Angehörigen der SS und der Wehrmacht. [The disclosure of the authoritarian attitude of former members of the SS and the Wehrmacht]. *Kölner Zeitschrift für Soziologie und Sozial Psychologie*, *22*, 551–566.

Steiner, J.M., & Fahrenberg, J. (1970b). The marks of authoritarian attitude in former members of the SS and the armed forces. *Abstracts on Criminology and Penology*, *10*(4), 351–362.

Stone, W.F. (1980). The myth of left-wing authoritarianism. *Political Psychology*, *2*(3–4), 3–19.

Stone, W.F. (1983). Left and right in personality and ideology: An attempt at clarification. *Journal of Mind and Behavior*, *4*, 211–220.

Stone, W.F. (1986). Personality and ideology: Empirical support for Tomkins's Polarity Theory. *Political Psychology*, *7*, 689–708.

Stone, W. (1991, July). *Right-wing authoritarianism and normative and humanistic personality orientations*. Paper presented at the meeting of the International Society of Political Psychology, Helsinki, Finland.

Stone, W.F., & Schaffner, P.E. (1988). *The Psychology of Politics* (2nd ed.). New York: Springer-Verlag.

Stouffer, S.A. (1955). *Communism, conformity, and civil liberties*. New York: Doubleday.

Sue, S., Smith, R.E., & Pedroza, G. (1975). Authoritarianism, pretrial publicity, and awareness of bias in simulated jurors. *Psychological Reports*, *37*, 1299–1302.

Suedfeld, P., & Rank, A.D. (1976). Revolutionary leaders: Long-term success as a function of changes in conceptual complexity. *Journal of Personality and Social Psychology*, *34*, 169–178.

Tajfel, H. (1981). *Human groups and social categories*. New York: Cambridge University Press.

Tajfel, H., & Turner, J.C. (1986). The social identity theory of intergroup behavior. In S. Worchel & W.G. Austin (Eds.), *Psychology of Intergroup Relations* (pp. 7–24). Chicago: Nelson-Hall.

Tarr, H., & Lorr, M. (1991). A comparison of right-wing authoritarianism, conformity, and conservatism. *Personality and Individual Differences*, *12*, 307–311.

Taylor, D.W., & McNemar, Q.W. (1955). Problem solving and thinking. In C.P. Stone & Q. McNemar (Eds.), *Annual Review of Psychology* (6, 455–482).

Tedeschi, J.I., Lindskold, S., & Rosenfeld, P. (1985). *Introduction to social psychology*. St. Paul, MN: West.

Temme, L.V. (1975). *Occupation: Meanings and measures*. Washington, DC: Bureau of Social Science Research.

Tetlock, P.E. (1983). Cognitive style and political ideology. *Journal of Personality and Social Psychology*, *45*, 118–126.

Tetlock, P.E. (1984). Cognitive style and political belief systems in the British House of Commons. *Journal of Personality and Social Psychology*, *46*, 365–375.

Tetlock, P.E. (1986). A value pluralism model of ideological reasoning. *Journal of Personality and Social Psychology*, *50*, 819–827.

Tolman, E.C. (1932). *Purposive behavior in animals and men*. New York: Century.

Tomkins, S.S. (1962). *Affect, imagery, consciousness* (Vol. 1–2). New York: Springer.

Tomkins, S.S. (1963). Left and right: A basic dimension of ideology and personality. In R.W. White (Ed.), *The Study of Lives* (pp. 388–411). Chicago: Atherton.

Tomkins, S.S. (1964). *Polarity Scale*. New York: Springer.

Tomkins, S.S. (1965). Affect and the psychology of knowledge. In S.S. Tomkins & C.E. Izard (Eds.), *Affect, Cognition, and Personality* (pp. 72–97). New York: Springer.

Tomkins, S.S. (1981). *Further thoughts on the left and the right*. Paper presented at the Fourth Annual Scientific Meeting of the International Society of Political Psychology, Mannheim, Germany.

Tomkins, S.S. (1987). Script theory. In J. Aronoff, A.I. Rabin, & R.A. Zucker. (Eds.), *The emergence of personality* (pp. 147–216). New York: Springer.

Tomkins, S.S. (1991). *Affect, imagery, consciousness: Vol. 3. The negative affects: Anger and fear*. New York: Springer.

Torney, J.V., Oppenheim, A.N., & Farnen, R.F. (1975). *Civic education in ten countries: An empirical study*. New York: Wiley-Halsted.

Toulmin, S.E. (1970). Does the distinction between normal and revolutionary science hold water? In I. Lakatos & A. Musgrave (Eds.), *Criticism and the growth of knowledge* (pp. 39–47). Cambridge, England: Cambridge University Press.

Trodahl, V.C., & Powell, F.A. (1965). A short form of the dogmatism scale for use in field situations. *Social Forces*, *49*, 211–214.

Vecchio, R.P. (1977). The parolee's dilemma: Effect of interpersonal attraction on recommendations for parole. *Psychological Reports*, *41*, 127–133.

Vidmar, N. (1974). Retributive and utilitarian motives and other correlates of Canadian attitudes toward the death penality. *Canadian Psychologist*, *15*, 337–356.

Waldman, E. (1963). *Soldat im Staat*. Boppard am Rhein, Germany: Harold Boldt Verlag.

Ward, D. (1982). [Review of *Right-wing authoritarianism*]. *American Political Science Review*, *76*, 737–738.

Ward, D. (1988). A critic's defense of the criticized. *Political Psychology, 9,* 317–320.

Wiggershaus, R. (1986). *Die Frankfurter Schule: Geschichte, theoretische Entwicklung, politische Bedeutung* [The Frankfurt School: History, theoretical development, political development]. Munich: Carl Hanser.

Williams, J.A. (1966). Regional differences in authoritarianism. *Social Forces, 45,* 273–277.

Wilson, G.D. (1973). *The psychology of conservatism.* London: Academic.

Winter, D.G. (1987). Leader appeal, leader performance, and the motive profile of leaders and followers: A study of American presidents and elections. *Journal of Personality and Social Psychology, 52,* 196–202.

Wright, J.M., & Harvey, O.J. (1965). Attitude change as a function of authoritarianism and punitiveness. *Journal of Personality and Social Psychology, 1,* 177–181.

Wrightsman, L.S. (1977). *Social psychology* (2nd ed.). Monterey, CA: Brooks/ Cole.

Young-Bruehl, E. (1988). *Anna Freud: A biography.* New York: Summit Books.

Zander, A., & Havelin, A. (1960). Social comparison and interpersonal attraction. *Human Relations, 13,* 21–32.

Zangle, (1978). *Einführung in die politische Sozialisationsforschung* [Introduction to research on political socialization]. Paderborn, Germany: Ferdinand Schoningh.

Zhuravlev, A.L., Rubakhin, V.P., & Shorin, V.G. (1976). *Individual leadership style in organizations* (in Russian). Moscow: Nauka.

Ziehe, T. (1975). *Pubertät und Narzissmus, Eurpaische Verlagsanstalt.* Frankfurt am Main: Europaische Verlagsanstalt.

Zimmer, J. (1972). Antiautoritare Erziehung: Theoretische Konzeption und Standorbestimmung. In Hans-werner Sasz (Ed.), *Antiautoritare Erziehung oder Die Erziehung der Erzieher.* Stuttgart: Metzler Verlag.

Zinnecker, J. (1985). Politik. Partien. Nationalismus. In A. Fischer, W. Fuchs, & J. Zinnecker (Eds.), *Jugendliche und Erwachsene '85: Generationen in Vergleich* [Youths and adults '85: Generations in comparison]. *Jugendwerk der Deutschen Shell* (Vol. 3, pp. 321–408). Opladen, Germany: Leske and Budrich.

ZUMA-Nachrichten (Zentrum für Umfragen, Methoden und Analysen e.V.). (The Center for Surveys, Methods and Analyses in Mannheim, Germany, publishes a bulletin about national and international survey work in May and November of each year).

ZUMA. Handbuch Sozialwissenschaftlicher Skalen [Handbook of Scales for the Social Sciences]. (1983). Mannheim, Germany: ZUMA.

ZUMA. Handbuch Sozialwissenschaftlicher Skalen [Handbook of Scales for the Social Sciences]. (1992, in press). J. Skalenhandbuch, Allmendinger, P. Schmidt, and B. Wegener (eds.), Bonn: Bad Godesberg, to be published in revised edition.

Zwillenberg, D.F. (1983). *Predicting biases in the punishment of criminals as a function of authoritarianism: The effects of severity of the crime, degree of mitigating circumstances, and status of the offender.* (Unpublished doctoral dissertation, Columbia University. (University Microfilms No. 8311876).

Index

Abalakina, M., 20, 40, 205–206, 232
Ackerman, N.W., 19, 120–121, 128–134, 142, 240
Acquiescence tendencies, 65
Adelson, J., 57
Adorno, T.W., 3, 6, 8–9, 12–17, 22, 34–36, 39, 48–50, 62–67, 70, 76–77, 99, 119, 122–123, 126–128, 135, 139, 144, 146, 156, 159, 170–172, 177, 184–185, 192, 194, 199, 201–202, 204, 229, 234, 244
A-E syndrome, *see* Authoritarianism-ethnocentrism (A-E)
Ageyev, V., 20, 40, 205–206, 225, 232
Ainsworth, M., 125, 135–136
Allport, G.W., 39, 238
Almond, G.A., 37, 196
Altemeyer, R., 14, 20, 22–23, 40, 47, 49, 61–62, 64–65, 67–68, 97, 106, 109–110, 113, 115, 117, 119–121, 125–126, 135, 139–141, 147–148, 151, 160–167, 181, 200–206, 210–215, 230, 234, 236–238, 241, 244
American Jewish Committee (AJC), 6, 18, 34, 37
Anomic Authoritarianism (AA) scale, 14, 102, 171–173
Antiauthoritarianism subscale, 100
Anti-intraception, 62, 166, 177, 232–233, 235
Anti-Semitism, 5–10, 17–18, 29, 34–36, 39, 42, 52, 60, 120–122, 128, 130–133, 144, 146, 159, 199, 201, 230, 232, 240

scale, 6, 34, 123
self-image and family background in, 130–134
Apartheid, 60, 67
Applezweig, D.G., 79, 84, 96–97
Arendt, H., 36
Aron, B., 12, 123
Articolo, D.J., 101
Asch, S., 72
Ashear, V.H., 102
Authoritarian
aggression, 22, 24, 160–161, 164–165, 174, 201, 230, 232–235, 237, 245
character, 27–28
leadership style, 199–200
personality, 3–6, 14, 20, 22, 28–29, 31, 35, 37, 68, 122, 128, 155–156, 161, 163, 166, 168, 170, 176–177, 179–180, 200–201, 220, 231, 241–244
submission, 22, 24, 160–161, 174, 201, 230, 232, 234–237, 245
term, 24, 121–122
Authoritarianism
attachment research and, 134–142
Austrian adolescents and, 191–193
as cognitive simplicity, 167–168
the dialectics of history and, 41–43
effect of education on, 66–67
ego development and, 170–171
-ethnocentrism (A-E), 70–72, 74, 93, 97, 202, 204, 209
experimentation and, 70–72, 99, 116–118
family and, 119–143

Printed in Great Britain
by Amazon